The *Pocket* Wadsworth Handbook

FOURTH EDITION

Laurie G. Kirszner
University of the Sciences in Philadelphia

Stephen R. Mandell
Drexel University

D0102516

WADSWORTH
CENGAGE Learning™

Australia • Brazil • Japan • Korea • Mexico • Singapore • Spain
United Kingdom • United States

WADSWORTH
CENGAGE Learning

**The Pocket Wadsworth Handbook,
Fourth Edition**
Laurie G. Kirszner, Stephen R. Mandell

Publisher: *Lyn Uhl*
Development Editor: *Karen Mauk*
Editorial Assistant: *Megan Power*
Technology Project Manager:
  Stephanie Gregoire
Executive Marketing Manager:
  Mandee Eckersley
Senior Marketing Communications
  Manager: *Stacey Purviance*
Senior Content Project Manager:
  Lianne Ames
Senior Art Director: *Cate Barr*
Manufacturing Manager: *Marcia Locke*
Permissions Editor: *Bob Kauser*
Production Service:
  Nesbitt Graphics, Inc.
Text Designer: *Nesbitt Graphics, Inc.*
Photo Researcher: *Sharon Donahue*
Cover Designer: *Brian Salisbury*
Compositor: *Nesbitt Graphics, Inc.*

For product information and
technology assistance, contact us
at **Cengage Learning Academic
Resource Center, 1-800-423-0563**

For permission to use material
from this text or product, submit
all requests online at
www.cengage.com/permissions
Further permissions questions
can be emailed to
permissionrequest@cengage.com

Library of Congress Control Number:
2007941621
ISBN-13: 978-1-4390-8181-5
ISBN-10: 1-4390-8181-6

Wadsworth Cengage Learning
20 Channel Center Street
Boston, MA 02210
USA

Cengage Learning products are repre-
sented in Canada by Nelson Education,
Ltd.

For your course and learning solutions,
visit **academic.cengage.com**

Purchase any of our products at your
local college store or at our preferred
online store **www.ichapters.com**

Printed in Canada
1 2 3 4 5 6 7 12 11 10 09

How to Use This Book

We would like to introduce you to *The Pocket Wadsworth Handbook*, Fourth Edition, a quick reference guide for college students. This book was designed to be a truly portable handbook that can fit easily in a backpack or pocket. Despite its compact size, *The Pocket Wadsworth Handbook* covers all the topics you'd expect to find in a much longer book: the writing process (illustrated by a model student paper); sentence grammar and style; punctuation and mechanics; the research process (illustrated by four model student research papers); and MLA, APA, Chicago, and CSE documentation styles. In addition, the book devotes a full chapter to writing an argumentative essay—and a full section to practical assignments (including Web site and document design, reading critically, writing for the workplace, and oral presentations). Finally, it includes an entire section that addresses the concerns of ESL writers.

The explanations and examples of writing in *The Pocket Wadsworth Handbook* can guide you not just in first-year courses but throughout your college career and beyond. Our goal throughout is to make the book clear, accessible, useful, and—most of all—easy to navigate. To achieve this goal, we incorporated distinctive design features throughout to make information easy to find and easy to use.

Design Features

- **Computer tips** highlight specific ways in which technology can help you throughout the writing, revising, and editing processes. Each computer tip includes the URL for the book's companion Web site, http://cengage.com/english/kirsznermandell, which contains a wealth of online resources.
- **Grammar checker boxes** illustrating sample errors show the advantages and limitations of using a grammar checker.
- **Numerous checklists** summarize key information that you can quickly access as needed.
- **Close-up boxes** provide an in-depth look at some of the more perplexing writing-related issues you will encounter.

- **Parts 7–8** include the most up-to-date documentation and format guidelines from the Modern Language Association, the American Psychological Association, the University of Chicago Press, and the Council of Science Editors.
- **A new Writing in the Disciplines chart** provides a quick overview of the different conventions, formats, and documentation styles called for in various academic disciplines.
- **A new MLA tab** makes it easy for you to flip directly to Part 7, "Documenting Sources: MLA Style."
- **Specially designed documentation directories** make it easy to locate models for various kinds of sources, including those found online from library subscription services such as InfoTrac® College Edition and Lexis-Nexis™. In addition, annotated diagrams of sample works-cited entries clearly illustrate the elements of proper documentation.
- **Marginal cross-references** throughout the book allow you to flip directly to other sections that treat topics in more detail.
- **Marginal ESL cross-references** throughout the book direct you to sections of Part 10, "Resources for Bilingual and ESL Writers," where concepts are presented as they apply specifically to second-language writers.
- **ESL tips** are woven throughout the text to explain concepts in relation to the unique experiences of bilingual students.

Acknowledgments

We thank the following reviewers for their advice, which helped us develop the fourth edition:

Candace Barrington, *Central Connecticut State University*

Melanie Brown, *St. Norbert College*

Judith Carter, *Amarillo College*

Leanne Frost, *Montana State University, Billings*

Lisa Goddard, *Long Beach City College*

Carol Gould, *Florida Atlantic University*

Michael Kapper, *Capital University*

Vincent Kayes, *Mount St. Mary College*

Fawn Knight, *Kentucky Christian University*

Laura Knight, *Mercer County Community College*

Mark Letourneau, *Weber State University*

Richard Levesque, *Fullerton College*

Erik Lofgren, *Bucknell University*

Mary Ellen Muesing, *University of North Carolina,
    Charlotte*

Kim Stallings, *University of North Carolina, Charlotte*

Barry Trachtenberg, *University at Albany*

Carlette Whitesides, *Mount Olive College*

Maria Zlateva, *Boston University*

As we have worked to develop a book that would give you the guidance you need to become self-reliant writers and to succeed in college and beyond, we have had the support of an outstanding team of creative professionals at Wadsworth: Publisher Lyn Uhl; Editorial Assistant Megan Power; Senior Content Project Manager Lianne Ames; and Executive Marketing Manager Mandee Eckersley.

We have also had the good fortune to work with an equally strong team outside Wadsworth: Development Editor Karen Mauk; the staff of Nesbitt Graphics, Inc.; our very talented Project Manager and Copyeditor, Susan McIntyre; and John McCullough, who created this book's clear and inviting design. To these people, and to all the others who worked with us on this project, we are very grateful.

Laurie Kirszner
Steve Mandell
January 2008

Teaching and Learning Resources

Infotrac® College Edition with InfoMarks™
ISBN: 0-534-55853-4　**ISBN-13:** 978-0-534-55853-6
InfoTrac® College Edition, an online research and learning center, offers over 20 million full-text articles from nearly 6,000 scholarly and popular periodicals. The articles cover a broad spectrum of disciplines and topics—ideal for every type of researcher.

Wadsworth's InSite for Writing and Research™
ISBN: 1-4130-0918-2　**ISBN-13:** 978-1-4130-0918-7
Finally, life just got easier—an online solution for both instructors and students, Wadsworth's InSite is a groundbreaking all-in-one tool that allows instructors the opportunity to manage the flow of papers online and allows students to submit papers and peer reviews online. For more helpful information on InSite, visit our new service/support Web site academic.cengage.com/tlc.

Turnitin®
ISBN: 1-4130-3018-1　**ISBN-13:** 978-1-4130-3018-1
Turnitin is proven plagiarism-prevention software that helps students improve their writing and research skills and allows instructors to confirm originality before reading and grading student papers. Take a tour at academic.engage.com/turnitin to see how Turnitin makes checking originality against billions of pages of Internet contents, millions of published works, and millions of student papers easy and almost instant.

English21 (and English21 Plus)
The largest compilation of online resources ever organized for composition and literature courses, English21 is a complete online support system that weaves robust, self-paced instruction with interactive assignments. Easily assignable, English 21 engages students as they become better-prepared and successful writers. English21 supports students through every step of the writing process, from assignment to final draft. English21 includes carefully crafted multimedia assignments; a collection of essays that amounts to a full-sized thematic reader; a full interactive handbook including hundreds of animations, exercises, and activities; a complete research guide with animated tutorials and a link to Gale's InfoTrac® data-

base; and a rich multimedia library with hand-selected images, audio clips, video clips, stories, poems, and plays.

Access to **English21 Plus** is available for a nominal fee when packaged with new copies of the text. **English21 Plus** includes all of the features mentioned above plus access to Wadsworth's **InSite for Writing and Research™.** InSite features an electronic peer-review system, an originality checker, a rich assignment library, and electronic grade marking. To learn more about **English21** and **English21 Plus,** please visit us online at academic.engage.com/english21.

Personal Tutor with SMARTHINKING
ISBN: 0-495-56385-4   **ISBN-13:** 978-0-495-56385-3
Personal Tutor with SMARTHINKING gives your students the help they need when they need it most. Cengage Learning has partnered with this leading service provider to give students the best in prepaid online tutoring. **Personal Tutor with SMARTHINKING** provides one-on-one tutoring and on-demand assignment help from experienced tutors in an easy-access online environment. Go to www.smarthinking.com to experience online tutoring. Contact your sales representative to learn more about **Personal Tutor.**

CengageNOW™ for Writing
ISBN: 1-4130-3245-1   **ISBN-13:** 978-1-4130-3245-1
CengageNOW™ for Writing is a powerful online teaching and learning system that contains diagnostic quizzing and multimedia tutorials that work with students to build personalized study strategies and help them master the basic concepts of writing. It features reliable solutions for delivering your course content and assignments along with time-saving ways to provide feedback. **CengageNOW** provides one-click-away results; the most common reporting tasks that instructors perform every day are always just one click away while they are working in the **CengageNOW** gradebook. For students, **CengageNOW** provides diagnostic self-assessment and personalized study plans that enable them to focus on what they need to learn and guides them in selecting activities that best match their learning styles.

Merriam Webster Dictionaries

Merriam-Webster's Collegiate® Dictionary, 11/e
1,664 pages | Casebound | **ISBN:** 0-87779-809-5
ISBN-13: 978-0-87779-809-5
Available only when packaged with a Wadsworth text, the new 11/e of America's best-selling hardcover dictionary merges print, CD-ROM, and Internet-based formats to deliver unprecedented accessibility and flexibility at one affordable price.

The Merriam-Webster Dictionary
960 pages | Paperbound | **ISBN:** 0-87779-930-X
ISBN-13: 978-0-87779-930-6
Available only when packaged with a Wadsworth text, this high-quality, economical language reference covers the core vocabulary of everyday life with over 70,000 definitions.

Merriam-Webster's Dictionary and Thesaurus
1,248 pages | Paperbound | **ISBN:** 0-87779-851-6
ISBN-13: 978-0-87779-851-4
Available only when packaged with a Wadsworth text, this dictionary and thesaurus are two essential language references in one handy volume. Included are nearly 60,000 alphabetical dictionary entries integrated with more than 13,000 thesaurus entries including extensive synonym lists, as well as abundant example phrases that provide clear and concise word guidance.

Companion Web Site

http://cengage.com/english/kirsznermandell
In addition to a great selection of password-protected instructor resources, the Companion Web Site contains many interactive resources for students, including libraries that offer animated tutorials and information on diction, grammar, mechanics, punctuation, and research, as well as examples of student papers.

PART 1

Writing Essays and Paragraphs

1 Understanding Purpose and Audience

Everyone who sets out to write confronts a series of choices. In the writing you do in school, on the job, and in your personal life, your understanding of **purpose** and **audience** is essential, influencing the choices you make about content, emphasis, organization, style, and tone.

1a Determining Your Purpose

In simple terms, your **purpose** for writing is what you want to accomplish:

- **Writing to Reflect** In diaries and journals, writers explore private ideas and feelings to make sense of their experiences; in autobiographical memoirs and in personal letters, they communicate their emotions and reactions to others.
- **Writing to Inform** In newspaper articles, writers report information, communicating factual details to readers; in reference books, instruction manuals, textbooks, and the like (as well as in Web sites sponsored by government or nonprofit organizations), writers provide definitions and explain concepts or processes, trying to help readers see relationships and understand ideas.
- **Writing to Persuade** In proposals and editorials, as well as in advertising and in some business communications, writers try to convince readers to accept their positions on various issues.
- **Writing to Evaluate** In reviews of books, films, or performances and in reports, critiques, and program evaluations, writers assess the validity, accuracy, and quality of information, ideas, techniques, products, procedures, or services, perhaps assessing the relative merits of two or more things.

Although writers write to reflect, to inform, to persuade, and to evaluate, these purposes are certainly not mutually exclusive, and writers may have other purposes as well. And, of course, in any piece of writing a writer may have a primary aim and one or more secondary purposes; in fact, a writer may even have different purposes in different sections—or different drafts—of a single document.

CHECKLIST

DETERMINING YOUR PURPOSE

Is your purpose:

- ☐ to express emotions?
- ☐ to inform?
- ☐ to persuade?
- ☐ to explain?
- ☐ to amuse or entertain?
- ☐ to evaluate?
- ☐ to discover?
- ☐ to analyze?
- ☐ to debunk?
- ☐ to draw comparisons?
- ☐ to make an analogy?
- ☐ to define?
- ☐ to criticize?
- ☐ to motivate?
- ☐ to satirize?
- ☐ to speculate?
- ☐ to warn?
- ☐ to reassure?
- ☐ to take a stand?
- ☐ to identify problems?
- ☐ to suggest solutions?
- ☐ to identify causes?
- ☐ to predict effects?
- ☐ to reflect?
- ☐ to interpret?
- ☐ to instruct?
- ☐ to inspire?

1b   Identifying Your Audience

Most of the writing you do is directed at an **audience,** a particular reader or group of readers.

1 Writing for an Audience

At different times, in different roles, you address a variety of audiences:

- **As a citizen,** consumer, or member of a community, civic, political, or religious group, you may respond to pressing social, economic, or political issues by writing emails or letters to a newspaper, a public official, or a representative of a special interest group.
- **In your personal life,** you may write notes, emails, or text messages to friends and family.
- **As an employee,** you may write letters, memos, and reports to your superiors, to staff members you supervise, or to coworkers; you may also be called on to address customers or critics, board members or stockholders, funding agencies or the general public.
- **As a student,** you write essays, reports, and other papers addressed to one or more instructors, and you may also participate in **peer review,** writing evaluations of See 1b2

classmates' essays and writing responses to their comments about your own work.

As you write, you shape your writing in terms of what you believe your audience needs and expects. Your assessment of your readers' interests, educational level, biases, and expectations determines what information you include, what you emphasize, and how you arrange your material.

2 The College Writer's Audience

Most of the writing you do in college is directed either at your instructors or at other students.

Writing for Your Instructor. As a student, you usually write for an audience of one: the instructor who assigns the paper. Instructors want to know what you know and whether you can express what you know clearly and accurately. They assign written work to encourage you to think, so the way you organize and express your ideas can be as important as the ideas themselves.

Because they are trained as careful readers and critics, your instructors expect accurate information, standard grammar and correct spelling, logically presented ideas, and a reasonable degree of stylistic fluency. They also expect you to define your terms and to support your generalizations with specific examples. Finally, every instructor also expects you to draw your own conclusions and to provide full and accurate **documentation** for ideas that are not your own.

See
Pts.
7–8

Writing for Other Students. Before you submit a paper to an instructor, you may have an opportunity to participate in **peer review,** sharing your work with your fellow students and responding in writing to their work:

■ **Writing Drafts** If you know that other students will read a draft of your paper, you need to consider how they might react to your ideas. For example, are they likely to agree with you? To be shocked or offended by your paper's language or content? To be confused, or even mystified, by any of your references? Even if your readers are your own age, you cannot assume that they share your values or your cultural frame of reference. It is therefore very important that you maintain an appropriate tone and use moderate language in your paper and that you explain any historical, geographical, or cultural references that might be unfamiliar to your audience.

■ **Writing Comments** When you respond in writing to another student's paper, you need to take into account how your audience will react to your comments. Here too, your tone is important: you want to be encouraging and polite, offering constructive comments that can help your classmate write a stronger essay.

CHECKLIST

AUDIENCE CONCERNS FOR PEER-REVIEW PARTICIPANTS

To get the most out of a peer-review session, keep the following guidelines in mind:

☐ **Know your audience.** To be sure you understand what the student writer needs from your comments, read the paper several times before you begin writing your response.

☐ **Focus on the big picture.** Don't get bogged down on minor problems with punctuation or mechanics or become distracted by a paper's proofreading errors.

☐ **Look for a positive feature.** Try to zero in on what you think is the paper's greatest strength.

☐ **Be positive throughout.** Try to avoid words like *weak*, *poor*, and *bad*; instead, try using a compliment before delivering the "bad news": "Paragraph 2 is very well developed; can you add this kind of support in paragraph 4?"

☐ **Show respect.** It is perfectly acceptable to tell a writer that something is confusing or inaccurate, but don't go on the attack.

☐ **Be specific.** Avoid generalizations like "needs more examples" or "could be more interesting"; instead, try to offer helpful, focused suggestions: "You could add an example after the second sentence in paragraph 2"; "Explaining how this process operates would make your discussion more interesting."

☐ **Don't give orders.** Ask questions, and make suggestions.

☐ **Include a few words of encouragement.** Try to emphasize the paper's strong points.

2 Writing Essays

Writing is a constant process of decision making—of selecting, deleting, and rearranging material as you plan, shape, draft and revise, and edit and proofread your paper.

2a Planning Your Essay

See Ch. 1 Once you understand your **purpose** and **audience**, you are ready to begin planning your essay: choosing a topic to write about and deciding what to say about it.

1 Choosing a Topic

Most of the time, your instructor will steer you toward a topic by giving you an assignment. This assignment will usually specify the required length and format and give you a general subject (or a list of subjects from which to choose); sometimes the assignment will pose a question for you to answer.

Assignment: Write a short essay about a problem students face in adjusting to college.

Topic: Overcoming computer illiteracy

Before you begin to write, be sure your topic is narrow enough for your purpose, your audience, and your page limit. If it is not, you will need to narrow it further.

2 Finding Something to Say

Once you decide on your topic, you can begin to collect ideas for your paper, using one (or several) of the strategies listed below:

- **Reading and Observing** As you read textbooks, magazines, and newspapers and browse the Internet, as you engage in conversation with friends and family, and as you watch films and TV shows, look for ideas you can use.
- **Keeping a Journal** Try recording your thoughts about your topic in a print or electronic journal, where

you can explore ideas, ask questions, and draw tentative conclusions.

■ **Freewriting** Try doing timed, unstructured writing. Writing informally for five to ten minutes without stopping may unlock ideas and encourage you to make free associations about your topic.

■ **Brainstorming** On an unlined sheet of paper, write down everything you can think of about your topic—comments, questions, lists, single words, and even symbols and diagrams.

■ **Asking Questions** If you prefer an orderly, systematic way of finding material to write about, apply the familiar journalistic questions—*who? what? why? where? when?* and *how?*—to your topic.

■ **Doing Research** Many assignments require you to do library or Internet research. **See Part 6** for information on writing with sources.

ESL TIP

Some ESL students spend little time generating ideas for their writing because they are primarily concerned about writing grammatically correct sentences. But remember, the purpose of writing is to communicate your ideas. If you want to find material to write about, you will need to devote plenty of time to the activities described above.

2b Using a Thesis to Shape Your Material

Once you have collected material for your essay, your next step is to **shape** your material into a thesis-and-support structure.

A **thesis-and-support essay** includes a **thesis statement** (which expresses the **thesis,** or main idea, of the essay) and the specific information that explains and develops that thesis.

As the diagram on page 8 shows, the essay you write will consist of an **introductory paragraph**, which opens your essay and includes your thesis; a **concluding paragraph**, which gives your essay a sense of closure, perhaps restating your thesis; and a number of **body paragraphs,** which provide the support for your thesis statement.

See 3d

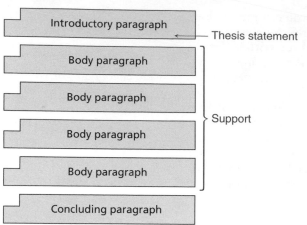

Introductory paragraph ← Thesis statement

Body paragraph

Body paragraph ⎫
Support
Body paragraph

Body paragraph ⎭

Concluding paragraph

CLOSE-UP

WRITING EFFECTIVE THESIS STATEMENTS

An effective thesis statement has four characteristics:

1. **An effective thesis statement clearly communicates your essay's main idea.** It tells your readers not only what your essay's topic is, but also how you will approach that topic and what you will say about it. Thus, your thesis statement reflects your essay's **purpose**.

See 1a

2. **An effective thesis statement is more than a general subject, a statement of fact, or an announcement of your intent.**

   Subject: Computers in college

   Statement of Fact: Computers are used extensively in college.

   Announcement: The essay that follows will show that computer literacy is important in college.

   Thesis Statement: Students who enter college with weak computer skills are at a significant disadvantage.

3. **An effective thesis statement is carefully worded.** Your thesis statement—usually expressed in a single concise sentence—should be direct and straightforward. Avoid vague phrases, such as *centers on, deals with, involves, revolves around,* or *is concerned with.* Do not include phrases like *As I will show, I plan to demonstrate,* and *It seems to me,* which weaken your

credibility by suggesting that your conclusions are based on opinion rather than on reading, observation, and experience.

4. **Finally, an effective thesis statement suggests your essay's direction, emphasis, and scope.** Your thesis statement should not make promises that your essay will not fulfill. It should suggest the major points you will cover and the order in which you will introduce them.

NOTE: As you write and rewrite, you may modify your essay's direction, emphasis, and scope; if you do so, you must also reword your thesis statement.

2c   Constructing an Informal Outline

Once you have decided on a thesis statement, you may want to construct an **informal outline** that arranges your essay's tentative main points and key supporting ideas in an orderly way. The following is an informal outline for the model student essay in **2f**.

College Students and Computer Literacy

Thesis statement: I was at a real disadvantage when I entered college because I lacked important computer skills.

Students' computer needs

- Basic word-processing programs
- Internet
- Email

Unprepared students

- No access at home
- No access at school

Consequences of computer illiteracy

- Difficulty with everyday tasks
- Embarrassment
- Missed opportunities

Possible solutions to problem

- Classes
- ??????

Personal experience

- Few computer skills
- Classes in computer lab

2d   Drafting and Revising

1 Writing a Rough Draft

When you write a rough draft, your goal is to get ideas down on paper so you can react to them. You will generally do several drafts of your essay, and you should expect to add or delete words, to reword sentences, to rethink ideas, and to reorder paragraphs. You should also expect to discover new ideas—or even to take an unexpected detour. At this point, concentrate on the body of your essay, and don't waste time writing the "perfect" introduction and conclusion.

To make revision easier, leave room on the page so that you can add material or rewrite. When you type, leave extra space between lines. Print out every draft, and edit by hand on the hard copy, typing in your changes on subsequent drafts.

2 Revising Your Drafts

When you revise, you "re-see" what you have written and write additional drafts. Everyone's revision process is different, but the following specific strategies can be helpful at this stage of the process:

See 29h1
- **Outline** your draft. An outline can help you check the logic of your paper's structure.
- **Use word-processing tools.** Use features like **Track Changes** and **Compare Drafts** to help you see how your revisions change your essay-in-progress.
- **Participate in peer review.** Ask a classmate to give you feedback on your draft.
- **Use instructors' comments.** Study your instructor's written comments on your draft, and arrange a conference if necessary.
- **Schedule a writing conference.** A writing center tutor can give you additional feedback on your draft.
- **Use a revision checklist.** Revise in stages, first looking at the whole essay and then turning your attention to the individual paragraphs, sentences, and words. Use the revision checklist that follows to guide you through the process.

CHECKLIST

REVISING YOUR ESSAY

The Whole Essay

☐ Are thesis and support logically related, with each body paragraph supporting your thesis statement? **(See 2b.)**

☐ Is your thesis statement clearly and specifically worded? **(See 2b.)**

☐ Have you discussed everything promised in your thesis statement? **(See 2b.)**

Paragraphs

☐ Does each body paragraph focus on one main idea, expressed in a clearly worded topic sentence? **(See 3a.)**

☐ Are the relationships of sentences within paragraphs clear? **(See 3b.)**

☐ Are your body paragraphs fully developed? **(See 3c.)**

☐ Does your introductory paragraph arouse interest and prepare readers for what is to come? **(See 3d1.)**

☐ Does your concluding paragraph sum up your essay's main idea? **(See 3d2.)**

Sentences

☐ Have you used correct sentence structure? **(See Chapters 5 and 6.)**

☐ Are your sentences varied? **(See Chapter 11.)**

☐ Have you eliminated wordiness and unnecessary repetition? **(See 12a–b.)**

☐ Have you avoided overloading your sentences with too many words, phrases, and clauses? **(See 12c.)**

☐ Have you avoided potentially confusing shifts in tense, voice, mood, person, or number? **(See 13a.)**

☐ Are your sentences constructed logically? **(See 13b–c.)**

☐ Have you strengthened your sentences by using parallel words, phrases, and clauses? **(See 14a.)**

☐ Have you placed modifiers clearly and logically? **(See Chapter 15.)**

Words

☐ Have you eliminated jargon, pretentious diction, clichés, and offensive language from your writing? **(See 16b–c.)**

CLOSE-UP

CHOOSING A TITLE

When you are ready to decide on a title for your essay, keep these criteria in mind:

- A title should convey your essay's focus, perhaps using key words and phrases from your essay or echoing the wording of your assignment.
- A title should arouse interest, perhaps with a provocative question, a quotation, or a controversial position.

Assignment: Write about a problem students face in adjusting to college.

Topic: Overcoming computer illiteracy

Possible Titles:

Computer Illiteracy: A Problem for College Students (echoes wording of assignment and uses key words from essay)

Can College Students Really Use Their Computers? (provocative question)

College Campuses and the "Digital Divide" (quotation)

The Plugged-In and the Unplugged: An Unfair Imbalance on College Campuses (controversial position)

2e Editing and Proofreading

When you **edit,** you concentrate on grammar, spelling, punctuation, and mechanics. When you **proofread,** you reread every word carefully to make sure you did not make any errors as you typed.

CLOSE-UP

PROOFREADING STRATEGIES

To help you proofread more effectively, try using these strategies:

- Read your paper aloud.
- Have a friend read your paper aloud to you.
- Read silently word by word, using your finger or a sheet of paper to help you keep your place.
- Read your paper's sentences in reverse order, beginning with the last sentence.

COMPUTER TIP   academic.cengage.com/eng/kirsznermandell

EDITING AND PROOFREADING

Here are some tips for effective editing and proofreading:

- As you edit, look at only a small portion of text at a time. Reduce the size of your window so that you can see only one or two lines of text at a time.
- Use the Search or Find command to look for words or phrases in usage errors that you commonly make—for instance, confusing *it's* with *its*. You can also uncover <u>sexist language</u> by searching for words such as *he, his, him,* or *man.*
- Remember that a spell checker will not catch a typo that creates a correctly spelled word—for example, *there* for *their* or *form* for *from.* Even after you run a spell check, you still must proofread your papers carefully.

See
16c2

2f **Model Student Paper**

Romney 1

Kimberly Romney
Professor Wilson
English 101
10 November 2006

Computer Illiteracy: A Problem for
College Students

Introduction   Today, most colleges expect entering students to be familiar with computers. From registering for courses to contacting professors, students are required to use computers on a daily basis. For this reason, students who enter college with weak

Thesis statement computer skills are at a significant disadvantage.

Importance of computers in society   Computers are increasingly important in today's society. As Henry Louis Gates, Jr., writes in his article "One Internet, Two Nations," many people are concerned that there is a division between those who have access to the Internet and those who do not. He writes, "Today we stand at the brink of becoming two societies, one largely white and plugged in and the other black and unplugged" (500). The gap between those who are technologically literate and those who are not (although it has narrowed since Gates wrote in 2002) extends beyond race and ethnicity to include the elderly, the disabled, and those who live in rural areas. This "digital divide" can cause serious problems for college students.

Importance of computers in college   Entering college students are expected to be familiar with a variety of software programs. Most

Romney 2

professors, for example, require their students to use *Microsoft Word* to write their papers, and many instructors expect their students to use *PowerPoint* to present their papers or research projects.

Students are also expected to be familiar with the Internet. For example, registration for classes is often conducted online. Professors and administrators use the Internet to post information about campuswide events, and many professors create their own Web pages where they post their syllabi and class assignments. Finally, professors expect their students to use the Internet when conducting research.

Importance of the Internet

A good understanding of how email works is also necessary for college success. If a student wants to communicate with someone in the class, email is one of the most efficient ways to do so. Email is also vital for communicating with professors. For example, if a student cannot attend office hours, he or she can still ask the professor a question.

Importance of email

Despite the importance of a strong working knowledge of computers and the Internet, many students (particularly older students who have been out of school for a few years) arrive at college with very little experience with either. In fact, computer illiteracy can be a real problem for entering college students. Some students have poor computer skills because they did not have access to a computer at home. Some families cannot afford computers, and others simply do not see a computer as a necessity.

Reason for students' poor skills: lack of access at home

Other students may not have been taught computer skills in elementary or high school. A recent

Romney 3

Reason for
students' poor
skills: lack of
access at
school

study of efforts to bridge the "digital divide" in
elementary and high schools reported that although
many schools are improving their access to computers,
teachers still might not use them in the classroom:

> Only 54 percent of respondents said
> they integrate computers into their
> daily curriculum, and more than 61
> percent of them said they do not have
> enough computers in their classrooms.
> More than half of teachers believe there
> should be one computer for each
> student, and nearly one-third of them
> say there should be one computer for
> every five students. (Jones)

Problems
caused by
weak
computer
skills

Those students who arrive at college with weak
computer skills face serious consequences. For
example, registering for classes on the Internet and
contacting professors or other students via email
become time-consuming (rather than timesaving)
tasks. Students may be so embarrassed by their weak
computer skills that they do not ask for help.
Without help, they have difficulty improving their
skills. As a result, they do not benefit from the
opportunities offered by the Internet (such as faster
and more thorough research) or by sophisticated
software programs (such as professional-looking
papers and presentations).

Possible
solution to
problems:
classes

Colleges and universities recognize the
problems these students face and offer programs to
help them. For example, our campus has an outreach
program aimed at students with sub-par computer

Romney 4

skills. Once a week, the computer lab offers classes
on software programs such as *Microsoft Word*,
PowerPoint, and *Dreamweaver*. A class about email
not only gives students basic information (such as
how to send and open attachments), but also tells
them how to use programs (such as *Outlook
Express*) to track their daily schedules and
appointments. The library also offers several
classes, both general and more discipline-specific,
about how to use the Internet for research.

However, while this outreach program can
provide students with opportunities to improve
their skills, many do not know about it. Students
are not given information about these classes at
orientation, and they are not well advertised in the
student newspaper, or even in the computer lab
and library. In addition, some staff members are
not very sensitive to the embarrassment that many
students feel about having poor computer skills.
Many students might avoid asking a librarian or
computer lab proctor for help, and this is a problem
that a good advertising campaign would remedy.

As a student from a small town where computer
classes were not a part of the high school curriculum,
I have personal experience with this problem. I came
to college with very limited computer skills.
Although I had some knowledge of *Microsoft Word*
and had used the Internet and email, I was not very
comfortable using computers. One of my first classes
here was a writing class that was held in a computer
lab. I was confronted with my problem every Monday,

Annotations in right margin:

Limitations
of classes

Personal
experience:
problems in
college

Romney 5

Wednesday, and Friday, and because I was embarrassed about my poor computer skills, I did not want to ask the professor for help. Trying to find help on my own was difficult. It took me two weeks to figure out when and where classes on *Microsoft Word* and the Internet were held. However, after taking these classes, my skills were greatly improved.

Personal experience: changes in high school

Through my own experience, I have come to realize that more efforts need to be made at the high school level to educate students about technology. In my own hometown, such efforts are already underway: my high school now has a computer lab, and the school district instituted a computer literacy class for all high school freshmen the year after I graduated.

According to my high school English teacher, Vicky Wellborn, students really enjoy this class: they go to the new computer lab during breaks or after school, and the lab is frequently full. In addition, the district now requires teachers to take a computer literacy class so that they are better prepared to answer students' questions (Wellborn).

Conclusion

Despite my own frustrating experiences, I am optimistic about the future. As high schools continue to make efforts to incorporate technology into the classroom, students entering college will be better prepared for the technological challenges they will face. And as they become more computer literate, the "digital divide" will close.

Romney 6

Works Cited

Gates, Henry Louis, Jr. "One Internet, Two Nations."
    The Blair Reader. Ed. Laurie G. Kirszner and
    Stephen R. Mandell. 4th ed. Upper Saddle
    River: Prentice, 2002. 499-501. Print.

Jones, K. C. "Survey Says." *Technology & Learning*
    26.3 (2005): 5. *Expanded Academic ASAP*.
    Web. 7 Oct. 2006.

Wellborn, Vicky. "Re: Computer Literacy." Message
    to the author. 23 Oct. 2006. E-mail.

3 Writing Paragraphs

A **paragraph** is a group of related sentences. It may be complete in itself or part of a longer piece of writing.

CHECKLIST

WHEN TO BEGIN A NEW PARAGRAPH

- ☐ Begin a new paragraph whenever you move from one major point to another.
- ☐ Begin a new paragraph whenever you move your readers from one time period or location to another.
- ☐ Begin a new paragraph whenever you introduce a major new step in a process or sequence.
- ☐ Begin a new paragraph when you want to emphasize an important idea.
- ☐ Begin a new paragraph every time a new person speaks.
- ☐ Begin a new paragraph to signal the end of your introduction and the beginning of your conclusion.

3a   Writing Unified Paragraphs

A paragraph is **unified** when it develops a single main idea. Each paragraph should have a **topic sentence** that states the main idea of the paragraph; the other sentences in the paragraph support that idea.

Topic sentence   I was a listening child, careful to hear the very different sounds of Spanish and English. Wide-eyed with hearing, I'd listen to sounds more than words. First, there were English (*gringo*) sounds. So many words were still unknown that when the butcher or the lady at the drugstore
Support   said something to me, exotic polysyllabic sounds would bloom in the midst of their sentences. Often the speech of people in public seemed to me very loud, booming with confidence. The man behind the counter would literally ask, "What can I do for you?" But by being so firm and so clear, the sound of his voice said that he was a *gringo;* he belonged in public society. (Richard Rodriguez, *Aria: A Memoir of a Bilingual Childhood*)

NOTE: A topic sentence usually comes at the beginning of a paragraph, but it may appear in the middle or at the end—or even be implied.

3b   Writing Coherent Paragraphs

A paragraph is **coherent** when all its sentences are logically related to one another. **Transitional words and phrases** clarify the relationships among sentences by establishing the spatial, chronological, and logical connections within a paragraph.

Topic sentence   Napoleon certainly made a change for the worse by leaving his small kingdom of Elba. After Waterloo, he went back to Paris, and he abdicated for a second time. A
Transitional words and phrases establish chronology of events   hundred days after his return from Elba, he fled to Rochefort in hope of escaping to America. Finally, he gave himself up to the English captain of the ship *Bellerophon.* Once again, he suggested that the Prince Regent grant him asylum, and once again, he was refused. In the end, all he saw of England was the Devon coast and Plymouth Sound as he passed on to the remote island of St. Helena. After six years of exile, he died on May 5, 1821, at the age of fifty-two. (Norman Mackenzie, *The Escape from Elba*)

USING TRANSITIONAL WORDS AND PHRASES

To Signal Sequence or Addition

again, also, besides, furthermore, moreover, in addition, first . . . second . . . third, one . . . another, too

To Signal Time

after, afterward, as soon as, at first, at the same time, before, earlier, finally, in the meantime, later, meanwhile, next, now, since, soon, subsequently, then, until

To Signal Comparison

also, by the same token, likewise, in comparison, similarly

To Signal Contrast

although, but, despite, even though, however, in contrast, instead, meanwhile, nevertheless, nonetheless, on the contrary, on the one hand . . . on the other hand, still, whereas, yet

To Introduce Examples

for example, for instance, namely, specifically

To Signal Narrowing of Focus

after all, indeed, in fact, in other words, in particular, specifically, that is

To Introduce Conclusions or Summaries

as a result, consequently, in summary, therefore, in conclusion, in other words, thus, to conclude

To Signal Concession

admittedly, certainly, granted, naturally, of course

To Introduce Causes or Effects

accordingly, as a result, because, consequently, hence, since, so, then, therefore

NOTE: <u>Parallel</u> words, phrases, and clauses ("<u>He was</u> a patriot. . . . <u>He was</u> a reformer. . . . <u>He was</u> an innovator. . . .") and repeated key words and phrases ("He invented a new type of <u>printing press</u>. . . . This <u>printing press</u>. . . .") can also help writers achieve coherence.

See 14a

3c   Writing Well-Developed Paragraphs

A paragraph is **well developed** when it includes all the support—examples, statistics, expert opinion, and so on—that readers need to understand and accept its main idea.

> Topic sentence

From Thanksgiving until Christmas, children are bombarded with ads for violent toys and games. Toy manufacturers persist in thinking that only toys that appeal to children's aggressiveness will sell. One television commercial praises the merits of a commando team that attacks and captures a miniature enemy base. Toy soldiers wear realistic uniforms and carry automatic rifles, pistols, knives, grenades, and ammunition. Another commercial shows laughing children shooting one another with plastic rocket fighters and tank-like vehicles. Despite claims that they (unlike action toys) have educational value, video games have increased the level of violence. The most popular video games involve children in strikingly realistic combat situations. One game lets children search out and destroy enemy fighters in outer space. Other best-selling games graphically simulate hand-to-hand combat on city streets. The real question is why parents buy these violent toys and games for their children. (student writer)

> Specific examples

> Specific examples

NOTE: Length alone does not determine whether a paragraph is well developed. The amount and kind of support you need depend on your audience, your purpose, and the scope of your paragraph's main idea.

3d   Writing Introductory and Concluding Paragraphs

1 Introductory Paragraphs

An **introductory paragraph** prepares readers for the essay to follow and makes them want to read further. Typically, it introduces the subject, narrows it, and then states the essay's thesis.

> Thesis statement

Although it has now faded from view, the telegraph lives on within the communications technologies that have subsequently built upon its foundations: the telephone, the fax machine, and, more recently, the Internet. And, ironically, it is the Internet—despite being regarded

> as a quintessentially modern means of communication—
> that has the most in common with its telegraphic ancestor.
> (Tom Standage, *The Victorian Internet*)

An introductory paragraph may also arouse readers' interest with a relevant quotation, a compelling question, a definition, or a controversial statement.

NOTE: Avoid introductions that simply announce your subject ("In my paper I will talk about Lady Macbeth") or that undercut your credibility ("I don't know much about alternative energy sources, but I would like to present my opinion").

CHECKLIST

REVISING INTRODUCTIONS

☐ Does your introduction include your essay's thesis statement?

☐ Does it lead naturally into the body of your essay?

☐ Does it arouse your readers' interest?

☐ Does it avoid statements that simply announce your subject or that undercut your credibility?

2 Concluding Paragraphs

A **concluding paragraph** reminds readers what they have read. Typically, it begins with specifics—for example, a review of the essay's main points—and then moves to more general statements.

> As an Arab-American, I feel I have the best of two worlds. I'm proud to be part of the melting pot, proud to contribute to the tremendous diversity of cultures, customs and traditions that make this country unique. But Arab-bashing—public acceptance of hatred and bigotry—is something no American can be proud of. (Ellen Mansoor Collier, "I Am Not a Terrorist")

A concluding paragraph may also offer a prediction, a warning, a recommendation, or a relevant quotation.

NOTE: Avoid conclusions that just repeat your introduction in different words or that undermine your concluding points ("I may not be an expert" or "At least this is my opinion"). If possible, end with a statement that readers will remember.

CHECKLIST

REVISING CONCLUSIONS

☐ Does your conclusion sum up your essay, perhaps by reviewing the essay's main points?

☐ Does it do more than just repeat the introduction?

☐ Does it avoid apologies?

☐ Does it end memorably?

4   Writing an Argumentative Essay

4a   Organizing an Argumentative Essay

In its simplest form, an argument consists of a thesis statement and supporting evidence. However, argumentative essays frequently use special strategies to win audience approval and to overcome potential opposition.

CLOSE-UP

ELEMENTS OF AN ARGUMENTATIVE ESSAY

See
3d1

Introduction

The <u>introduction</u> of your argumentative essay acquaints readers with your subject. Here you show how your subject concerns your audience and establish common ground with your readers.

See
2b

Thesis Statement

Most often, you present your <u>thesis statement</u> in your introduction. However, if you are presenting a highly controversial argument, you may postpone stating your thesis until later in your essay.

Background

In this section, you can summarize others' opinions on the issue, give definitions of key terms, or review basic facts.

Arguments in Support of Your Thesis

Here you present your points along with the evidence to support them. Most often, you begin with your weakest argument and work up to your strongest.

Refutation of Opposing Arguments

In an argumentative essay, you should summarize and **refute**—disprove or call into question—the major arguments against your thesis.

Conclusion

Often, the <u>conclusion</u> restates the major arguments in support of your thesis. Your conclusion can also summarize key points, restate your thesis, or remind readers of the weaknesses of opposing arguments. Many writers like to end their arguments with a statement that sums up their main point.

See 3d2

4b Model Argumentative Essay

The following argumentative essay includes many of the elements discussed in the Close-up box above. The student draws her supporting evidence from her own knowledge and experience as well as from research.

Samantha Masterton

Professor Egler

English 102

4 April 2007

The Returning Student: Older Is Definitely Better

Introduction

After graduating from high school, young people must decide what they want to do with the rest of their lives. Many graduates (often without much thought) decide to continue their education uninterrupted, and they go on to college. This group of teenagers makes up what many see as typical first-year college students. Recently, however, this stereotype has been challenged by an influx of older students, including myself, into American colleges and universities. Not only do these students make a valuable contribution to the schools they attend, but they also offer an alternative to young people who go to college simply because they do not know what else

Thesis statement

to do. A few years off between high school and college can give many students the life experience they need to appreciate the value of higher education.

Background

The college experience of an eighteen-year-old is quite different from that of an older "nontraditional" student. The typical high school graduate is often concerned with things other than cracking books—for example, going to parties, dating, and testing personal limits. However, older students—those who are twenty-five years of age or older—take seriously the idea of returning to college. Although many high school students do not think twice about whether or not to attend college, older

Masterton 2

students have much more to consider when they think about returning to college. For example, they must decide how much time they can spend getting their degree and consider the impact attending college will have on their family and their finances.

Most older students return to school with clear goals. A US Department of Education report called *Nontraditional Undergraduates* shows that more than one-third of nontraditional students decided to attend college because it was required by their job, and eighty-seven percent enrolled in order to gain skills (10). Getting a college degree is often a requirement for professional advancement, and older students are therefore more likely to take college seriously. For older students, college is often an extension of work rather than a place to discover what they want to be when they graduate. A study by psychologists R. Eric Landrum, Je T'aime Hood, and Jerry M. McAdams concluded, "Nontraditional students seemed to be more appreciative of their opportunities, as indicated by their higher enjoyment of school and appreciation of professors' efforts in the classroom" (744).

Older students also understand the actual benefits of doing well in school and successfully completing a degree program. Older students I have known rarely cut lectures or put off studying. This is because older students are often balancing the demands of home and work, and they know how important it is to do well. The difficulties of juggling school, family, and work force older

Argument in support of thesis

Argument in support of thesis

students to be disciplined and focused. As a result, older students spend more hours per week studying and tend to have a higher GPA than younger students do (Landrum, Hood, and McAdams 742-43).

Personal experience used as evidence in support of thesis

My observations of older students have convinced me that many students would benefit from delaying entry into college. Given their greater maturity and experience, older students bring more into the classroom than younger students do. Eighteen-year-olds are often immature and inexperienced. They have not formulated definite goals or developed firm ideas about themselves or about the world in which they live. In contrast, older students have had a variety of real-life experiences. Most have worked for several years, and many have started families. As a result, they are better prepared for college than they would have been when they were young.

Refutation of opposing argument

Of course, postponing college for a few years is not for everyone. Certainly some teenagers have a definite sense of purpose and maturity, and these individuals would benefit from an early college experience. For example, Charles Woodward, a law librarian, went to college directly after high school, and for him the experience was positive. "I was serious about learning, and I loved my subject," he said. "I felt fortunate that I knew what I wanted from college and from life." Many younger students, however, are not like Woodward; they graduate from high school without any clear sense of purpose. For this reason, they should postpone college until they are mature enough to benefit from the experience.

Masterton 4

Granted, some older students have difficulties when they return to college. Because these students have been out of school so long, they may have difficulty studying. As I have seen, though, these problems disappear after a period of adjustment, and older students quickly adapt to college. Of course, it is true that many older students have trouble balancing the needs of their family with the demands of college. However, this challenge is becoming easier with the growing number of online courses, the availability of distance education, and the introduction of governmental programs, such as educational tax credits (Agbo 164-65).

Refutation of opposing argument

All things considered, higher education is often wasted on the young, who are either too immature or too unfocused to take advantage of it. Taking a few years off between high school and college would give these students the time they need to make the most of a college education. The increasing number of older students returning to college seems to indicate that many students are taking this path. According to a US Department of Education report, *Digest of Education Statistics, 2001*, forty percent of students enrolled in American colleges in 2000 were twenty-five years of age or older. Older students such as these have taken time off to serve in the military, to gain valuable work experience, or to raise a family. By the time they get to college, they have defined their goals and made a firm commitment to achieve them. It is clear that postponing college a few years can result in a better educational experience.

Conclusion

Masterton 5

Works-cited
list begins
new page

Works Cited

Agbo, S. "The United States: Heterogeneity of the
Student Body and the Meaning of
'Nontraditional' in U.S. Higher Education."
*Higher Education and Lifelong Learners:
International Perspectives on Change*. Ed.
Hans G. Schuetze and Maria Slowey. London:
Routledge, 2000. 149-69. Print.

Landrum, R. Eric, Je T'aime Hood, and Jerry M.
McAdams. "Satisfaction with College by
Traditional and Nontraditional College
Students." *Psychological Reports* 89.3 (2001):
740-46. Print.

United States. Dept. of Educ. Office of Educ.
Research and Improvement. Natl. Center for
Educ. Statistics. *Digest of Education Statistics,
2001*. By Thomas D. Snyder. 2002. *National
Center for Education Statistics*. Web. 27 Feb.
2007.

Four sets of
unspaced
hyphens
indicate that
*United States,
Dept. of
Educ., Office
of Educ.
Research and
Improvement,
and Natl.
Center for
Educ.
Statistics* are
repeated from
previous entry

---. ---. ---. ---. *Nontraditional Undergraduates*.
By Susan Choy. 2002. *National Center for
Education Statistics*. Web. 27 Feb. 2007.

Woodward, Charles B. Personal interview. 21 Mar.
2007.

PART 2

Writing Grammatical Sentences

See
A2.3
A **run-on** is an error that occurs when two **independent clauses** are joined incorrectly. There are two kinds of run-ons.

A **comma splice** is a run-on that occurs when two independent clauses are joined with just a comma. A **fused sentence** is a run-on that occurs when two independent clauses are joined with no punctuation.

> **Comma Splice:** Charles Dickens created the character of Mr. Micawber, he also created Uriah Heep.

> **Fused Sentence:** Charles Dickens created the character of Mr. Micawber he also created Uriah Heep.

GRAMMAR CHECKER

IDENTIFYING COMMA SPLICES

Your word processor's grammar checker will highlight comma splices and prompt you to revise them. It may also offer suggestions for revision.

> Comma Use:
> I went to the mall, she went to the beach.

CLOSE-UP

REVISING COMMA SPLICES AND FUSED SENTENCES

To revise a comma splice or fused sentence, use one of the following four strategies:

1. Add a period between the clauses, creating two separate sentences.
2. Add a semicolon between the clauses, creating a compound sentence.
3. Add an appropriate coordinating conjunction, creating a compound sentence.
4. Add a subordinating conjunction or relative pronoun, creating a complex sentence.

5b Correcting Comma Splices and Fused Sentences

1 Adding a Period

You can add a period between the independent clauses, creating two separate sentences. This is a good strategy to use when the clauses are long or when they are not closely related.

In 1894 Frenchman Alfred Dreyfus was falsely con-
victed of treason, his struggle for justice pitted the
army against the civil libertarians.

(edit: period inserted after "treason"; "his" capitalized to "His")

2 Adding a Semicolon

You can add a **semicolon** between two closely related clauses that convey parallel or contrasting information.

See 19a

Chippendale chairs have straight legs however, Queen Anne chairs have curved legs.

(edit: semicolon inserted after "legs")

NOTE: When you use a **transitional word or phrase** (such as *however*, *therefore*, or *for example*) to connect two independent clauses, the transitional element must be preceded by a semicolon and followed by a comma. If you use a comma alone, you create a comma splice. If you omit punctuation entirely, you create a fused sentence.

See 3b

3 Adding a Coordinating Conjunction

You can use a coordinating conjunction (*and, or, but, nor, for, so, yet*) to join two closely related clauses of equal importance into one **compound sentence**. The coordinating conjunction you choose indicates the relationship between the clauses: addition (*and*), contrast (*but, yet*), causality (*for, so*), or a choice of alternatives (*or, nor*). Be sure to add a comma before the coordinating conjunction.

See 11a1

Elias Howe invented the sewing machine, and Julia Ward Howe was a poet and social reformer.

(edit: "and" inserted after comma)

4 Adding a Subordinating Conjunction or Relative Pronoun

When the ideas in two independent clauses are not of equal importance, you can use an appropriate subordinating

See
11a2
conjunction or a relative pronoun to join the clauses into one **complex sentence**, placing the less important idea in the dependent clause.

> Stravinsky's ballet *The Rite of Spring* shocked Parisians
> in 1913, *because* its rhythms seemed erotic.

> Lady Mary Wortley Montagu *, who* had suffered from
> smallpox herself, ~~she~~ helped spread the practice of
> inoculation.

6 Revising Sentence Fragments

6a Recognizing Sentence Fragments

A **sentence fragment** is an incomplete sentence—a clause or a phrase—that is punctuated as if it were a sentence. A sentence may be incomplete for any of the following reasons:

■ **It lacks a subject.**

> Many astrophysicists now believe that galaxies are
> distributed in clusters. <u>And even form supercluster
> complexes.</u>

■ **It lacks a verb.**

> Every generation has its defining moments. <u>Usu-
> ally the events with the most news coverage.</u>

■ **It lacks both a subject and a verb.**

See
A1.3
> Researchers are engaged in a variety of studies.
> <u>Suggesting a link between alcoholism and heredity.</u>
> (*Suggesting* is a **verbal**, which cannot serve as a
> sentence's main verb.)

See
A2.3
■ **It is a <u>dependent clause</u>.**

> Bishop Desmond Tutu was awarded the 1984 Nobel
> Peace Prize. <u>Because he struggled to end apartheid.</u>

> The pH meter and the spectrophotometer are two
> scientific instruments. <u>That changed the chemistry
> laboratory dramatically.</u>

NOTE: A sentence cannot consist of a single clause that begins with a subordinating conjunction (such as *because*) or a relative pronoun (such as *that*); moreover, unless it is a question, a sentence cannot consist of a single clause beginning with *when, where, who, which, what, why,* or *how.*

GRAMMAR CHECKER

IDENTIFYING FRAGMENTS

Your grammar checker will identify many (although not all) sentence fragments. However, not every word group identified as a fragment will actually be a fragment. You, not your grammar checker, will have to make the final decision about whether or not a sentence is grammatically complete—and how to correct it.

> Fragment:
> Present and past, town and country, familiar and foreign.

6b Correcting Sentence Fragments

If you identify a fragment in your writing, use one of the following strategies to correct it.

1 Attaching the Fragment to an Independent Clause

In most cases, the simplest way to correct a fragment is by attaching it to an adjacent independent clause that contains the missing words.

President Johnson did not seek reelection, ~~For~~ *for* a number of reasons. (**prepositional phrase** fragment)
See A2.3

Students sometimes take a leave of absence, ~~To~~ *to* decide on definite career goals. (**verbal phrase** fragment)
See A2.3

The pilot changed course, *realizing* ~~Realizing~~ that the weather was worsening. (verbal phrase fragment)

Brian was the star forward of the Blue Devils, *the* ~~The~~ team with the best record. (**appositive** fragment)
See 9b3

Fairy tales are full of damsels in distress, such as
Rapunzel. (appositive fragment)

People with dyslexia have trouble reading, and may also
find it difficult to write. (part of compound predicate)

They took only a compass and a canteen, and some
trail mix. (part of compound object)

See
A2.3
Property taxes rose sharply, although city services
declined. (**dependent clause** fragment)

The battery is dead, which means the car won't
start. (dependent clause fragment)

CLOSE-UP

LISTS

See
22a1
When a fragment takes the form of a **list**, add a colon to
connect the list to the independent clause that introduces it.

Tourists often outnumber residents in at least four
European cities: Venice, Florence, Canterbury, and Bath.

---

2 Deleting the Subordinating Conjunction or Relative Pronoun

When a fragment consists of a dependent clause that is
punctuated as though it were a complete sentence, you
can correct it by attaching it to an adjacent independent clause, as illustrated in **6b1**. Alternatively, you can
simply delete the subordinating conjunction or relative
pronoun.

Property taxes rose sharply. ~~Although~~ City services
declined. (subordinating conjunction *although* deleted)

The battery is dead. ~~Which~~ This means the car won't start.
(relative pronoun *which* replaced by *this*, a word that
can serve as the sentence's subject)

NOTE: Simply deleting the subordinating conjunction or relative pronoun, as in the two examples on page 36, is usually the least desirable way to revise a sentence fragment because it is likely to create two choppy sentences and obscure the connection between them.

3 Supplying the Missing Subject or Verb

Another way to correct a fragment is to add the missing words (a subject or a verb or both) that are needed to make the fragment a sentence.

> In 1948, India became independent. ~~Divided~~ *It was divided* into the nations of India and Pakistan. (verbal phrase fragment)

> A familiar trademark can increase a product's sales. ~~Reminding~~ *It reminds* shoppers that the product has a longstanding reputation. (verbal phrase fragment)

CLOSE-UP

FRAGMENTS INTRODUCED BY TRANSITIONS

Some fragments are word groups that are introduced by **transitional words and phrases**, such as *also*, *finally*, *in addition*, and *now*, but are missing subjects and verbs. To correct such a fragment, you need to add the missing subject and verb.

See 3b

> Finally, *he found* a new home for the family.

> In addition, *we need* three new keyboards for the computer lab.

6c Using Fragments Intentionally

Fragments are often used in speech and informal writing as well as in journalism, creative writing, and advertising. In professional and academic writing, however, sentence fragments are generally not acceptable.

CHECKLIST

USING FRAGMENTS INTENTIONALLY

It is permissable to use fragments in the following special situations:

- [ ] In lists
- [ ] In captions that accompany visuals
- [ ] In topic outlines
- [ ] In quoted dialogue
- [ ] In bulleted or numbered lists in *PowerPoint* presentations
- [ ] In titles and subtitles of papers and reports

---

7 Understanding Agreement

Agreement is the correspondence between words in number, gender, or person. Subjects and verbs agree in **number** (singular or plural) and **person** (first, second, or third); pronouns and their antecedents agree in number, person, and gender.

See 13a4

7a Making Subjects and Verbs Agree

Singular subjects take singular verbs, and plural subjects take plural verbs.

See 8b1

Present tense verbs, except *be* and *have*, add *-s* or *-es* when the subject is third-person singular. (Third-person singular subjects include nouns; the personal pronouns *he*, *she*, *it*, and *one*; and many **indefinite pronouns**.)

See 7a4

The <u>President</u> <u>has</u> the power to veto congressional legislation.

<u>She</u> frequently <u>cites</u> statistics to support her points.

In every group <u>somebody</u> <u>emerges</u> as a natural leader.

Present tense verbs do not add *-s* or *-es* when the subject is a plural noun, a first-person or second-person pronoun (*I*, *we*, *you*), or a third-person plural pronoun (*they*).

<u>Experts</u> <u>recommend</u> that dieters avoid processed meat.

At this stratum, <u>we</u> <u>see</u> rocks dating back ten million years.

<u>They</u> <u>say</u> that some wealthy people have defaulted on their student loans.

In some situations, making subjects and verbs agree can cause problems for writers.

1 Words between Subject and Verb

If a modifying phrase comes between the subject and the verb, the verb should agree with the subject, not with a word in the modifying phrase.

The <u>sound</u> of the drumbeats <u>builds</u> in intensity in Eugene O'Neill's play *The Emperor Jones.*

The <u>games</u> won by the intramural team <u>are</u> few and far between.

This rule also applies to phrases introduced by *along with, as well as, in addition to, including,* and *together with.*

Heavy <u>rain</u>, along with high winds, <u>causes</u> hazardous driving conditions.

2 Compound Subjects Joined by *And*

Compound subjects joined by *and* usually take plural verbs.

<u>Air bags and antilock brakes</u> <u>are</u> standard on all new models.

There are, however, two exceptions to this rule. First, when a compound subject joined by *and* stands for a single idea or person, it is treated as a unit and takes a singular verb: *<u>Rhythm and blues</u> <u>is</u> a forerunner of rock and roll.*

Second, when *each* or *every* precedes a compound subject joined by *and,* the subject takes a singular verb: *<u>Every desk and file cabinet</u> <u>was</u> searched before the letter was found.*

3 Compound Subjects Joined by *Or*

Compound subjects joined by *or* may take either singular or plural verbs.

If both subjects are singular, use a singular verb; if both are plural, use a plural verb. If a singular and a plural subject are linked by *or* (or by *either . . . or, neither . . . nor,* or *not only . . . but also*), the verb agrees with the subject that is nearer to it.

<u>Either radiation treatments or chemotherapy</u> <u>is</u> combined with surgery for effective results.

<u>Either chemotherapy or radiation treatments</u> <u>are</u> combined with surgery for effective results.

4 Indefinite Pronouns

ESL
45c3 Most **indefinite pronouns**—*another, anyone, everyone, one, each, either, neither, anything, everything, something, nothing, nobody,* and *somebody*—are singular and take singular verbs.

<u>Anyone</u> <u>is</u> welcome to apply for this grant.

Some indefinite pronouns—*both, many, few, several, others*—are plural and take plural verbs.

<u>Several</u> of the articles <u>are</u> useful.

A few indefinite pronouns—*some, all, any, more, most,* and *none*—can be singular or plural, depending on the noun they refer to.

<u>Some</u> of this trouble <u>is</u> to be expected. (*Some* refers to *trouble*.)

<u>Some</u> of the spectators <u>are</u> getting restless. (*Some* refers to *spectators*.)

GRAMMAR CHECKER

SUBJECT-VERB AGREEMENT

Your word processor's grammar checker will highlight and offer revision suggestions for many subject-verb agreement errors, including errors in sentences that have indefinite pronoun subjects.

Subject-Verb Agreement:

All of these little details makes the contract hard to understand.

Suggestions:

make

---

5 Collective Nouns

A **collective noun** names a group of persons or things—for instance, *navy, union, association, band.* When a collective noun refers to the group as a unit (as it usually does), it takes a singular verb; when it refers to the individuals or items that make up the group, it takes a plural verb.

To many people, <u>the royal family</u> <u>symbolizes</u> Great Britain. (The family, as a unit, is the symbol.)

The family all eat at different times. (Each member eats separately.)

Phrases that name fixed amounts—*three-quarters, twenty dollars, the majority*—are treated like collective nouns. When the amount denotes a unit, it takes a singular verb; when it denotes part of the whole, it takes a plural verb.

Three-quarters of his usual salary is not enough to live on.

Three-quarters of the patients improve dramatically after treatment.

NOTE: *The number is always singular, and a number is always plural: The number of voters has declined; A number of students have missed the opportunity to preregister.*

6 Singular Subjects with Plural Forms

A singular subject takes a singular verb even if the form of the subject is plural.

Statistics deals with the collection and analysis of data.

When such a word has a plural meaning, however, use a plural verb.

The statistics prove him wrong.

7 Inverted Subject-Verb Order

Even when **word order** is inverted so that the verb comes before the subject (as it does in questions and in sentences beginning with *there is* or *there are*), the subject and verb must agree. ESL 45f

Is either answer correct?

There are currently thirteen circuit courts of appeals in the federal system.

8 Linking Verbs

A **linking verb** should agree with its subject, not with the subject complement. See 10a

The problem was termites.

Termites were the problem.

9 Relative Pronouns

See
A1.2
When you use a **relative pronoun** (*who, which, that,* and so on) to introduce a dependent clause, the verb in the dependent clause should agree in number with the pronoun's **antecedent,** the word to which the pronoun refers.

> The farmer is among the <u>ones</u> who <u>suffer</u> during a grain embargo.

> The farmer is the only <u>one</u> who <u>suffers</u> during a grain embargo.

7b Making Pronouns and Antecedents Agree

Singular pronouns—such as *he, him, she, her, it, me, myself,* and *oneself*—should refer to singular antecedents. Plural pronouns—such as *we, us, they, them,* and *their*—should refer to plural antecedents.

1 Compound Antecedents

In most cases, use a plural pronoun to refer to a **compound antecedent** (two or more antecedents connected by *and*).

> <u>Mormonism and Christian Science</u> were similar in <u>their</u> beginnings.

However, there are several exceptions to this general rule:

■ Use a singular pronoun when a compound antecedent is preceded by *each* or *every.*

> <u>Every programming language and software package</u> has <u>its</u> limitations.

■ Use a singular pronoun to refer to two or more singular antecedents linked by *or* or *nor.*

> <u>Neither Thoreau nor Whitman</u> lived to see <u>his</u> work read widely.

■ When one part of a compound antecedent is singular and one part is plural, the pronoun agrees in person and number with the antecedent that is nearer to it.

Neither the boy nor his parents had fastened their seatbelts.

2 Collective Noun Antecedents

If the meaning of a collective noun antecedent is singular (as it will be in most cases), use a singular pronoun. If the meaning is plural, use a plural pronoun.

The teachers' union announced its plan to strike. (The members acted as a unit.)

The team moved to their positions. (Each member acted individually.)

3 Indefinite Pronoun Antecedents

See 7a4

Most **indefinite pronouns**—*each, either, neither, one, anyone,* and the like—are singular and take singular pronouns.

Neither of the men had his proposal ready by the deadline.

Each of these neighborhoods has its own traditions and values.

A few indefinite pronouns are plural; others can be singular or plural.

CLOSE-UP

Pronoun-Antecedent Agreement

In speech and in informal writing, many people use the plural pronouns *they* or *their* with singular indefinite pronouns that refer to people, such as *someone, everyone,* and *nobody.*

Everyone can present their own viewpoint.

In college writing, however, you should avoid using a plural pronoun with a singular subject. Instead, you can use both the masculine and the feminine pronoun.

(continued)

See
16c2

> **PRONOUN-ANTECEDENT AGREEMENT** *(continued)*
>
> <u>Everyone</u> can present <u>his or her</u> own viewpoint.
>
> Or, you can make the sentence's subject plural.
>
> <u>All participants</u> can present <u>their</u> own viewpoints.
>
> The use of *his* to refer to a singular indefinite pronoun is considered **sexist language**: *<u>Everyone</u> can present <u>his</u> own viewpoint.*

GRAMMAR CHECKER

PRONOUN-ANTECEDENT AGREEMENT

Your word processor's grammar checker will highlight and offer revision suggestions for many pronoun-antecedent agreement errors.

Pronoun Use:

Someone should take responsibility for their actions.

Suggestions:

his or her

---

8 Using Verbs

8a Using Irregular Verbs

A **regular verb** forms both its past tense and its past participle by adding *-d* or *-ed* to the **base form** of the verb (the present tense form of the verb that is used with *I*).

PRINCIPAL PARTS OF REGULAR VERBS		
Base Form	**Past Tense Form**	**Past Participle**
smile	smiled	smiled
talk	talked	talked

Irregular verbs do not follow this pattern. The chart that follows lists the principal parts of the most frequently used irregular verbs.

FREQUENTLY USED IRREGULAR VERBS

Base Form	Past Tense Form	Past Participle
arise	arose	arisen
awake	awoke, awaked	awoke, awaked
be	was/were	been
beat	beat	beaten
begin	began	begun
bend	bent	bent
bet	bet, betted	bet
bite	bit	bitten
blow	blew	blown
break	broke	broken
bring	brought	brought
build	built	built
burst	burst	burst
buy	bought	bought
catch	caught	caught
choose	chose	chosen
cling	clung	clung
come	came	come
cost	cost	cost
deal	dealt	dealt
dig	dug	dug
dive	dived, dove	dived
do	did	done
drag	dragged	dragged
draw	drew	drawn
drink	drank	drunk
drive	drove	driven
eat	ate	eaten
fall	fell	fallen
fight	fought	fought
find	found	found
fly	flew	flown
forget	forgot	forgotten, forgot
freeze	froze	frozen
get	got	gotten
give	gave	given
go	went	gone
grow	grew	grown
hang (suspend)	hung	hung
have	had	had
hear	heard	heard
keep	kept	kept
know	knew	known
lay (place/put)	laid	laid
lead	led	led
lend	lent	lent

(continued)

FREQUENTLY USED IRREGULAR VERBS *(continued)*

Base Form	Past Tense Form	Past Participle
let	let	let
lie (recline)	lay	lain
make	made	made
prove	proved	proved, proven
read	read	read
ride	rode	ridden
ring	rang	rung
rise	rose	risen
run	ran	run
say	said	said
see	saw	seen
set (place)	set	set
shake	shook	shaken
shrink	shrank, shrunk	shrunk, shrunken
sing	sang	sung
sink	sank	sunk
sit	sat	sat
speak	spoke	spoken
speed	sped, speeded	sped, speeded
spin	spun	spun
spring	sprang	sprung
stand	stood	stood
steal	stole	stolen
strike	struck	struck, stricken
swear	swore	sworn
swim	swam	swum
swing	swung	swung
take	took	taken
teach	taught	taught
throw	threw	thrown
wake	woke, waked	waked, woken
wear	wore	worn
wring	wrung	wrung
write	wrote	written

CLOSE-UP

LIE/LAY AND SIT/SET

Lie means "to recline" and does not take an object ("He likes to *lie* on the floor"); *lay* means "to place" or "to put" and does take an object ("He wants to *lay* a rug on the floor").

Base Form	Past Tense Form	Past Participle
lie	lay	lain
lay	laid	laid

Sit means "to assume a seated position" and does not take an object ("She wants to *sit* on the table"); *set* means "to place" or "to put" and usually takes an object ("She wants to *set* a vase on the table").

Base Form	Past Tense Form	Past Participle
sit	sat	sat
set	set	set

8b Understanding Tense

Tense is the form a verb takes to indicate when an action occurred or when a condition existed.

ESL
45a2

ENGLISH VERB TENSES

Simple Tenses

Present (I *finish*, he or she *finishes*)

Past (I *finished*)

Future (I *will finish*)

Perfect Tenses

Present perfect (I *have finished*, he or she *has finished*)

Past perfect (I *had finished*)

Future perfect (I *will have finished*)

Progressive Tenses

Present progressive (I *am finishing*, he or she *is finishing*)

Past progressive (I *was finishing*)

Future progressive (I *will be finishing*)

Present perfect progressive (I *have been finishing*)

Past perfect progressive (I *had been finishing*)

Future perfect progressive (I *will have been finishing*)

1 Using the Simple Tenses

The **simple tenses** include *present*, *past*, and *future:*

■ The **present tense** usually indicates an action that is taking place at the time it is expressed or an action that occurs regularly.

> I <u>see</u> your point. (an action taking place when it is expressed)
>
> We <u>wear</u> wool in the winter. (an action that occurs regularly)

CLOSE-UP

SPECIAL USES OF THE PRESENT TENSE

The present tense has four special uses.

To Indicate Future Time: The grades <u>arrive</u> next Thursday.

To State a Generally Held Belief: Studying <u>pays</u> off.

To State a Scientific Truth: An object at rest <u>tends</u> to stay at rest.

To Discuss a Literary Work: *Family Installments* <u>tells</u> the story of a Puerto Rican family.

■ The **past tense** indicates that an action has already taken place.

> John Glenn <u>orbited</u> the Earth three times on February 20, 1962. (an action completed in the past)
>
> As a young man, Mark Twain <u>traveled</u> through the Southwest. (an action that occurred once or many times in the past but did not extend into the present)

■ The **future tense** indicates that an action will or is likely to take place.

> Halley's Comet <u>will reappear</u> in 2061. (a future action that will definitely occur)
>
> The housing boom in Nevada <u>will</u> probably <u>continue</u>. (a future action that is likely to occur)

2 Using the Perfect Tenses

The **perfect tenses** indicate actions that were or will be completed before other actions or conditions. The perfect tenses are formed with the appropriate tense form of the auxiliary verb *have* plus the past participle:

- The **present perfect** tense can indicate either of two kinds of continuing action beginning in the past.

  Dr. Kim <u>has finished</u> studying the effects of BHA on rats. (an action that began in the past and is finished at the present time)

  My mother <u>has invested</u> her money wisely. (an action that began in the past and extends into the present)

- The **past perfect** tense indicates an action occurring before a certain time in the past.

  By 1946, engineers <u>had built</u> the first electronic digital computer.

- The **future perfect** tense indicates that an action will be finished by a certain future time.

  By Tuesday, the transit authority <u>will have run</u> out of money.

3 Using the Progressive Tenses

The **progressive tenses** indicate continuing action. They are formed with the appropriate tense of the verb *be* plus the present participle:

- The **present progressive** tense indicates that something is happening at the time it is expressed in speech or writing.

  The volcano <u>is erupting</u>, and lava <u>is flowing</u> toward the town.

- The **past progressive** tense can indicate either of two kinds of past action.

  Roderick Usher's actions <u>were becoming</u> increasingly bizarre. (a continuing action in the past)

  The French revolutionary Marat was stabbed to death while he <u>was bathing</u>. (an action occurring at the same time in the past as another action)

- The **future progressive** tense indicates a continuing action in the future.

    The treasury secretary <u>will be monitoring</u> the money supply very carefully.

- The **present perfect progressive** tense indicates action continuing from the past into the present and possibly into the future.

    Rescuers <u>have been working</u> around the clock.

- The **past perfect progressive** tense indicates that a past action went on until another one occurred.

    President Kennedy <u>had been working</u> on civil rights legislation before he was assassinated.

- The **future perfect progressive** tense indicates that an action will continue until a certain future time.

    By eleven o'clock, we <u>will have been driving</u> for seven hours.

8c Understanding Mood

Mood is the form a verb takes to indicate whether a writer is making a statement, asking a question, giving a command, or expressing a wish or a contrary-to-fact statement. There are three moods in English: the *indicative*, the *imperative*, and the *subjunctive*.

The **indicative** mood states a fact, expresses an opinion, or asks a question: *Jackie Robinson <u>had</u> a great impact on professional baseball.*

The **imperative** mood is used in commands and direct requests: <u>*Use*</u> *a dictionary.*

The **subjunctive** mood is used to express wishes, contrary-to-fact conditions, and requests or recommendations:

- The **present subjunctive** is used in *that* clauses after words such as *ask, demand, suggest, require,* and *recommend.* The present subjunctive uses the base form of the verb, regardless of the subject.

    Captain Ahab demanded that his crew <u>hunt</u> the white whale.

    The report recommended that doctors <u>be</u> more flexible.

- The **past subjunctive** is used in **conditional statements** (statements beginning with *if, as if,* or *as though* that are contrary to fact and statements that express a wish). The past subjunctive has the same form as the past tense of the verb, except for the verb *be,* which uses *were,* even with singular subjects.

> If John <u>went</u> home, he could see Marsha. (John is not home.)

> The father acted as if he <u>were</u> having the baby. (The father couldn't be having the baby.)

> I wish I <u>were</u> more organized. (expresses a wish)

8d Understanding Voice

Voice is the form a verb takes to indicate whether the subject of a sentence acts or is acted upon. When the subject of a verb does something—that is, acts—the verb is in the **active voice.** When something is done to the subject of a verb—that is, the subject is acted upon—the verb is in the **passive voice.**

Active Voice: Hart Crane <u>wrote</u> *The Bridge.*

Passive Voice: *The Bridge* <u>was written</u> by Hart Crane.

Because the active voice emphasizes the person or thing performing an action, it is usually clearer and more emphatic than the passive voice. Whenever possible, use active voice in your college writing.

> *The students chose investigative*
> <del>Investigative</del> reporter Bob Woodward <del>was chosen by the students</del> as the graduation speaker.

Some situations, however, require the use of the passive voice—for example, when the actor is unknown or when the action itself is more important than the actor.

> Grits <u>are eaten</u> throughout the South. (Passive voice emphasizes the fact that grits are eaten; who eats them is not important.)

> DDT <u>was found</u> in soil samples. (Passive voice emphasizes the discovery of DDT; who found it is not important.)

9 Using Pronouns

9a Understanding Pronoun Case

Pronouns change **case** to indicate their function in a sentence. English has three cases: *subjective*, *objective*, and *possessive*.

PRONOUN CASE FORMS							
Subjective							
I	he, she	it	we	you	they	who	whoever
Objective							
me	him, her	it	us	you	them	whom	whomever
Possessive							
my mine	his, her hers	its	our ours	your yours	their theirs	whose	

1 Subjective Case

A pronoun takes the **subjective case** in these situations.

Subject of a Verb: <u>I</u> bought a new mountain bike.

Subject Complement: It was <u>he</u> for whom the men were looking.

2 Objective Case

A pronoun takes the **objective case** in these situations.

Direct Object: Our sociology teacher asked Adam and <u>me</u> to work on the project.

Indirect Object: The plumber's bill gave <u>him</u> quite a shock.

Object of a Preposition: Between <u>us</u> we own ten shares of stock.

> ## CLOSE-UP
>
> ### PRONOUN CASE WITH PREPOSITIONS
>
> *I* is not necessarily more appropriate than *me*. In the following situation, *me* is correct.
>
> Just between you and <u>me</u> [not *I*], I think the data are incomplete. (*Me* is the object of the preposition *between*.)

3 Possessive Case

A pronoun takes the **possessive case** when it indicates ownership (*our* car, *your* book). The possessive case is also used before a **gerund**.

See A1.3

Napoleon approved of <u>their</u> [not *them*] ruling Naples. (*Ruling* is a gerund.)

9b Determining Pronoun Case in Special Situations

1 Comparisons with *Than* or *As*

When a comparison ends with a pronoun, the pronoun's function in the sentence determines your choice of pronoun case. If the pronoun functions as a subject, use the subjective case; if it functions as an object, use the objective case. You can determine the function of the pronoun by completing the comparison.

Darcy likes John more than <u>I</u>. (*I* is the subject: more than *I* like John.)

Darcy likes John more than <u>me</u>. (*Me* is the object: more than she likes *me*.)

2 *Who* and *Whom*

The case of the pronouns *who* and *whom* depends on their function *within their own clause*. When a pronoun serves as the subject of its clause, use *who* or *whoever*; when it functions as an object, use *whom* or *whomever*.

The Salvation Army gives food and shelter to <u>whoever</u> is in need. (*Whoever* is the subject of the dependent clause.)

I wonder <u>whom</u> jazz musician Miles Davis influenced. (*Whom* is the object of *influenced* in the dependent clause.)

CLOSE-UP

PRONOUN CASE IN QUESTIONS

To determine the case of *who* at the beginning of a question, use a personal pronoun to answer the question. The case of *who* should be the same as the case of the personal pronoun.

<u>Who</u> wrote *The Age of Innocence?* <u>She</u> wrote it. (subject)

<u>Whom</u> do you support for mayor? I support <u>her</u>. (object)

---

3 Appositives

ESL
45c4 An **appositive** is a noun or noun phrase that identifies or renames an adjacent noun or pronoun. The case of a pronoun in an appositive depends on the function of the word the appositive identifies or renames.

Two artists, <u>he</u> and Smokey Robinson, recorded for Motown Records. (*Artists* is the subject of the sentence, so the pronoun in the appositive *he and Smokey Robinson* takes the subjective case.)

We heard two Motown recording artists, Smokey Robinson and <u>him</u>. (*Artists* is the object of the verb *heard*, so the pronoun in the appositive *Smokey Robinson and him* takes the objective case.)

4 *We* and *Us* before a Noun

When a first-person plural pronoun directly precedes a noun, the case of the pronoun depends on the way the noun functions in the sentence.

<u>We</u> women must stick together. (*Women* is the subject of the sentence, so the pronoun *we* takes the subjective case.)

Good teachers make learning easy for <u>us</u> students. (*Students* is the object of the preposition *for*; so the pronoun *us* takes the objective case.)

9c Revising Pronoun Reference Errors

ESL
45c1 An **antecedent** is the word or word group to which a pronoun refers. The connection between a pronoun and its antecedent should always be clear.

1 Ambiguous Antecedents

Sometimes it is not clear to which antecedent a pro-noun—for example, *this, that, which,* or *it*—refers. In such cases, eliminate the ambiguity by substituting a noun for the pronoun.

The accountant took out his calculator and completed
the tax return. Then, he put ~~it~~ *the calculator* into his briefcase. (The pronoun *it* can refer either to *calculator* or to *tax return.*)

Sometimes a pronoun—for example, *this*—does not seem to refer to any specific antecedent. In such cases, supply a noun to clarify the reference.

Some one-celled organisms contain chlorophyll yet
are considered animals. This *paradox* illustrates the difficulty

of classifying single-celled organisms. (Exactly what
does *this* refer to?)

2 Remote Antecedents

The farther a pronoun is from its antecedent, the more difficult it is for readers to make a connection between them. If a pronoun's antecedent is far away from it, re-place the pronoun with a noun.

During the mid-1800s, many Czechs began to immi-

grate to America. By 1860, about 23,000 Czechs had

left their country. By 1900, 13,000 Czech immigrants
America's
were coming to ~~its~~ shores each year.

3 Nonexistent Antecedents

Sometimes a pronoun refers to an antecedent that does not appear in the sentence. In such cases, replace the pro-noun with a noun.

Our township has decided to build a computer lab in
Teachers
the elementary school. ~~They~~ feel that fourth-graders

should begin using computers. (*They* refers to an antecedent the writer has failed to mention.)

CLOSE-UP

WHO, WHICH, AND *THAT*

In general, *who* refers to people or to animals that have names. *Which* and *that* refer to objects, events, or unnamed animals. When referring to an antecedent, be sure to choose the appropriate pronoun (*who, which,* or *that*).

David Henry Hwang, <u>who</u> wrote the Tony Award–winning play *M. Butterfly,* also wrote *Family Devotions* and *FOB.*

The spotted owl, <u>which</u> lives in old-growth forests, is in danger of extinction.

Houses <u>that</u> are built today are usually more energy efficient than those built twenty years ago.

Never use *that* to refer to a person:

The man ~~that~~ *who* won the trophy is my neighbor.

See 18d1 **NOTE:** *Which* introduces **nonrestrictive clauses**, which are set off by commas. *That* introduces **restrictive clauses**, which are not set off by commas. *Who* can introduce either restrictive or nonrestrictive clauses.

10   Using Adjectives and Adverbs

Adjectives and adverbs describe, limit, or qualify other words, phrases, or clauses. **Adjectives** modify nouns and pronouns. **Adverbs** modify verbs, adjectives, or other adverbs—or entire phrases, clauses, or sentences.

The function of a word, not its form, determines whether it is an adjective or an adverb. Although many adverbs (such as *immediately* and *hopelessly*) end in *-ly,* others (such as *almost* and *very*) do not. Moreover, some words that end in *-ly* (such as *lively*) are adjectives. To determine whether a modifier is an adjective or an adverb, you must locate the word it modifies and determine what part of speech the word is.

ESL TIP

For information on correct placement of adjectives and adverbs in a sentence, **see 45d1**. For information on correct order of adjectives in a series, **see 45d2**.

10a Using Adjectives

Be sure to use an adjective, not an adverb, as a subject complement. A **subject complement** is a word that follows a linking verb and modifies the sentence's subject, not its verb. A **linking verb** does not show physical or emotional action. *Seem, appear, believe, become, grow, turn, remain, prove, look, sound, smell, taste, feel,* and the forms of the verb *be* are (or can be used as) linking verbs.

See
A1.3

> Michelle seemed <u>brave</u>. (*Seemed* shows no action, so it is a linking verb. Because *brave* is a subject complement that modifies the noun *Michelle*, it takes the adjective form.)

> Michelle smiled <u>bravely</u>. (*Smiled* shows action, so it is not a linking verb. Because *bravely* modifies *smiled*, it takes the adverb form.)

NOTE: Some verbs can function as either linking verbs or action verbs.

> He looked <u>hungry</u>. (*Looked* is a linking verb; *hungry* modifies the subject.)

> He looked <u>hungrily</u> at the sandwich. (*Looked* is an action verb; *hungrily* modifies the verb.)

10b Using Adverbs

Be sure to use an adverb, not an adjective, to modify verbs, adjectives, or other adverbs—or entire phrases, clauses, or sentences.

> Most students did ~~great~~ ^{very well} on the midterm.

> My parents dress a lot more ~~conservative~~ ^{conservatively} than my friends do.

CLOSE-UP

USING ADJECTIVES AND ADVERBS

In informal speech, adjective forms such as *good, bad, sure, real, slow, quick,* and *loud* are often used to modify verbs, adjectives, and adverbs. Avoid these informal modifiers in college writing.

The program ran ~~real good~~ the first time we tried it,
but the new system performed ~~bad~~.

(corrections: "really well" above "real good"; "badly" above "bad")

10c Using Comparative and Superlative Forms

Most adjectives and adverbs have **comparative** and **superlative** forms that are used to indicate degree.

COMPARATIVE AND SUPERLATIVE FORMS		
Form	**Function**	**Example**
Positive	Describes a quality; indicates no comparisons	big, easily
Comparative	Indicates comparisons between two qualities (greater or lesser)	bigger, more easily
Superlative	Indicates comparisons among more than two qualities (greatest or least)	biggest, most easily

NOTE: Some adverbs, particularly those indicating time, place, and degree (*almost, very, here, yesterday,* and *immediately*), do not have comparative or superlative forms.

1 Regular Comparative and Superlative Forms

To form the comparative and superlative, all one-syllable adjectives and many two-syllable adjectives (particularly those that end in *-y, -ly, -le, -er,* and *-ow*) add *-er* or *-est*: slow*er*, funni*er*; slow*est*, funni*est*. (Note that a final *y* becomes *i* before the *-er* or *-est* is added.)

Other two-syllable adjectives and all long adjectives form the comparative with *more* and the superlative with *most:* <u>more</u> famous, <u>more</u> incredible; <u>most</u> famous, <u>most</u> incredible.

Adverbs ending in *-ly* also form the comparative with *more* and the superlative with *most:* <u>more</u> slowly; <u>most</u> slowly. Other adverbs use the *-er* and *-est* endings: soon<u>er</u>; soon<u>est</u>.

All adjectives and adverbs indicate a lesser degree with *less* (<u>less</u> lovely; <u>less</u> slowly) and the least degree with *least* (<u>least</u> lovely; <u>least</u> slowly).

CLOSE-UP

USING COMPARATIVES AND SUPERLATIVES

■ Never use both *more* and *-er* to form the comparative, and never use both *most* and *-est* to form the superlative.

Nothing could have been ~~more~~ easier.

Jack is the ~~most~~ meanest person in town.

■ Never use the superlative when comparing only two things.

     older
Stacy is the ~~oldest~~ of the two sisters.
        ^

■ Never use the comparative when comparing more than two things.

    earliest
We chose the ~~earlier~~ of the four appointments.
      ^

---

2 Irregular Comparative and Superlative Forms

Some adjectives and adverbs have irregular comparative and superlative forms.

IRREGULAR COMPARATIVE AND SUPERLATIVE FORMS			
	Positive	**Comparative**	**Superlative**
Adjectives:	good	better	best
	bad	worse	worst
	a little	less	least
	many, some much	more	most
Adverbs:	well	better	best
	badly	worse	worst

CLOSE-UP

ILLOGICAL COMPARATIVE AND SUPERLATIVE FORMS

Adjectives that denote absolute states can logically exist only in the positive degree. For example, words such as *perfect, unique, empty, excellent, impossible, parallel,* and *dead* cannot have comparative or superlative forms.

I read ~~the most~~ ^an^ excellent story.

The bobbleheads in her collection were ~~very~~ unique.

These words can, however, be modified by words that suggest approaching the absolute state—*nearly* or *almost,* for example.

He revised until his draft was <u>almost perfect</u>.

PART 3

Writing Effective Sentences

11 Writing Varied Sentences

11a Using Compound and Complex Sentences

See A2.2 Paragraphs that mix <u>simple sentences</u> with compound and complex sentences are more varied—and therefore more interesting—than those that do not.

1 Compound Sentences

A **compound sentence** consists of two or more independent clauses joined with *coordinating conjunctions, transitional words and phrases, correlative conjunctions, semicolons,* or *colons.*

Coordinating Conjunctions

> The pianist made some mistakes, <u>but</u> the concert was a success.

NOTE: Use a comma before the coordinating conjunction—See A2.3 *and, or, nor, but, for, so,* and *yet*—that joins the two <u>independent clauses</u>.

Transitional Words and Phrases

> The saxophone does not belong to the brass family; <u>in fact</u>, it is a member of the woodwind family.

NOTE: Use a semicolon—not a comma—before the transitional word or phrase that joins the two independent See 3b clauses. Frequently used **transitional words and phrases** include conjunctive adverbs such as *consequently, finally, still,* and *thus* as well as expressions such as *for example, in fact,* and *for instance.*

Correlative Conjunctions

> <u>Either</u> he left his coat in his locker, <u>or</u> he left it on the bus.

Semicolons

> Alaska is the largest state; Rhode Island is the smallest.

Colons

> He got his orders: he was to leave for Iraq on Sunday.

2 Complex Sentences

A **complex sentence** consists of one independent clause and at least one <u>**dependent clause**</u>. In a complex sentence, a **subordinating conjunction** or **relative pronoun** links the independent and dependent clauses and indicates the relationship between them.

See A2.3

      (dependent clause)   (independent clause)
[<u>After</u> the town was evacuated], [the hurricane began].

    (independent clause)   (dependent clause)
[Officials watched the storm] [<u>that</u> threatened to destroy the town].

                  (dependent clause)
Town officials, [<u>who</u> were very concerned], watched the storm.

FREQUENTLY USED SUBORDINATING CONJUNCTIONS		
after	before	until
although	if	when
as	once	whenever
as if	since	where
as though	that	wherever
because	unless	while

RELATIVE PRONOUNS		
that	whatever	who (whose, whom)
what	which	whoever (whomever)

11b Varying Sentence Length

Strings of short simple sentences can be tedious—and sometimes hard to follow, as the following paragraph indicates.

> John Peter Zenger was a newspaper editor. He waged and won an important battle for freedom of the press in America. He criticized the policies of the British governor. He was charged with criminal libel as a result. Zenger's lawyers were disbarred by the governor. Andrew Hamilton defended him. Hamilton convinced the jury that Zenger's criticisms were true. Therefore, the statements were not libelous.

You can revise choppy sentences like these by using *coordination, subordination,* or *embedding* to combine them with adjacent sentences.

Coordination pairs similar elements—words, phrases, or clauses—giving equal weight to each.

Two choppy sentences linked with *and,* creating compound sentence

John Peter Zenger was a newspaper editor. He waged and won an important battle for freedom of the press in America. He criticized the policies of the British governor and he was charged with criminal libel as a result. Zenger's lawyers were disbarred by the governor. Andrew Hamilton defended him. Hamilton convinced the jury that Zenger's criticisms were true. Therefore, the statements were not libelous.

ESL TIP

Some ESL students rely on simple sentences and coordination in their writing because they are afraid of making sentence structure errors. The result is a monotonous style. To add variety, try using **subordination** and **embedding** (explained below) in your sentences.

Subordination places the more important idea in an independent clause and the less important idea in a dependent clause.

Simple sentences become dependent clauses, creating two complex sentences

John Peter Zenger was a newspaper editor who waged and won an important battle for freedom of the press in America. He criticized the policies of the British governor, and he was charged with criminal libel as a result. When Zenger's lawyers were disbarred by the governor, Andrew Hamilton defended him. Hamilton convinced the jury that Zenger's criticisms were true. Therefore, the statements were not libelous.

Embedding is the working of additional words and phrases into sentences.

The sentence *Hamilton convinced the jury . . .* becomes the phrase *convincing the jury*

John Peter Zenger was a newspaper editor who waged and won an important battle for freedom of the press in America. He criticized the policies of the British governor, and he was charged with criminal libel as a result. When Zenger's lawyers were disbarred by the governor, Andrew Hamilton defended him, convincing the jury that Zenger's criticisms were true. Therefore, the statements were not libelous.

This final revision of the original paragraph's choppy sentences is interesting and readable because it is now composed of varied and logically linked sentences. The final short simple sentence has been retained for emphasis.

11c Varying Sentence Openings

Rather than beginning every sentence with the subject (*I*, *He*, or *It*, for example), begin some sentences with modifying words, phrases, or clauses.

Words

<u>Proud</u> and <u>relieved</u>, they watched their daughter receive her diploma.

<u>Hungrily</u>, he devoured his lunch.

Phrases

<u>For better or for worse</u>, credit cards are now widely available to college students.

<u>Located on the west coast of Great Britain</u>, Wales is part of the United Kingdom.

<u>His interests widening</u>, Picasso designed ballet sets and illustrated books.

Clauses

<u>After Woodrow Wilson was incapacitated by a stroke</u>, his wife unofficially performed many presidential duties.

12 Writing Concise Sentences

A sentence is not concise simply because it is short; a **concise** sentence contains only the words necessary to make its point.

12a Eliminating Wordiness

Whenever possible, delete nonessential words—*deadwood*, *utility words*, and *circumlocution*—from your writing.

1 Eliminating Deadwood

The term **deadwood** refers to unnecessary phrases that take up space and add nothing to meaning.

Many
~~There were many~~ factors ~~that~~ influenced his decision to become a priest.

The two plots are ~~both~~ similar in ~~the way~~ that they trace the characters' increasing rage.

is
The only truly tragic character in *Hamlet*, ~~would have to be~~ Ophelia.

This
~~In this~~ article ~~it~~ discusses lead poisoning.

Deadwood also includes unnecessary statements of opinion, such as *I feel, it seems to me, I believe,* and *in my opinion.*

The
~~In my opinion, I believe the~~ characters seem undeveloped.

This
~~As far as I'm concerned, this~~ course looks interesting.

2 Eliminating Utility Words

Utility words function as filler; they contribute nothing to the meaning of a sentence. Utility words include nouns with imprecise meanings (*factor, situation, type, aspect,* and so on); adjectives so general that they are almost meaningless (*good, bad, important*); and common adverbs denoting degree (*basically, actually, quite, very, definitely*). Often, you can just delete a utility word; if you cannot, replace it with a more precise word.

Registration
~~The registration situation~~ was disorganized.

an
The scholarship ~~basically~~ offered Fran ~~a good~~ opportunity to study Spanish.

It was ~~actually~~ a worthwhile book, but I didn't ~~completely~~ finish it.

3 Avoiding Circumlocution

Circumlocution is taking a roundabout way to say something (using ten words when five will do). Instead of complicated constructions, use concise, specific words and phrases that come right to the point.

~~It is not unlikely that the~~ *The* trend toward lower consumer spending will *probably* continue.

Joe was in the army *while* ~~during the same time that~~ I was in college.

CLOSE-UP

REVISING WORDY PHRASES

If you cannot edit a wordy construction, substitute a more concise, more direct term.

Wordy	Concise
at the present time	now
due to the fact that	because
in the vicinity of	near
have the ability to	be able to

12b Eliminating Unnecessary Repetition

Redundant word groups (repeated words or phrases that say the same thing, such as *unanticipated surprise*) and other kinds of unnecessary repetition can annoy readers and obscure your meaning. Correct unnecessary repetition by using one of the following strategies.

1 Deleting Redundancy

People's clothing ~~attire~~ can reveal a good deal about their personalities.

The two candidates share several positions ~~in common~~.

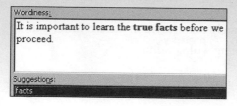

GRAMMAR CHECKER

DELETING REDUNDANCY

Your word processor's grammar checker will often highlight redundant expressions and offer suggestions for revision.

2 Substituting a Pronoun

Fictional detective Miss Marple has solved many crimes. *The Murder at the Vicarage* was one of ∧*her* ~~Miss Marple's~~ most challenging cases.

3 Creating an Appositive

Red Barber,′ ~~was~~ a sportscaster,′∧~~He~~ was known for his colorful expressions.

4 Creating a Compound

John F. Kennedy was the youngest man ever elected president,∧*and* ~~He was~~ the first Catholic to hold this office.

5 Creating a Complex Sentence

Americans value freedom of speech,∧*, which* ~~Freedom of speech~~ is guaranteed by the First Amendment.

12c　Tightening Rambling Sentences

The combination of nonessential words, unnecessary repetition, and complicated syntax creates **rambling sentences.** Revising rambling sentences frequently requires extensive editing.

1 Eliminating Excessive Coordination

When you string a series of clauses together with coordinating conjunctions, you create a rambling, unfocused **compound sentence**. To revise such sentences, first identify the main idea, and state it in an independent clause; then, subordinate the supporting details. See 11a1

> **Wordy:** Puerto Rico is a large island in the Caribbean, and it is very mountainous, and it has steep slopes, and they fall to gentle plains along the coast.

> **Concise:** A large island in the Caribbean, Puerto Rico is very mountainous, with steep slopes falling to gentle plains along the coast. (Puerto Rico's mountainous terrain is the sentence's main idea.)

2 Eliminating Adjective Clauses

A series of **adjective clauses** is also likely to produce a rambling sentence. To revise, substitute concise modifying words or phrases for adjective clauses. See A2.3

> **Wordy:** *Moby-Dick*, <u>which is a novel about a white whale</u>, was written by Herman Melville, <u>who was friendly with Nathaniel Hawthorne</u>, <u>who urged him to revise the first draft</u>.

> **Concise:** *Moby-Dick*, a novel about a white whale, was written by Herman Melville, who revised the first draft at the urging of his friend Nathaniel Hawthorne.

3 Eliminating Passive Constructions

Excessive use of the **passive voice** can create rambling sentences. Correct this problem by changing passive voice to active voice. See 8d

> ~~Water rights are being fought for in court by~~ Indian tribes like the Papago in Arizona and the Pyramid Lake Paiute in Nevada. *are fighting in court for water rights.*

GRAMMAR CHECKER

ELIMINATING PASSIVE CONSTRUCTIONS

Your word processor's grammar checker will highlight passive voice constructions in your writing and offer revision suggestions.

Passive Voice:

High test scores that will improve his grade point average are being achieved by the student.

Suggestions:

The student is achieving high test scores that will improve his grade point average

---

4 Eliminating Wordy Prepositional Phrases

See A2.3

When you revise, substitute adjectives or adverbs for wordy **prepositional phrases**.

The trip was ~~one of danger~~ *dangerous* but also *exciting.* ~~one of excitement.~~

He spoke ~~in a confident manner~~ *confidently* and ~~with a lot of authority.~~ *authoritatively.*

5 Eliminating Wordy Noun Constructions

See A2.3

Substitute strong verbs for wordy **noun phrases**.

We have ~~made the decision~~ *decided* to postpone the meeting until ~~the appearance of~~ all the board members *appear*.

13 Revising Awkward or Confusing Sentences

The most common causes of awkward or confusing sentences are *unnecessary shifts, mixed constructions, faulty predication,* and *illogical comparisons.*

13a Revising Unnecessary Shifts

1 Shifts in Tense

Verb **tense** in a sentence or in a related group of sentences should shift only for good reason—to indicate changes of time, for example. Unnecessary shifts in tense can be confusing.

See 8b; ESL 45a2

> I registered for the advanced philosophy seminar be-
> cause I wanted a challenge. However, by the first week
> *started*
> I ~~start~~ having trouble understanding the reading. (un-
> necessary shift from past to present)

2 Shifts in Voice

Unnecessary shifts from active to passive **voice** (or from passive to active) can be confusing.

See 8d; ESL 45a6

> F. Scott Fitzgerald wrote *This Side of Paradise*, and
> *wrote*
> later *The Great Gatsby* ~~was written.~~ (unnecessary shift
> from active to passive)

3 Shifts in Mood

Unnecessary shifts in **mood** can also create awkward sentences.

See 8c

> *be*
> Next, heat the mixture in a test tube, and ~~you should~~
> ~~make~~ sure it does not boil. (unnecessary shift from
> imperative to indicative)

4 Shifts in Person and Number

Person indicates who is speaking (first person—*I, we*), who is spoken to (second person—*you*), and who is spoken about (third person—*he, she, it,* and *they*). Most often, unnecessary shifts between the second and the third person are responsible for awkward sentences.

ESL 45a1

> *you*
> When ~~one~~ ~~looks~~ for a car loan, you compare the in-
> terest rates of several banks. (unnecessary shift from
> third to second person)

Number indicates one (singular—*novel, it*) or more than one (plural—*novels, they, them*). Singular pronouns

See 9c; ESL 45c1

should refer to singular **antecedents** and plural pronouns to plural antecedents.

If a person does not study regularly, ~~they~~ *he or she* will have a difficult time passing Spanish. (unnecessary shift from singular to plural)

13b Revising Mixed Constructions

A **mixed construction** occurs when a dependent clause, prepositional phrase, or independent clause is incorrectly used as the subject of a sentence.

Because she studies every day, ~~explains why~~ she gets good grades. (dependent clause incorrectly used as subject)

By calling for information, ~~is the way to~~ *you can* learn more about the benefits of ROTC. (prepositional phrase incorrectly used as subject)

Being ~~He was~~ late ~~was what~~ made him miss Act 1. (independent clause incorrectly used as subject)

13c Revising Faulty Predication

Faulty predication occurs when a sentence's predicate does not logically complete its subject. Faulty predication often occurs in sentences that contain a linking verb—a form of the verb *be*, for example—and a subject complement.

Mounting costs and decreasing revenues ~~were~~ *caused* the downfall of the hospital.

Faulty predication also occurs in one-sentence definitions that contain the construction *is where* or *is when*. In a definition, *is* must be preceded and followed by a noun or noun phrase.

Taxidermy is *the construction of* ~~where you construct~~ a lifelike representation of an animal from its preserved skin.

Finally, faulty predication occurs when the phrase *the reason is* precedes *because*. In this situation, *because* (which means "for the reason that") is redundant and should be deleted.

The reason we drive is *that* ~~because~~ we are afraid to fly.

14 Using Parallelism

Parallelism—the use of matching words, phrases, or clauses to express equivalent ideas—adds unity, balance, and coherence to your writing. Effective parallelism makes sentences easier to follow and emphasizes connections among equivalent ideas, but faulty parallelism can create awkward sentences that obscure your meaning and confuse readers.

14a Using Parallelism Effectively

1 With Items in a Series

Items in a series should be presented in parallel terms.

<u>Eat</u>, <u>drink</u>, and <u>be</u> merry.

<u>Baby food consumption</u>, <u>toy production</u>, and <u>minivan sales</u> are likely to decline as the U.S. population ages.

2 With Paired Items

Paired words, phrases, or clauses should be presented in parallel terms.

The thank-you note was <u>short</u> but <u>sweet</u>.

<u>Ask not what your country can do for you</u>; <u>ask what you can do for your country</u>. (John F. Kennedy)

Paired items linked by **correlative conjunctions** (such as *not only . . . but also* and *either . . . or*) should always be parallel.

The designer paid attention not only <u>to color</u> but also <u>to texture</u>.

Either <u>repeat physics</u> or <u>take calculus</u>.

Parallelism is also used with paired elements linked by *than* or *as*.

Richard Wright and James Baldwin chose <u>to live in Paris</u> rather than <u>to remain in the United States</u>.

NOTE: Elements in **outlines** and **lists** should also be parallel.

See 29h1, 40c

14b Revising Faulty Parallelism

Faulty parallelism occurs when matching words, phrases, or clauses are not used to express equivalent ideas.

> Many developing countries lack sufficient housing, sufficient food, and ~~their~~ <u>sufficient</u> health-care facilities ~~are also insufficient~~.

To correct faulty parallelism, match nouns with nouns, verbs with verbs, and phrases or clauses with similarly constructed phrases or clauses.

> Popular exercises for men and women include spinning, weight <u>lifting</u> ~~lifters~~, and jogging.

> I look forward to hearing from you and to <u>having</u> ~~have~~ an opportunity to tell you more about myself.

CLOSE-UP

REPEATING KEY WORDS

Although the use of similar grammatical structures may be enough to convey parallelism, sometimes sentences are even clearer if certain key words (for example, articles, prepositions, and the *to* in infinitives) are also repeated in each element of a pair or series. In the following sentence, repeating the preposition *by* makes it clear that *not* applies only to the first phrase.

> Computerization has helped industry by not allowing labor costs to skyrocket, <u>by</u> increasing the speed of production, and <u>by</u> improving efficiency.

GRAMMAR CHECKER

REVISING FAULTY PARALLELISM

Grammar checkers are not very useful for identifying faulty parallelism. Although your grammar checker may highlight some nonparallel constructions, it may miss others.

15 Placing Modifiers Carefully

A **modifier** is a word, phrase, or clause that describes, limits, or qualifies another word in the sentence. A modifier should be placed close to the word it modifies.

Wendy watched the storm, <u>fierce and threatening</u>. (*fierce and threatening* modifies *storm*)

Faulty modification is the awkward or confusing placement of modifiers or the modification of nonexistent words.

GRAMMAR CHECKER

REVISING FAULTY MODIFICATION

Your grammar checker will identify some modification problems, including certain awkward **split infinitives**. However, the grammar checker will not offer revision suggestions.

See 15b

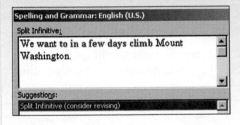

15a Revising Misplaced Modifiers

A **misplaced modifier** is a word or word group whose placement suggests that it modifies one word when it is intended to modify another.

Confusing: <u>With an IQ of just 52</u>, the lawyer argued that his client should not get the death penalty. (Does the lawyer have an IQ of 52?)

Revised: The lawyer argued that his client, <u>with an IQ of just 52</u>, should not get the death penalty.

75

1 Placing Modifying Words Precisely

Limiting modifiers—such as *almost*, *only*, *even*, *hardly*, *just*, *merely*, *nearly*, *exactly*, *scarcely*, and *simply*—should always immediately precede the words they modify. Different placements change the meaning of the sentence.

> Nick *just* set up camp at the edge of town. (He did it just now.)
>
> *Just* Nick set up camp at the edge of town. (He did it alone.)
>
> Nick set up camp *just* at the edge of town. (His camp was precisely at the edge.)

When a limiting modifier is placed so that it is not clear whether it modifies a word before it or one after it, it is called a **squinting modifier**.

> The life that everyone thought would fulfill her <u>totally</u> bored her.

To correct a squinting modifier, place the modifier so that it is clear which word it modifies.

> The life that everyone thought would <u>totally</u> fulfill her bored her. (She was expected to be totally fulfilled.)
>
> The life that everyone thought would fulfill her bored her <u>totally</u>. (She was totally bored.)

2 Relocating Misplaced Phrases

To avoid ambiguity, place **phrases** as close as possible to the words they modify:

■ Place verbal phrases directly before or directly after the words they modify.

> *Roller-skating along the shore,*
> Jane watched the boats. ~~roller skating along the shore.~~

■ Place prepositional phrase modifiers immediately after the words they modify.

> *with no arms*
> *Venus de Milo* is a statue created by a famous artist. ~~with no arms.~~

3 Relocating Misplaced Dependent Clauses

A dependent clause that serves as a modifier must be clearly related to the word it modifies.

■ An **adjective clause** usually appears immediately after the word it modifies.

> This diet program *,which will benefit everyone,* will limit the consumption of possible carcinogens ~~, which will benefit everyone.~~

■ An **adverb clause** may appear in various positions, as long as its relationship to the word it modifies is clear.

> When Lincoln was president, the Civil War raged.

> The Civil War raged when Lincoln was president.

15b Revising Intrusive Modifiers

An **intrusive modifier** awkwardly interrupts a sentence, making the sentence difficult to understand.

Revise when a long modifying phrase comes between an auxiliary verb and a main verb.

> *Without*
> ~~She had, without~~ giving it a second thought or considering the consequences, *she had* ~~planned~~ to reenlist.

Revise when a modifier creates an awkward **split infinitive**—that is, when the modifier comes between (*splits*) the word *to* and the base form of the verb.

> *defeat his opponent*
> He hoped to quickly and easily ~~defeat his opponent.~~

NOTE: A split infinitive is acceptable when the intervening modifier is short, especially if the alternative would be awkward or ambiguous: *She expected to almost beat her previous record.*

15c Revising Dangling Modifiers

A **dangling modifier** is a word or phrase that cannot logically modify any word in the sentence.

> Using this drug, many undesirable side effects are experienced. (Who is using this drug?)

One way to correct this dangling modifier is to supply a subject that *using this drug* can modify.

Using this drug, <u>patients</u> experience many undesirable side effects.

Another way to correct the dangling modifier is to change it into a dependent clause.

Many undesirable side effects are experienced <u>when this drug is used</u>.

CLOSE-UP

DANGLING MODIFIERS AND THE PASSIVE VOICE

See 8d; ESL 45a6
Many sentences that include dangling modifiers are in the passive voice. Changing the **passive voice** to the **active voice** corrects the dangling modifier by changing the subject of the sentence's main clause (*side effects*) to a word that the dangling modifier can logically modify (*patients*).

---

16 Choosing Words

16a Choosing the Right Word

1 Denotation and Connotation

A word's **denotation** is its basic dictionary meaning— what it stands for without any emotional associations. A word's **connotations** are the emotional, social, and political associations it has in addition to its denotative meaning.

Word	Denotation	Connotation
politician	someone who holds a political office	opportunist; wheeler-dealer

If you use terms without considering their connotations, you risk confusing and possibly angering your readers.

ESL TIP

Dictionary entries sometimes give a word's connotations as well as its denotations. You can increase your understanding of a word's connotations by paying attention to the context in which the word appears.

2 Euphemisms

A **euphemism** is a mild or polite term used in place of a blunt term that describes something that is unpleasant or embarrassing. College writing is no place for euphemisms. Say what you mean—*pregnant*, not *expecting*; *died*, not *passed away*; and *strike*, not *work stoppage*.

3 Specific and General Words

Specific words refer to particular persons, items, or events; **general** words denote entire classes or groups. *Queen Elizabeth II*, for example, is more specific than *ruler*; *jeans* is more specific than *clothing*; and *hybrid car* is more specific than *vehicle*. You can use general words to describe entire classes of items, but you should use specific words to clarify such generalizations.

CLOSE-UP

USING SPECIFIC WORDS

Avoid general words such as *nice*, *great*, and *terrific* that say nothing and could be used in almost any sentence. These <u>utility words</u> convey only enthusiasm, not precise meanings. Replace them with more specific words.

See 12a2

4 Abstract and Concrete Words

Abstract words—*beauty*, *truth*, *justice*, and so on—refer to ideas, qualities, or conditions that cannot be perceived by the senses. **Concrete** words name things that readers can see, hear, taste, smell, or touch. The more concrete your words and phrases, the more vivid the images you evoke in the reader.

5 Commonly Confused Words (Homophones)

Some words, such as *accept* and *except*, are pronounced alike but spelled differently. Because they are often confused, you should be careful when you use them.

accept	to receive
except	other than
affect	to have an influence on (*verb*)
effect	result (*noun*); to cause (*verb*)
its	possessive of *it*
it's	contraction of *it is*

For a full list of these and other homophones, along with their meanings and sentences illustrating their use, **see Appendix B.**

16b Avoiding Inappropriate Language

When you write, use language that is appropriate for your audience and purpose.

1 Jargon

Jargon, the specialized or technical vocabulary of a trade, profession, or academic discipline, is useful for communicating in the field for which it was developed, but outside that field it can be confusing.

The patient had ~~an acute myocardial infarction.~~ *a heart attack.*

2 Pretentious Diction

Good writing is clear writing, and pompous or flowery language is no substitute for clarity. Revise to eliminate **pretentious diction,** inappropriately elevated and wordy language.

As I fell ~~into slumber~~ *asleep*, I ~~cogitated~~ *thought* about my day ~~ambling~~ *hiking* through ~~the splendor of~~ the Appalachian Mountains.

3 Clichés

Clichés are tired expressions that have lost all meaning because they have been so overused. Familiar sayings like "last but not least," "crystal clear," and "what goes around comes around," for example, do little to enhance your writing. Avoid the temptation to use clichés in your college writing.

16c Avoiding Offensive Language

1 Stereotypes

When referring to a racial, ethnic, or religious group, use words with neutral connotations or words that the group itself uses in *formal* speech or writing. Also avoid potentially offensive labels related to age, class, occupation, physical ability, or sexual orientation.

2 Sexist Language

Avoid **sexist language**, language that promotes gender stereotypes. Sexist language entails much more than the use of derogatory words. Assuming that some professions are exclusive to one gender—for instance, that *nurse* denotes only women or that *engineer* denotes only men—is also sexist. So is the use of job titles such as *mailman* for *letter carrier* and *stewardess* for *flight attendant*.

Sexist language also occurs when a writer fails to apply the same terminology to both men and women. For example, you should refer to two scientists with PhDs not as Dr. Sagan and Mrs. Yallow, but as Dr. Sagan and Dr. Yallow.

In your writing, always use *women*—not *girls* or *ladies*—when referring to adult females. Also avoid using the generic *he* or *him* when your subject could be either male or female. Instead, use the third-person plural or the phrase *he or she* (not *he/she*).

Sexist: Before boarding, each <u>passenger</u> should make certain that <u>he</u> has <u>his</u> ticket.

Revised: Before boarding, <u>passengers</u> should make certain that <u>they</u> have <u>their</u> tickets.

Revised: Before boarding, each <u>passenger</u> should make certain that <u>he</u> or <u>she</u> has a ticket.

NOTE: Be careful not to use *they* or *their* to refer to a singular antecedent.

Drivers
^~~Any driver~~ caught speeding should have their driving
privileges suspended.

CLOSE-UP

ELIMINATING SEXIST LANGUAGE

For most sexist usages, there are nonsexist alternatives.

Sexist Usage	Possible Revisions
1. Mankind	People, human beings
Man's accomplishments	Human accomplishments
Man-made	Synthetic
2. Female engineer (lawyer, accountant, etc.), male model	Engineer (lawyer, accountant, etc.), model
3. Policeman/woman	Police officer
Salesman/woman/girl	Salesperson/sales representative
Businessman/woman	Businessperson, executive
4. <u>Everyone</u> should complete <u>his</u> application by Tuesday.	Everyone should complete <u>his or her</u> application by Tuesday.
	<u>All students</u> should complete <u>their</u> applications by Tuesday.

PART 4

Understanding Punctuation

17 Using End Punctuation

17a Using Periods

Use a period to signal the end of most sentences, including indirect questions.

> Something is rotten in Denmark.

> They wondered whether the water was safe to drink.

Also use periods in most abbreviations.

> Mr. Spock   Aug.   Dr. Livingstone
>
> 9 p.m.   etc.   1600 Pennsylvania Ave.

If an abbreviation ends the sentence, do not add another period.

> He promised to be there at 6 a.m./

However, do add a question mark if the sentence is a question.

> Did he arrive at 6 p.m.?

If the abbreviation falls *within* a sentence, use normal punctuation after the period.

> He promised to be there at 6 p.m., but he forgot.

CLOSE-UP

ABBREVIATIONS WITHOUT PERIODS

Abbreviations composed of all capital letters do not usually require periods unless they stand for initials of people's names (E. B. White).

> MD   RN   BC

Familiar abbreviations of names of corporations or government agencies and abbreviations of scientific and technical terms do not require periods.

CD-ROM   NYU   DNA   CIA   WCAU-FM

Acronyms—new words formed from the initial letters or first few letters of a series of words—do not include periods.

hazmat   AIDS   NAFTA   modem   CAT scan

Clipped forms (commonly accepted shortened forms of words, such as *gym*, *dorm*, *math*, and *fax*) do not use periods. Postal abbreviations do not include periods.

TX   CA   MS   PA   FL   NY

Use periods to mark divisions in dramatic, poetic, and biblical references.

Hamlet 2.2.1–5 (act, scene, lines)

Paradise Lost 7.163–167 (book, lines)

Judges 4.14 (chapter, verse)

NOTE: In **MLA parenthetical references**, titles of literary and biblical works are often abbreviated: *Ham.* **2.2.1-5**; **Judg. 4.14**.

See 34a1

CLOSE-UP

ELECTRONIC ADDRESSES

Periods, along with other punctuation marks (such as slashes and colons), are frequently used in electronic addresses (URLs).

academic.cengage.com/eng/kirsznermandell/

NOTE: When you type an electronic address, do not end it with a period, and do not add spaces after periods within the address.

17b Using Question Marks

Use a question mark to signal the end of a direct question.

Who was that man at the door?

Use a question mark in parentheses to indicate that a date or number is uncertain.

Aristophanes, the Greek playwright, was born in 448 (?) BC and died in 380 (?) BC.

CLOSE-UP

EDITING MISUSED QUESTION MARKS

■ Use a period, not a question mark, with an indirect question.

The personnel officer asked whether he knew how to
type?̣

■ Do not use a question mark to convey sarcasm. Instead, suggest your attitude through your choice of words.

I refused his ^*not very* generous (?) offer.

17c   Using Exclamation Points

An exclamation point is used to signal the end of an emotional or emphatic statement, an emphatic interjection, or a forceful command.

Remember the Maine!

"No! Don't leave!" he cried.

CLOSE-UP

EDITING MISUSED EXCLAMATION POINTS

Except for recording dialogue, do not use exclamation points in college writing. Even in informal writing, use exclamation points sparingly—and never use two or more in a row.

---

18   Using Commas

18a   Setting Off Independent Clauses

Use a comma when you form a compound sentence by linking two independent clauses with a **coordinating
_{See}
_{A1.7} conjunction** (*and, but, or, nor, for, yet, so*) or a pair of **correlative conjunctions**.

The House approved the bill, but the Senate rejected it.

Either the hard drive is full, or the modem is too slow.

NOTE: You may omit the comma if two clauses connected by a coordinating conjunction are very short: *Love it or leave it.*

18b   Setting Off Items in a Series

Use commas between items in a series of three or more **coordinate elements** (words, phrases, or clauses joined by a coordinating conjunction).

> _Chipmunk_, _raccoon_, and _Mugwump_ are Native American words.

> You may pay <u>by check</u>, <u>with a credit card</u>, or <u>in cash</u>.

> <u>Brazilians speak Portuguese</u>, <u>Colombians speak Spanish</u>, and <u>Haitians speak French and Creole</u>.

NOTE: To avoid ambiguity, always use a comma before the *and* (or other coordinating conjunction) that separates the last two items in a series: *The downtown area includes a bakery, a florist, a small supermarket with an excellent butcher, and a bookstore.*

Do not use a comma to introduce or to close a series.

> Three important criteria are⁄ fat content, salt content, and taste.

> The provinces Quebec, Ontario, and Alberta⁄ are in Canada.

Use a comma between items in a series of two or more **coordinate adjectives**—adjectives that modify the same word or word group—unless they are joined by a conjunction.

> She brushed her <u>long</u>, <u>shining</u> hair.

> The baby was <u>tired</u> and <u>cranky</u> and <u>wet</u>. (no commas required)

CHECKLIST

PUNCTUATING ADJECTIVES IN A SERIES

☐ If you can reverse the order of the adjectives or insert *and* between the adjectives without changing the meaning, the adjectives are coordinate, and you should use a comma.

She brushed her long, shining hair.

She brushed her shining, long hair.

She brushed her long [and] shining hair.

(continued)

> **PUNCTUATING ADJECTIVES IN A SERIES**
> (*continued*)
>
> ☐ If you cannot reverse the order, the adjectives are not
> coordinate, and you should not use a comma.
>
> Ten red balloons fell from the ceiling.
>
> Red ten balloons fell from the ceiling.
>
> Ten [and] red balloons fell from the ceiling.

18c Setting Off Introductory Elements

An introductory dependent clause, verbal phrase, or prepositional phrase is generally set off from the rest of the sentence by a comma.

<u>When war came to Baghdad,</u> many victims were chil-
dren. (dependent clause)

<u>Pushing onward,</u> Scott struggled toward the South
Pole. (verbal phrase)

<u>During the Depression,</u> movie attendance rose.
(prepositional phrase)

If an introductory prepositional phrase is short and no
ambiguity is possible, you may omit the comma: *After
lunch I took a four-hour nap.*

CLOSE-UP

TRANSITIONAL WORDS AND PHRASES

See
3b
When a <u>transitional word or phrase</u> begins a sentence, it
is usually set off with a comma.

<u>However,</u> any plan that is enacted must be fair.

<u>In other words,</u> we cannot act hastily.

18d Setting Off Nonessential Material

Use commas to set off nonessential material whether it
appears at the beginning, in the middle, or at the end of a
sentence.

1 Nonrestrictive Modifiers

Use commas to set off **nonrestrictive modifiers,** which supply information that is not essential to the meaning of the words they modify. (Do *not* use commas to set off **restrictive modifiers,** which supply information essential to the meaning of the words they modify.)

Nonrestrictive (commas required): Actors, <u>who have inflated egos</u>, are often insecure. (*All* actors—not just those with inflated egos—are insecure.)

Restrictive (no commas): Actors <u>who have inflated egos</u> are often insecure. (Only those actors with inflated egos—not all actors—are insecure.)

In the following examples, commas set off only nonrestrictive modifiers—those that supply nonessential information. Commas do not set off restrictive modifiers, which supply essential information.

Adjective Clauses

Restrictive: Speaking in public is something <u>that most people fear</u>.

Nonrestrictive: He ran for the bus, <u>which was late as usual</u>.

Prepositional Phrases

Restrictive: The man <u>with the gun</u> demanded their money.

Nonrestrictive: The clerk, <u>with a nod</u>, dismissed me.

Verbal Phrases

Restrictive: The candidates <u>running for mayor</u> have agreed to a debate.

Nonrestrictive: The marathoner, <u>running his fastest</u>, beat his previous record.

Appositives

Restrictive: The film <u>*Citizen Kane*</u> made Orson Welles famous.

Nonrestrictive: *Citizen Kane*, <u>Orson Welles's first film</u>, made him famous.

CHECKLIST

RESTRICTIVE AND NONRESTRICTIVE MODIFIERS

To determine whether a modifier is restrictive or nonrestrictive, answer these questions:

☐ Is the modifier essential to the meaning of the noun it modifies (*The man with the gun,* not just any man)? If so, it is restrictive and does not take commas.

☐ Is the modifier introduced by *that* (*something that most people fear*)? If so, it is restrictive. *That* cannot introduce a nonrestrictive clause.

☐ Can you delete the relative pronoun without causing ambiguity or confusion (*something [that] most people fear*)? If so, the clause is restrictive.

☐ Is the appositive more specific than the noun that precedes it (*the film* Citizen Kane)? If so, it is restrictive.

CLOSE-UP

USING COMMAS WITH *THAT* AND *WHICH*

■ *That* introduces only restrictive clauses, which are not set off by commas.

I bought a used car that cost $2,000.

■ *Which* generally introduces only nonrestrictive clauses, which are set off by commas.

The used car I bought, which cost $2,000, broke down after a week.

GRAMMAR CHECKER

THAT OR *WHICH*

Your word processor's grammar checker may identify *which* as an error when it introduces a restrictive clause. It will prompt you to add commas, using *which* to introduce a nonrestrictive clause, or to change *which* to *that.* Review the meaning of your sentence, and revise accordingly.

"That" or "Which":
Only the books which are in the attic must be moved.

Suggestions:
books, which are in the attic,
————OR————
books that are in the attic

2 Transitional Words and Phrases

<u>Transitional words and phrases</u> qualify, clarify, and make connections. Because they are not essential to meaning, however, they are always set off by commas when they interrupt a clause or when they begin or end a sentence.

> The Outward Bound program, <u>for example,</u> is considered safe.

> <u>In fact,</u> Outward Bound has an excellent reputation.

> Other programs are not so safe, <u>however</u>.

See 3b

CLOSE-UP

PUNCTUATION WITH TRANSITIONAL WORDS AND PHRASES

When a transitional word or phrase joins two independent clauses, it must be preceded by a semicolon and followed by a comma.

> Laughter is the best medicine; <u>of course,</u> penicillin also comes in handy sometimes.

---

3 Contradictory Phrases

A phrase that expresses a contradiction is usually set off from the rest of the sentence by one or more commas.

> This medicine is taken after meals, <u>never on an empty stomach</u>.

> Mark McGwire, <u>not Sammy Sosa,</u> was the first to break Roger Maris's home-run record.

4 Miscellaneous Nonessential Elements

Other nonessential elements usually set off by commas include tag questions, names in direct address, mild interjections, and *yes* and *no*.

> This is your first day on the job, <u>isn't it</u>?

> I wonder, <u>Mr. Honeywell,</u> whether Mr. Albright deserves a raise.

> <u>Well,</u> it's about time.

> <u>Yes,</u> that's what I thought.

18e Using Commas in Other Conventional Contexts

1 With Direct Quotations

In most cases, use commas to set off a direct quotation from the **identifying tag** (*he said, she answered*, and so on).

Emerson said, "I greet you at the beginning of a great career."

"I greet you at the beginning of a great career," Emerson said.

"I greet you," Emerson said, "at the beginning of a great career."

When the identifying tag comes between two complete sentences, however, the tag is introduced by a comma but followed by a period.

"Winning isn't everything," Coach Vince Lombardi once said, "It's the only thing."

2 With Titles or Degrees Following a Name

Michael Crichton, MD, wrote *Jurassic Park*.

Hamlet, Prince of Denmark, is Shakespeare's most famous character.

3 In Dates and Addresses

On August 30, 1983, the space shuttle *Challenger* was launched.

Her address is 600 West End Avenue, New York, NY 10024.

NOTE: When only the month and year are given, do not use a comma to separate the month from the year: *May 1968*. Do not use a comma to separate the street number from the street or the state name from the zip code.

18f Using Commas to Prevent Misreading

In some cases, a comma is used to avoid ambiguity. For example, consider the following sentence.

Those who can, sprint the final lap.

Without the comma, *can* appears to be an auxiliary verb ("Those who can sprint. . . ."), and the sentence seems incomplete. The comma tells readers to pause and thus prevents confusion.

Also use a comma to acknowledge the omission of a repeated word, usually a verb, and to separate words repeated consecutively.

Pam carried the box; Tim, the suitcase.

Everything bad that could have happened, happened.

18g Editing Misused Commas

Do not use commas in the following situations.

1 To Set Off Restrictive Modifiers

The film, *Malcolm X*, was directed by Spike Lee.

They planned a picnic, in the park.

2 Between a Subject and Its Predicate

A woman with dark red hair, opened the door.

3 Between a Verb and an Indirect Quotation or Indirect Question

General Douglas MacArthur vowed, that he would return.

The landlord asked, if we would sign a two-year lease.

4 In Compounds That Are Not Composed of Independent Clauses

During the 1400s plagues, and pestilence were common. (compound subject)

Many women thirty-five and older are returning to college, and tend to be good students. (compound predicate)

5 Before a Dependent Clause at the End of a Sentence

Jane Addams founded Hull House, because she wanted to help Chicago's poor.

19 Using Semicolons

The **semicolon** is used only between items of equal grammatical rank: two independent clauses, two phrases, and so on.

19a Separating Independent Clauses

Use a semicolon between closely related independent clauses that convey parallel or contrasting information but are not joined by a coordinating conjunction.

> Paul Revere's *The Boston Massacre* is an early example of American protest art; Edward Hicks's later "primitive" paintings are socially conscious art with a religious strain.

CLOSE-UP

USING SEMICOLONS

See
Ch. 5

Using only a comma or no punctuation at all between independent clauses creates a <u>run-on</u>.

Use a semicolon between two independent clauses when the second clause is introduced by a transitional word or phrase (the transitional element is followed by a comma).

> Thomas Jefferson brought two hundred vanilla beans and a recipe for vanilla ice cream back from France; <u>thus</u>, he gave America its all-time favorite ice cream flavor.

19b Separating Items in a Series

Use semicolons between items in a series when one or more of these items include commas.

> Three papers are posted on the bulletin board outside the building: a description of the exams; a list of appeal

procedures for students who fail; and an employment ad from an automobile factory, addressed specifically to candidates whose appeals are turned down. (Andrea Lee, *Russian Journal*)

Laramie, Wyoming; Wyoming, Delaware; and Delaware, Ohio, were three of the places they visited.

19c Editing Misused Semicolons

Do not use semicolons in the following situations.

1 Between a Dependent and an Independent Clause

Because drugs can now suppress the body's immune reaction; fewer organ transplants are rejected.

2 To Introduce a List

Despite the presence of CNN and FOX News, the evening news remains a battleground for the three major television networks; CBS, NBC, and ABC.

GRAMMAR CHECKER

EDITING MISUSED SEMICOLONS

Your word processor's grammar checker will highlight certain misused semicolons and frequently offer suggestions for revision.

Comma Use:

Although the library is usually open year-round; it will be closed this fall for renovations.

Suggestions:

year-round,

20 Using Apostrophes

Use an apostrophe to form the possessive case, to indicate omissions in contractions, and to form certain plurals.

20a Forming the Possessive Case

The possessive case indicates ownership. In English, the possessive case of nouns and indefinite pronouns is indicated either with a phrase that includes the word *of* (the hands *of* the clock) or with an apostrophe and, in most cases, an *s* (the clock's hands).

1 Singular Nouns and Indefinite Pronouns

To form the possessive case of singular nouns and indefinite pronouns, add -'*s*.

"The Monk's Tale" is one of Chaucer's *Canterbury Tales*.

When we would arrive was anyone's guess.

NOTE: With some singular nouns that end in -*s*, pronouncing the possessive ending as a separate syllable can sound awkward. In such cases, it is acceptable to use just an apostrophe: *Crispus Attucks' death, Aristophanes' play.*

2 Plural Nouns

To form the possessive case of regular plural nouns (those that end in -*s* or -*es*), add only an apostrophe.

Laid-off employees received two weeks' severance pay and three months' medical benefits.

The Lopezes' three children are triplets.

To form the possessive case of nouns that have irregular plurals, add -'*s*.

The Children's Hour is a play by Lillian Hellman.

3 Compound Nouns or Groups of Words

To form the possessive case of compound words or groups of words, add -'*s* to the last word.

The President accepted the Secretary of Defense's resignation.

This is someone else's responsibility.

4 Two or More Items

To indicate individual ownership of two or more items, add -'s to each item.

Ernest Hemingway's and Gertrude Stein's writing styles have some similarities.

To indicate joint ownership, add -'s only to the last item.

Lewis and Clark's expedition has been the subject of several books.

20b Indicating Omissions in Contractions

Apostrophes replace omitted letters in contractions that combine a pronoun and a verb (*he* + *will* = *he'll*) or the elements of a verb phrase (*do* + *not* = *don't*).

FREQUENTLY USED CONTRACTIONS	
don't (do not)	they're (they are)
I'm (I am)	we'll (we will)
isn't (is not)	we've (we have)
it's (it is)	won't (will not)
let's (let us)	wouldn't (would not)

GRAMMAR CHECKER

REVISING CONTRACTIONS

Contractions are generally too informal for use in college writing. If you set your word processor's writing style to Formal or Technical, the grammar checker will highlight contractions and offer suggestions for revision.

Contraction Use:

You'll want to be sure to bring your laptop and external DVD drive.

Suggestions:

You will

CLOSE-UP

USING APOSTROPHES

Be careful not to confuse contractions (which always include apostrophes) with the possessive forms of personal pronouns (which never include apostrophes).

Contractions	**Possessive Forms**
Who's on first?	Whose book is this?
They're playing our song.	Their team is winning.
It's raining.	Its paws were muddy.
You're a real pal.	Your résumé is very impressive.

CLOSE-UP

INDICATING OMITTED NUMBERS

In informal writing, an apostrophe may also be used to represent the century in a year: *Class of '97, the '60s.* In college writing, however, write out the year in full.

20c Forming Plurals

In a few special situations, add *-'s* to form plurals.

FORMING PLURALS WITH APOSTROPHES

Plurals of Letters

> The Italian language has no *j*'s, *k*'s, or *w*'s.

Plurals of Words Referred to as Words

> The supervisor would accept no *if*'s, *and*'s, or *but*'s.

See 25c

NOTE: <u>**Elements spoken of as themselves**</u> (letters, numerals, or words) are set in italic type; the plural ending, however, is not.

20d Editing Misused Apostrophes

Do not use apostrophes in the following situations.

1 With Plural Nouns That Are Not Possessive

The Thompson's are not at home.

Down vest's are very warm.

The Philadelphia Seventy Sixer's have had good years and bad.

2 To Form the Possessive Case of Personal Pronouns

This ticket must be your's or her's.

The next turn is their's.

Her doll had lost it's right eye.

The next great moment in history is our's.

21 Using Quotation Marks

Use quotation marks to set off brief passages of quoted speech or writing, to set off titles, and to set off words used in special ways. Do not use quotation marks when quoting long passages of prose or poetry.

21a Setting Off Quoted Speech or Writing

When you quote a word, phrase, or brief passage of someone's speech or writing, enclose the quoted material in a pair of quotation marks.

Gloria Steinem said, "We are becoming the men we once hoped to marry."

Galsworthy writes, "Aunt Juley stayed in her room, prostrated by the blow" (329). (Note that in this example from a student paper, the end punctuation follows the parenthetical documentation.)

CLOSE-UP

USING QUOTATION MARKS WITH DIALOGUE

When you record **dialogue** (conversation between two or more people), enclose the quoted words in quotation marks. Begin a new paragraph each time a new speaker is introduced.

When you are quoting several paragraphs of dialogue by one speaker, begin each new paragraph with quotation marks. However, use closing quotation marks only at the end of the entire passage (not at the end of each paragraph).

Special rules govern the punctuation of a quotation when it is used with an **identifying tag**—a phrase (such as *he said*) that identifies the speaker or writer.

1 Identifying Tag in the Middle of a Quoted Passage

Use a pair of commas to set off an identifying tag that interrupts a quoted passage.

"In the future," pop artist Andy Warhol once said, "everyone will be world famous for fifteen minutes."

If the identifying tag follows a complete sentence but the quoted passage continues, use a period after the tag. Begin the new sentence with a capital letter, and enclose it in quotation marks.

"Be careful," Erin warned. "Reptiles can be tricky."

2 Identifying Tag at the Beginning of a Quoted Passage

Use a comma after an identifying tag that introduces quoted speech or writing.

The Raven repeated, "Nevermore."

See 22a Use a <u>colon</u> instead of a comma before a quotation if the identifying tag is a complete sentence.

She gave her final answer: "No."

GRAMMAR CHECKER

USING PUNCTUATION WITH QUOTATION MARKS

Your word processor's grammar checker will often highlight missing punctuation in sentences containing quotation marks and offer suggestions for revision.

> Punctuation with Quotations:
>
> In *The Varieties of Religious Experience*, William James writes "The lustre of the present hour is always borrowed from the background of possibilities it goes with" (141).
>
> Suggestions:
>
> writes,

3 Identifying Tag at the End of a Quoted Passage

Use a comma to set off a quotation from an identifying tag that follows it.

"Be careful out there," the sergeant warned.

If the quotation ends with a question mark or an exclamation point, use that punctuation mark instead of the comma. In this situation, the identifying tag begins with a lowercase letter even though it follows end punctuation.

"Is Ankara the capital of Turkey?" she asked.

"Oh boy!" he cried.

NOTE: Commas and periods are always placed inside quotation marks. For information on placement of other punctuation marks with quotation marks, **see 21d.**

CLOSE-UP

QUOTING LONG PROSE PASSAGES

Do *not* enclose a **long prose passage** (more than four lines) in quotation marks. Instead, set it off by indenting the entire passage one inch from the left-hand margin. Treat the passage like regular text: double-space between lines, and double-space above and below it. Introduce the passage with a colon, and place parenthetical documentation one space after the end punctuation.

(continued)

QUOTING LONG PROSE PASSAGES *(continued)*

The following portrait of Aunt Juley illustrates several of the devices Galsworthy uses throughout *The Forsyte Saga*, such as a journalistic detachment, a sense of the grotesque, and an ironic stance:

> Aunt Juley stayed in her room, prostrated by the blow. Her face, discoloured by tears, was divided into compartments by the little ridges of pouting flesh which had swollen with emotion. . . . Her warm heart could not bear the thought that Ann was lying there so cold. (329)

Many similar portraits of characters appear throughout the novel.

When you quote a long prose passage that is a single paragraph, do not indent the first line. When quoting two or more paragraphs, however, indent the first line of each paragraph (including the first) an additional three spaces. If the first sentence of the quoted passage does not begin a paragraph in the source, do not indent it—but do indent the first line of each subsequent paragraph. If the passage you are quoting includes material set in quotation marks, keep those quotation marks.

NOTE: The guidelines presented here conform to MLA style.

CLOSE-UP

QUOTING POETRY

See 22e

Treat one line of poetry like a short prose passage: enclose it in quotation marks and run it into the text. If you quote two or three lines of poetry, separate the lines with **slashes**, and run the quotation into the text. (Leave one space before and one space after the slash.) If you quote more than three lines of poetry, set them off like a long prose passage. (For special emphasis, you may set off fewer lines in this way.) Be sure to reproduce *exactly* the spelling, capitalization, and indentation of the quoted lines.

> Wilfred Owen, a poet who was killed in action in World
> War I, expressed the horrors of war with vivid imagery:
>> Bent double, like old beggars under sacks.
>> Knock-kneed, coughing like hags, we cursed
>>> through sludge.
>> Till on the haunting flares we turned our backs
>> And towards our distant rest began to trudge.
>>> (lines 1-4)

21b Setting Off Titles

Titles of short works and titles of parts of long works are enclosed in quotation marks. Other titles are **italicized**.

See 25a

TITLES REQUIRING QUOTATION MARKS

Articles in Magazines, Newspapers, and Professional Journals
   "Why Johnny Can't Write"

Essays, Short Stories, Short Poems, and Songs
   "Fenimore Cooper's Literary Offenses"
   "Flying Home"
   "The Road Not Taken"
   "The Star-Spangled Banner"

Chapters or Sections of Books
   "Miss Sharp Begins to Make Friends"

Episodes of Radio or Television Series
   "Lucy Goes to the Hospital"

NOTE: Current MLA style recommends italicizing in place of underlining.

21c Setting Off Words Used in Special Ways

Enclose a word used in a special or unusual way in quotation marks. (If you use *so-called* before the word, do not use quotation marks as well.)

It was clear that adults approved of children who were "readers," but it was not at all clear why this was so. (Annie Dillard)

Also enclose a **coinage**—an invented word—in quotation marks.

After the twins were born, the minivan became a "babymobile."

21d Using Quotation Marks with Other Punctuation

At the end of a quotation, punctuation is sometimes placed before the quotation marks and sometimes placed after the quotation marks:

■ Place quotation marks *after* the comma or period at the end of a quotation.

Many, like poet Robert Frost, think about "the road not taken," but not many have taken "the one less traveled by."

■ Place quotation marks *before* a semicolon or colon at the end of a quotation.

Students who do not pass the test receive "certificates of completion"; those who pass are awarded diplomas.

Taxpayers were pleased with the first of the candidate's promised "sweeping new reforms": a balanced budget.

■ If a question mark, exclamation point, or dash is part of the quotation, place the quotation marks *after* the punctuation.

"Who's there?" she demanded.

"Stop!" he cried.

"Should we leave now, or—" Vicki paused, unable to continue.

■ If a question mark, exclamation point, or dash is not part of the quotation, place the quotation marks *before* the punctuation.

Did you finish reading "The Black Cat"?

Whatever you do, don't yell "Uncle"!

The first story—Updike's "*A & P*"—provoked
discussion.

CLOSE-UP

QUOTATIONS WITHIN QUOTATIONS

Use *single* quotation marks to enclose a quotation within a
quotation.

> Claire noted, "Liberace always said, 'I cried all the way
> to the bank.' "

Also use single quotation marks within a quotation to
set off a title that would normally be enclosed in double
quotation marks.

> I think what she said was, "Play it, Sam. Play 'As Time
> Goes By.' "

Use *double* quotation marks around quotations or titles
within a **long prose passage**.

See
21a

21e Editing Misused Quotation Marks

Do not use quotation marks in the following situations.

1 To Set Off Indirect Quotations

Do not use quotation marks to set off someone else's
written or spoken words that are not quoted exactly.

> Freud wondered "what women wanted."

2 To Set Off Slang or Technical Terms

> Dawn is "into" running.

> "Biofeedback" is sometimes used to treat migraines.

CLOSE-UP

TITLES OF YOUR OWN PAPERS

Do not use quotation marks (or italics) to set off the title of
your own paper.

22 Using Other Punctuation Marks

22a Using Colons

The **colon** is a strong punctuation mark that points readers ahead to the rest of the sentence. When a colon introduces a list or series, explanatory material, or a quotation, it must be preceded by a complete sentence.

1 Introducing Lists or Series

Use colons to set off lists or series, including those introduced by phrases like *the following* or *as follows.*

> Waiting tables requires three skills: memory, speed, and balance.

2 Introducing Explanatory Material

Use colons to introduce material that explains, exemplifies, or summarizes.

> She had one dream: to play professional basketball.

Sometimes a colon separates two independent clauses, the second illustrating or clarifying the first.

> The survey presents an interesting finding: Americans do not trust the news media.

CLOSE-UP

USING COLONS

When a complete sentence follows a colon, the sentence may begin with either a capital or a lowercase letter. However, if the sentence is a quotation, the first word is always capitalized (unless it was not capitalized in the source).

---

3 Introducing Quotations

See 21a When you quote a <u>long prose passage</u>, always introduce it with a colon. Also use a colon before a short quotation when it is introduced by a complete sentence.

> With dignity, Bartleby repeated the words again: "I prefer not to."

OTHER CONVENTIONAL USES OF COLONS

To Separate Titles from Subtitles

Family Installments: Memories of Growing Up Hispanic

To Separate Minutes from Hours

6:15 a.m.

After Salutations in <u>formal letters</u>

Dear Dr. Evans:

See
42a

**To Separate Place of Publication from Name of
Publisher in a <u>works-cited list</u>**

Boston: Wadsworth, 2007.

See
34a2

---

4 Editing Misused Colons

Do not use colons after expressions such as *namely, for
example, such as,* or *that is.*

The Eye Institute treats patients with a wide variety of
conditions, such as: myopia, glaucoma, and cataracts.

Do not place colons between verbs and their objects or
complements or between prepositions and their objects.

James Michener wrote: *Hawaii, Centennial, Space,* and
Poland.

Hitler's armies marched through: the Netherlands,
Belgium, and France.

22b Using Dashes

1 Setting Off Nonessential Material

Like commas, **dashes** can set off <u>nonessential material</u>,
but unlike commas, dashes call attention to the material
they set off. Indicate a dash with two unspaced hyphens
(which your word-processing program will automatically
convert to a dash).

See
18d

For emphasis, you may use dashes to set off explanations, qualifications, examples, definitions, and appositives.

Neither of the boys—both nine-year-olds—had any
history of violence.

Too many parents learn the dangers of swimming
pools the hard way—after their toddler has drowned.

2 Introducing a Summary

Use a dash to introduce a statement that summarizes a list or series that appears before it.

"Study hard," "Respect your elders," "Don't talk with your mouth full"—Sharon had often heard her parents say these things.

3 Indicating an Interruption

In dialogue, a dash may indicate a hesitation or an unfinished thought.

"I think—no, I know—this is the worst day of my life," Julie sighed.

NOTE: Because too many dashes can make a passage seem disorganized and out of control, you should be careful not to overuse them.

22c Using Parentheses

1 Setting Off Nonessential Material

Use **parentheses** to enclose material that is relatively unimportant in a sentence—for example, material that expands, clarifies, illustrates, or supplements.

In some European countries (notably Sweden and France), superb daycare is offered at little or no cost to parents.

Also use parentheses to set off digressions and afterthoughts.

Last Sunday we went to the new stadium (it was only half-filled) to see the game.

When a complete sentence set off by parentheses falls within another sentence, it should not begin with a capital letter or end with a period.

Because the area is so cold (temperatures average in the low twenties), it is virtually uninhabitable.

If the parenthetical sentence does *not* fall within another sentence, however, it must begin with a capital letter and end with appropriate punctuation.

The region is very cold. (Temperatures average in the low twenties.)

2 Using Parentheses in Other Situations

Use parentheses around letters and numbers that identify points on a list, dates, cross-references, and documentation.

All reports must include the following components: (1) an opening summary, (2) a background statement, and (3) a list of conclusions.

Russia defeated Sweden in the Great Northern War (1700–1721).

Other scholars also make this point (see p. 54).

One critic has called the novel "puerile" (Arvin 72).

22d Using Brackets

When one set of parentheses falls within another, use **brackets** in place of the inner set.

In her study of American education between 1945 and 1960 (*The Troubled Crusade* [New York: Basic, 1963]), Diane Ravitch addresses issues like progressive education, race, educational reforms, and campus unrest.

Also use brackets within quotations to indicate to readers that the bracketed words are yours and not those of your source. You can bracket an explanation, a clarification, a correction, or an opinion.

"Even at Princeton he [F. Scott Fitzgerald] felt like an outsider."

If a quotation contains an error, indicate that the error is not yours by following it with the Latin word *sic* ("thus") in brackets.

"The octopuss [sic] is a cephalopod mollusk with eight arms."

NOTE: Use brackets to indicate changes you make in order to fit a **quotation** smoothly into your sentence. See 32a

22e   Using Slashes

1 Separating One Option from Another

The either/or fallacy is a common error in logic.

Writer/director M. Night Shyamalan spoke at the film festival.

Note that there is no space before or after the slash.

2 Separating Lines of Poetry Run into the Text

The poet James Schevill writes, "I study my defects / And learn how to perfect them."

In this case, leave one space before and one space after the slash.

22f   Using Ellipses

Use ellipses in the following situations.

1 Indicating an Omission in Quoted Prose

Use an **ellipsis**—three *spaced* periods—to indicate that you have omitted words from a prose quotation. Note that an ellipsis in the middle of a quoted passage can indicate the omission of a word, a sentence or two, or even a whole paragraph or more. When deleting material from a quotation, be very careful not to change the meaning of the original passage.

> **Original:** "When I was a young man, being anxious to distinguish myself, I was perpetually starting new propositions." (Samuel Johnson)

> **With Omission:** "When I was a young man, . . . I was perpetually starting new propositions."

Note that when you delete words immediately after an internal punctuation mark (such as the comma in the above example), you retain the punctuation before the ellipsis.

When you delete material at the end of a sentence, place the sentence's period or other end punctuation before the ellipsis.

According to humorist Dave Barry, "from outer space Europe appears to be shaped like a large ketchup stain. ●●●" (period followed by ellipsis)

NOTE: Never begin a quoted passage with an ellipsis.

When you delete material between sentences, any punctuation should precede the ellipsis.

Deletion from Middle of One Sentence to End of Another: According to Donald Hall, "Everywhere one meets the idea that reading is an activity desirable in itself. ●●● People surround the idea of reading with piety and do not take into account the purpose of reading." (period followed by ellipsis)

Deletion from Middle of One Sentence to Middle of Another: "When I was a young man, ●●● I found that generally what was new was false." (Samuel Johnson) (comma followed by ellipsis)

NOTE: If a quoted passage already contains an ellipsis, MLA recommends that you enclose your own ellipses in brackets to distinguish them from those that appear in the original quotation.

CLOSE-UP

USING ELLIPSES

If a quotation ending with an ellipsis is followed by parenthetical documentation, the final punctuation comes after the documentation.

As Jarman argues, "Compromise was impossible . . ." (161).

---

2 Indicating an Omission in Quoted Poetry

Use an ellipsis when you omit a word or phrase from a line of poetry. When you omit one or more lines of poetry, use a line of spaced periods. (The length may be equal either to the line above it or to the missing line— but it should not be longer than the longest line of the poem.)

Original:

> Stitch! Stitch! Stitch!
> In poverty, hunger, and dirt,
> And still with a voice of dolorous pitch,
> Would that its tone could reach the Rich,
> She sang this "Song of the Shirt"!
>
> (Thomas Hood)

With Omission:

> Stitch! Stitch! Stitch!
> In poverty, hunger, and dirt,
>
> ....
>
> She sang this "Song of the Shirt"!

PART 5

Understanding Spelling and Mechanics

23 Improving Spelling

23a Understanding Spelling and Pronunciation

Because pronunciation in English often provides few clues to spelling, you need to pay particular attention to the three problem areas that cause most misspellings.

1 Vowels in Unstressed Positions

Many unstressed vowels sound exactly alike. For instance, the unstressed vowels *a*, *e*, and *i* are impossible to distinguish by pronunciation alone in the suffixes *-able* and *-ible*, *-ance* and *-ence*, and *-ant* and *-ent*.

comfort<u>able</u>	brilli<u>ance</u>	serv<u>ant</u>
compat<u>ible</u>	excell<u>ence</u>	independ<u>ent</u>

2 Silent Letters

Some English words contain silent letters, such as the *b* in *climb* and the *t* in *mortgage*.

ai<u>s</u>le	depo<u>t</u>
condem<u>n</u>	<u>k</u>night
de<u>s</u>cend	<u>p</u>neumonia

3 Words That Are Often Pronounced Carelessly

Words like the following are often misspelled because when we pronounce them, we add, omit, or transpose letters.

can<u>d</u>idate	nuc<u>l</u>ear	recogni<u>z</u>e
enviro<u>n</u>ment	lib<u>r</u>ary	suppose<u>d</u> to
Feb<u>r</u>uary	quan<u>t</u>ity	use<u>d</u> to

23b Learning Spelling Rules

Memorizing a few spelling rules can help you overcome problems caused by inconsistencies between pronunciation and spelling.

1 The *ie/ei* Combinations

Use *i* before *e* (*belief*, *chief*) except after *c* (*ceiling*, *receive*) or when pronounced *ay*, as in *neighbor* or *weigh*. **Exceptions:** *either*, *neither*, *foreign*, *leisure*, *weird*, and *seize*. In addition, if the *ie* combination is not pronounced as a unit, the rule does not apply: *atheist*, *science*.

2 Doubling Final Consonants

The only words that double their consonants before a suffix that begins with a vowel (*-ed* or *-ing*) are those that pass the following three tests:

1. They have one syllable or are stressed on the last syllable.
2. They have only one vowel in the last syllable.
3. They end in a single consonant.

The word *tap* satisfies all three conditions: it has only one syllable, it has only one vowel (*a*), and it ends in a single consonant (*p*). Therefore, the final consonant doubles before a suffix beginning with a vowel (*tapped*, *tapping*).

3 Silent *e* before a Suffix

When a suffix that begins with a consonant is added to a word ending in a silent *e*, the *e* is usually kept: *hope/hopeful*. **Exceptions:** *argument*, *truly*, *ninth*, *judgment*, and *abridgment*.

When a suffix that begins with a vowel is added to a word ending in a silent *e*, the *e* is usually dropped: *hope/hoping*. **Exceptions:** *changeable*, *noticeable*, and *courageous*.

4 *y* before a Suffix

When a word ends in a consonant plus *y*, the *y* usually changes to an *i* when a suffix is added (*beauty* + *ful* = *beautiful*). The *y* is kept, however, when the suffix *-ing* is added (*tally* + *ing* = *tallying*) and in some one-syllable words (*dry* + *ness* = *dryness*).

When a word ends in a vowel plus *y*, the *y* is kept (*joy* + *ful* = *joyful*). **Exception:** *day* + *ly* = *daily*.

5 *seed* Endings

Endings with the sound *seed* are nearly always spelled *cede*, as in *precede*. **Exceptions:** *supersede*, *exceed*, *proceed*, and *succeed*.

6 -able, -ible

If the root of a word is itself a word, the suffix *-able* is most commonly used (*comfortable, agreeable*). If the root of a word is not a word, the suffix *-ible* is most often used (*compatible, incredible*).

7 Plurals

Most nouns form plurals by adding *-s: tortilla/tortillas, boat/boats*. There are, however, a number of exceptions:

■ **Words Ending in -f or -fe** Some words ending in *-f* or *-fe* form plurals by changing the *f* to *v* and adding *-es* or *-s: life/lives, self/selves*. Others add just *-s: belief/beliefs, safe/safes*.

■ **Words Ending in -y** Most words that end in a consonant followed by *y* form plurals by changing the *y* to *i* and adding *-es: baby/babies*. **Exceptions:** proper nouns such as *Kennedy* (plural *Kennedys*).

■ **Words Ending in -o** Most words that end in a consonant followed by *o* add *-es* to form the plural: *tomato/tomatoes, hero/heroes*. **Exceptions:** *silo/silos, piano/pianos, memo/memos, soprano/sopranos*.

■ **Words Ending in -s, -ss, -sh, -ch, -x, and -z** Words ending in *-s, -ss, -sh, -ch, -x,* and *-z* form plurals by adding *-es: Jones/Joneses, kiss/kisses, rash/rashes, lunch/lunches, box/boxes, buzz/buzzes*. **Exceptions:** Some one-syllable words that end in *-s* or *-z* double their final consonants when forming plurals: *quiz/quizzes*.

■ **Compound Nouns** Hyphenated compound nouns whose first element is more important than the others form the plural with the first element: *sister-in-law/sisters-in-law*.

■ **Foreign Plurals** Some words, especially those borrowed from Latin or Greek, keep their foreign plurals.

Singular	Plural
basis	bases
criterion	criteria
datum	data
memorandum	memoranda
stimulus	stimuli

COMPUTER TIP   academic.cengage.com/eng/kirsznermandell

RUNNING A SPELL CHECK

Remember that your spell checker will not identify a word that is spelled correctly but used incorrectly—*then* for *than* or *its* for *it's*, for example—or a typo that creates another word, such as *word* for *work*. For this reason, you still need to proofread your papers.

24 Knowing When to Capitalize

In addition to capitalizing the first word of a sentence (including a quoted sentence) and the pronoun *I*, always capitalize proper nouns and important words in titles.

COMPUTER TIP   academic.cengage.com/eng/kirsznermandell

REVISING CAPITALIZATION ERRORS

In *Microsoft Word*, the AutoCorrect tool will automatically capitalize certain words—such as the first word of a sentence or the days of the week. Be sure to proofread your work after using the AutoCorrect tool, though, since it can sometimes introduce capitalization errors into your writing.

24a Capitalizing Proper Nouns

Proper nouns—the names of specific persons, places, or things—are capitalized, and so are adjectives formed from proper nouns.

1 Specific People's Names

Eleanor Roosevelt   Medgar Evers

Capitalize a title when it precedes a person's name or replaces the name (Senator Barack Obama, Dad). Do not capitalize titles that *follow* names or that refer to the general position, not to the particular person who holds it

(Barack Obama, the senator), except for very high-ranking positions: President of the United States. Never capitalize a title denoting a family relationship when it follows an article or a possessive pronoun: an aunt, my uncle.

Capitalize titles or abbreviations of academic degrees, even when they follow a name: Dr. Benjamin Spock, Benjamin Spock, MD.

2 Names of Particular Structures, Special Events, Monuments, and So On

the *Titanic*   the World Series

the Brooklyn Bridge   Mount Rushmore

3 Places and Geographical Regions

Saturn   the Straits of Magellan

Budapest   the Western Hemisphere

NOTE: Capitalize *north*, *south*, *east*, and *west* when they denote particular geographical regions (the West), but not when they designate directions (west of town).

4 Days of the Week, Months, and Holidays

Saturday   Rosh Hashanah

January   Ramadan

5 Historical Periods and Events, Documents, and Names of Legal Cases

the Battle of Gettysburg   Romanticism

Brown v. *Board of Education*   the Treaty of Versailles

6 Races, Ethnic Groups, Nationalities, and Languages

African American   Korean

Latino/Latina   Dutch

NOTE: When the words *black* and *white* refer to races, they have traditionally not been capitalized. Current usage is divided on whether to capitalize *black*.

7 Religions and Their Followers; Sacred Books and Figures

Mormons   the Talmud   Buddha

Islam   God   the Scriptures

8 Specific Organizations

the New York Yankees

League of Women Voters

the American Bar Association

the Anti-Defamation League

9 Businesses, Government Agencies, and Other Institutions

Congress

the Environmental Protection Agency

Lincoln High School

the University of Maryland

10 Brand Names and Words Formed from Them

Coke   Astroturf   Rollerblades   Post-it

11 Specific Academic Courses and Departments

Sociology 201   Department of English

NOTE: Do not capitalize a general subject area (sociology, zoology) unless it is the name of a language.

12 Adjectives Formed from Proper Nouns

Keynesian economics   Elizabethan era

Freudian slip   Shakespearean sonnet

NOTE: When words derived from proper nouns have lost their specialized meanings, do not capitalize them: *china* pattern.

24b Capitalizing Important Words in Titles

In general, capitalize all words in titles with the exception of articles (*a*, *an*, and *the*), prepositions, coordinating conjunctions, and the *to* in infinitives. If an article, preposition, or coordinating conjunction is the *first* or *last* word in the title, however, do capitalize it.

The Declaration of Independence

Across the River and into the Trees

A Man and a Woman

"What Friends Are For"

CLOSE-UP

EDITING MISUSED CAPITALS

Do not capitalize the following:

■ Seasons (summer, fall, winter, spring)
■ Names of centuries (the twenty-first century)
■ Names of general historical periods (the automobile age)
■ Diseases and other medical terms (unless a proper noun is part of the name): mumps, smallpox, polio

ESL TIP

Do not capitalize a word simply because you want to emphasize its importance. If you are not sure whether a word should be capitalized, look it up in a dictionary.

25 Using Italics

25a Setting Off Titles and Names

See 21b Use italics for the titles and names in the box below. All other titles are set off with **quotation marks**.

TITLES AND NAMES SET IN ITALICS

Books: *David Copperfield*, *The Kite Runner*

Newspapers: the *Washington Post*, the *Philadelphia Inquirer* (According to MLA style, the word *the* is not italicized— or capitalized—in titles of newspapers.)

Magazines and Professional or Academic Journals: *Rolling Stone*, *Scientific American*, *PMLA*

Online Magazines and Journals: *salon.com*, *theonion.com*

Web Sites or Home Pages: *urbanlegends.com*, *movie-mistakes.com*

Pamphlets: *Common Sense*

Films: *Casablanca*, *Citizen Kane*

Television Programs: *American Idol*, *The Simpsons*

Radio Programs: *All Things Considered*, *The Tavis Smiley Show*

Long Poems: *John Brown's Body*, *The Faerie Queen*

Plays: *Macbeth*, *A Raisin in the Sun*

Long Musical Works: *Rigoletto*, *Eroica*

Software Programs: *Word*, *PowerPoint*

Paintings and Sculpture: *Guernica*, *Pietà*

Ships: *Lusitania*, U.S.S. *Saratoga* (S.S. and U.S.S. are not italicized.)

Trains: *City of New Orleans*, *The Orient Express*

Aircraft: *The Hindenburg*, *Enola Gay* (Only particular aircraft, not makes or types such as Piper Cub and Boeing 757, are italicized.)

Spacecraft: *Challenger*, *Enterprise*

NOTE: Names of sacred books, such as the Bible, and well-known documents, such as the Constitution and the Declaration of Independence, are neither italicized nor placed within quotation marks.

CLOSE-UP

USING ITALICS

Current MLA guidelines recommend that you use italics in place of underlining.

25b Setting Off Foreign Words and Phrases

Use italics to set off foreign words and phrases that have not become part of the English language.

> "*C'est la vie,*" Madeleine said when she saw the long line for basketball tickets.
>
> *Spirochaeta plicatilis* is a corkscrew-like bacterium.

If you are not sure whether a foreign word has been assimilated into English, consult a dictionary.

25c Setting Off Elements Spoken of as Themselves and Terms Being Defined

Use italics to set off letters, numerals, and words that refer to the letters, numerals, and words themselves.

> Is that a *p* or a *g*?
>
> I forget the exact address, but I know it has a *3* in it.
>
> Does *through* rhyme with *cough*?

Also use italics to set off words and phrases that you go on to define.

> A *closet drama* is a play meant to be read, not performed.

NOTE: When you quote a dictionary definition, put the word you are defining in italics and the definition itself in quotation marks.

> To *infer* means "to draw a conclusion"; to *imply* means "to suggest."

25d Using Italics for Emphasis

Italics may occasionally be used for emphasis.

> Initially, poetry might be defined as a kind of language that says *more* and says it *more intensely* than does ordinary language. (Lawrence Perrine, *Sound and Sense*)

However, overuse of italics is distracting. Instead of italicizing, indicate emphasis with word choice and sentence structure.

26 Using Hyphens

Hyphens have two conventional uses: to break a word at the end of a line and to link words in certain compounds.

26a Breaking a Word at the End of a Line

A computer never breaks a word at the end of a line; if the full word will not fit, it is brought down to the next line. Sometimes, however, you will want to break a word with a hyphen—for example, to fill in space at the end of a line.

When you break a word at the end of a line, divide it only between syllables, consulting a dictionary if necessary. Never divide a word at the end of a page, and never hyphenate a one-syllable word. In addition, never leave a single letter at the end of a line or carry only one or two letters to the next line.

If you divide a **compound word** at the end of a line, put the hyphen between the elements of the compound (*snow-mobile*, not *snowmo-bile*).

See 26b

COMPUTER TIP   academic.cengage.com/eng/kirsznermandell

DIVIDING ELECTRONIC ADDRESSES (URLS)

Never insert a hyphen to divide an electronic address (URL) at the end of a line. (Readers might think the hyphen is part of the address.) MLA style recommends that you break the URL after a slash. If this is not possible, break it in a logical place—after a period, for example—or avoid the problem altogether by moving the entire URL to the next line.

26b Dividing Compound Words

A **compound word** is composed of two or more words. Some familiar compound words are always hyphenated: *no-hitter, helter-skelter*. Other compounds are always written as one word (*fireplace*) and others as two separate words (*bunk bed*). Your dictionary can tell you whether or not a particular compound requires a hyphen.

GRAMMAR CHECKER

HYPHENATING COMPOUND WORDS

Your word processor's grammar checker will highlight certain compound words with incorrect or missing hyphenation and offer suggestions for revision.

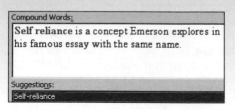

Compound Words:
Self reliance is a concept Emerson explores in his famous essay with the same name.

Suggestions:
Self-reliance

Hyphens are generally used in the following compounds.

1 In Compound Adjectives

A **compound adjective** is a series of two or more words that function together as an adjective. When a compound adjective *precedes* the noun it modifies, use hyphens to join its elements.

> The research team tried to use <u>nineteenth●century</u> technology to design a <u>space●age</u> project.

When a compound adjective *follows* the noun it modifies, do not use hyphens to join its elements.

> The three <u>government●operated</u> programs were run smoothly, but the one that was not <u>government●operated</u> was short of funds.

NOTE: A compound adjective formed with an adverb ending in *-ly* is not hyphenated even when it precedes the noun: *Many <u>upwardly●mobile</u> families are on tight budgets.*

Use **suspended hyphens**—hyphens followed by a space or by appropriate punctuation and a space—in a series of compounds that have the same principal elements.

> Graduates of <u>two●</u> and <u>four●year</u> colleges were eligible for the grants.

> The exam called for <u>sentence●</u>, <u>paragraph●</u>, and <u>essay● length</u> answers.

2 With Certain Prefixes or Suffixes

Use a hyphen between a prefix and a proper noun or adjective.

mid-July   pre-Columbian

Use a hyphen to connect the prefixes *all-*, *ex-*, *half-*, *quarter-*, *quasi-*, and *self-* and the suffix *-elect* to a noun.

ex-senator   self-centered   president-elect

Also hyphenate to avoid certain hard-to-read combinations, such as two *i*'s (*semi-illiterate*) or more than two of the same consonant (*shell-less*).

3 In Compound Numerals and Fractions

Hyphenate compounds that represent numbers below one hundred (even if they are part of a larger number).

the <u>twenty-first</u> century   three hundred <u>sixty-five</u> days

Also hyphenate the written form of a fraction when it modifies a noun.

a <u>two-thirds</u> share of the business

27 Using Abbreviations

Generally speaking, **abbreviations** are not appropriate in college writing except in tables, charts, and works-cited lists. Some abbreviations are acceptable only in scientific, technical, or business writing or only in a particular discipline. If you have questions about the appropriateness of a particular abbreviation, consult a style manual in your field.

COMPUTER TIP   academic.cengage.com/eng/kirsznermandell

ABBREVIATIONS IN ELECTRONIC COMMUNICATIONS

Shorthand abbreviations and symbols—such as GR8 (great) and 2NITE (tonight)—are common in text messages. Although they are acceptable in informal electronic communication, such abbreviations are not appropriate in college writing (or in business communication).

27a Abbreviating Titles

Titles before and after proper names are usually abbreviated.

Mr. Homer Simpson   Rep. John Lewis

Henry Kissinger, PhD   Dr. Martin Luther King, Jr.

Do not, however, use an abbreviated title without a name.

The ~~Dr.~~ ^{doctor} diagnosed hepatitis.

27b Abbreviating Organization Names and Technical Terms

See 17a

Well-known businesses and government, social, and civic organizations are frequently referred to by capitalized initials. These **abbreviations** fall into two categories: those in which the initials are pronounced as separate units (MTV) and **acronyms,** in which the initials are pronounced as a word (NATO).

To save space, you may use accepted abbreviations for complex technical terms that are not well known, but be sure to spell out the full term the first time you mention it, followed by the abbreviation in parentheses.

Citrus farmers have been using ethylene dibromide (EDB), a chemical pesticide, for more than twenty years. Now, however, EDB has contaminated water supplies.

27c Abbreviating Dates, Times of Day, Temperatures, and Numbers

50 BC (*BC* follows the date)

3:03 p.m. (lowercase)

AD 432 (*AD* precedes the date)

180° F (Fahrenheit)

Always capitalize *BC* and *AD*. (The alternatives *BCE*, for "before the Common Era," and *CE*, for "Common Era," are also capitalized.) The abbreviations *a.m.* and *p.m.* are used only when they are accompanied by numbers: *I'll see you in the morning* (not *in the a.m.*).

Avoid the abbreviation *no.* except in technical writing, and then use it only before a specific number: *The unidentified substance was labeled no. 52.*

CLOSE-UP

ABBREVIATIONS IN MLA DOCUMENTATION

See 34a2

<u>MLA documentation style</u> requires abbreviations of publishers' company names—for example, **Columbia UP** for *Columbia University Press*—in the works-cited list. Do not, however, use such abbreviations in the body of your paper. MLA style also permits the use of abbreviations that designate parts of written works (**ch. 3, sec. 7**)—but only in the works-cited list and parenthetical documentation. MLA also recommends abbreviating citations for very well-known literary works and for books of the Bible in parenthetical citations: *Oth.* (*Othello*), **Exod.** (Exodus). These words should not be abbreviated in the text of your paper or in the works-cited list.

27d Editing Misused Abbreviations

In college writing, abbreviations are not used in the following cases.

1 Latin Expressions

Poe wrote "The Gold Bug," "The Tell-Tale Heart," ~~etc.~~ *and so on.*

Many musicians (~~e.g.,~~ *for example,* Bruce Springsteen) have been influenced by Bob Dylan.

2 Names of Days, Months, or Holidays

On ~~Sat., Dec.~~ *Saturday, December* 23, I started my ~~Xmas~~ *Christmas* shopping.

3 Names of Streets and Places

He lives on Riverside ~~Dr.~~ *Drive* in ~~NYC.~~ *New York City.*

Exceptions: The abbreviations *U.S.* (*U.S. Coast Guard*), *St.* (*St. Albans*), and *Mt.* (*Mt. Etna*) are acceptable, as is *DC* in *Washington, DC*.

4 Names of Academic Subjects

Psychology   literature
~~Psych.~~ and English ~~lit.~~ are required courses.
   ^   ^

5 Units of Measurement

MLA style does not permit abbreviations for units of measurement and requires that you spell out words such as *inches, feet, years, miles, pints, quarts,* and *gallons.*

In technical and business writing, however, some units of measurement are abbreviated when they are preceded by a numeral.

The hurricane had winds of 35 mph.

One new hybrid gets over 50 mpg.

6 Symbols

The symbols =, +, and # are acceptable in technical and scientific writing but not in nontechnical college writing. The symbols % and $ are acceptable only when used with **numerals** (15%, $15,000), not with spelled-out numbers.

See
28b

28 Using Numbers

Convention determines when to use a **numeral** (22) and when to spell out a number (twenty-two). Numerals are commonly used in scientific and technical writing and in journalism, but they are used less often in academic or literary writing.

NOTE: The guidelines in this chapter are based on the *MLA Handbook for Writers of Research Papers,* 7th ed. (2009). **APA style,** however, requires that all numbers below ten be spelled out if they do not represent specific measurements and that the numbers ten and above be expressed in numerals.

See
Ch. 35

28a Spelled-Out Numbers versus Numerals

Unless a number falls into one of the categories listed in **28b,** spell it out *if you can do so in one or two words.*

The Hawaiian alphabet has only <u>twelve</u> letters.

Class size stabilized at <u>twenty-eight</u> students.

The subsidies are expected to total about <u>two million</u> dollars.

Numbers *more than two words* long are expressed in figures.

The dietitian prepared <u>125</u> sample menus.

The developer of the community purchased <u>300,000</u> doorknobs and <u>153,000</u> faucets.

Never begin a sentence with a numeral. If necessary, reword the sentence.

Faulty: 250 students are currently enrolled in World History 106.

Revised: Current enrollment in World History 106 is 250 students.

NOTE: When one number immediately precedes another in a sentence, spell out the first, and use a numeral for the second: *five 3-quart containers.*

GRAMMAR CHECKER

SPELLED-OUT NUMBERS VERSUS NUMERALS

Your word processor's grammar checker will often highlight numerals in your writing and suggest that you spell them out. Before clicking Change, be sure that the number does not fall into one of the categories listed in **28b.**

Spell Out Number:

This essay by Walter Benjamin focuses on 2 groups of people: the victors and the vanquished.

Suggestions:

two

28b Conventional Uses of Numerals

■ **Addresses:** 111 Fifth Avenue, New York, NY 10003
■ **Dates:** January 15, 1929   1914–1919
■ **Exact Times:** 9:16   10 a.m. or 10:00 a.m. (but spell out times of day when they are used with *o'clock:* ten o'clock)
■ **Exact Sums of Money:** $25.11 $6,752.00
■ **Divisions of Works:** Act 5   lines 17–28   page 42
■ **Percentages and Decimals:** 80%   3.14

NOTE: You may spell out a percentage (*eighty percent*) if you use percentages infrequently in your paper, provided the percentage can be expressed in two or three words. Always use a numeral (not a spelled-out number) with a % symbol.

■ **Measurements with Symbols or Abbreviations:** 32°   15 cc
■ **Ratios and Statistics:** 20 to 1   a mean of 40
■ **Scores:** a lead of 6 to 0
■ **Identification Numbers:** Route 66   Track 8 Channel 12

PART 6

Writing with Sources

29 Writing Research Papers

Research is the systematic investigation of a topic outside your own knowledge and experience. However, doing research means more than just reading about other people's ideas. When you undertake a research project, you become involved in a process that requires you to **think critically:** to evaluate and interpret the ideas explored in your sources and to formulate ideas of your own. Whether you are working with print sources (books, journals, magazines) or **electronic resources** (online catalogs, databases, the Internet), in the library or at your home computer, your research will be most efficient if you follow a systematic process.

See 30a2

CHECKLIST

THE RESEARCH PROCESS

☐ Choose a topic. (**See 29a.**)

☐ Do exploratory research and formulate a research question. (**See 29b.**)

☐ Assemble a working bibliography. (**See 29c.**)

☐ Develop a tentative thesis. (**See 29d.**)

☐ Do focused research. (**See 29e.**)

☐ Take notes. (**See 29f.**)

☐ Fine-tune your thesis. (**See 29g.**)

☐ Outline your paper. (**See 29h1.**)

☐ Draft your paper. (**See 29h2.**)

☐ Revise your paper. (**See 29h3.**)

☐ Prepare a final draft. (**See 29i.**)

29a Choosing a Topic

The first step in the research process is finding a topic to write about. In many cases, your instructor will help you to choose a topic, either by providing a list of suitable topics or by suggesting a general subject area—for example, a famous trial, an event that happened on the day you were born, a social problem on college campuses, or an issue related to the Internet. Even in these cases, you will still need to choose one of the topics or narrow the subject area—deciding, for example, on one trial, one event, one problem, or one issue.

If your instructor prefers that you select a topic on your own, you should consider a number of possible topics and weigh both their suitability for research and your interest in them. You decide on a topic for your research paper in much the same way as you decide on a topic for a short essay: you read, brainstorm, talk to people, and ask questions. Specifically, you talk to friends and family members, coworkers, and perhaps your instructor; you read magazines and newspapers; you take stock of your interests; you consider possible topics suggested by your other courses—historical events, scientific developments, and so on; and, of course, you search the Internet. (Your search engine's **subject guides** can be particularly helpful as you look for a promising topic or narrow a broad subject.) See 31a3

29b Doing Exploratory Research and Formulating a Research Question

Doing **exploratory research**—searching the Internet and looking through general reference works, such as encyclopedias, bibliographies, and specialized dictionaries (either in print or online)—helps you to get an overview of your topic. Your goal at this stage is to formulate a **research question,** the question you want your research paper to answer. A research question helps you to decide which sources to seek out, which to examine first, which to examine in depth, and which to skip entirely. (The answer to your research question will be your paper's **thesis statement**.) See 2b

29c Assembling a Working Bibliography

As soon as you start your exploratory research, you begin to assemble a **working bibliography** for your paper. (This working bibliography will be the basis for your **works-cited list**, which will include all the sources you cite in your paper.) See 34a2

CLOSE-UP

ASSEMBLING A WORKING BIBLIOGRAPHY

As you record bibliographic information for your sources, include the following information:

(continued)

ASSEMBLING A WORKING BIBLIOGRAPHY
(continued)

Book Author(s); title (italicized in computer file, underlined on index card); call number (for future reference); city of publication; publisher; date of publication; medium; brief evaluation

Article Author(s); title of article (in quotation marks); title of journal (italicized in computer file, underlined on index card); volume and issue numbers; date; inclusive page numbers; medium; date downloaded (if applicable); URL (if applicable); brief evaluation

---

As you consider each potential source, keep track of your sources by recording full and accurate bibliographic information—author, title, page numbers, and complete publication information—in a separate computer file designated "Bibliography" or, if you prefer, on individual index cards.

Information for Working Bibliography (in Computer File)

Author —	Pekow, Charles
Title —	"Community Technology Program in Crosshairs of Congress"
Publication information and medium —	*Community College Week.* 15 Aug. 2005: n. pag. *Academic Search Premier.* Web. Accessed January 30, 2006.
Evaluation —	Good summary of the different positions that the members of Congress have on whether the federal government should provide funding for the Community Technology Centers program.

Information for Working Bibliography (on Index Card)

Call number —	HN49.I56 N69 2001
Author —	Norris, Pippa
Title —	Digital Divide: Civic Engagement, Information Poverty, and the Internet Worldwide
Publication information and medium —	Cambridge: Cambridge UP, 2001. Print.
Evaluation —	A book about the digital divide that explains its history and its relationship to economics and class. Published in 2001; may be outdated.

Keep records of interviews (including telephone and email interviews), meetings, lectures, films, and electronic sources as well as of books and articles. For each source, include not only basic identifying details—such as the date of an interview, the call number of a library book, the electronic address (URL) of an Internet source, or the author of an article accessed from a library's subscription database—but also a brief **evaluation** that includes comments about the kind of information the source contains, the amount of information offered, its relevance to your topic, and its limitations.

As you go about collecting sources and building your working bibliography, monitor the quality and relevance of all the materials you examine. Making informed choices early in the research process will save you a lot of time in the long run. (For more on evaluating library sources, **see 30b;** for guidelines on evaluating Internet sources, **see 31c.**)

`29d` Developing a Tentative Thesis

Your **tentative thesis** is a preliminary statement of the main point you think your research will support. This statement, which you will eventually refine into a **thesis statement**, should be the tentative answer to your research question.

See 29g

DEVELOPING A TENTATIVE THESIS

Subject Area
Issue related to the Internet

Topic
Access to the Internet

Research Question
Do all Americans have equal access to the Internet?

Tentative Thesis
Not all Americans have equal access to the Internet, and this is a potentially serious problem.

Because it suggests the specific direction your research will take as well as the scope and emphasis of your argument, the tentative thesis you come up with at this point can help you generate a list of the main ideas you plan to develop in your paper. This list can help you to narrow the focus of your research so that you can zero in on a few specific categories to explore as you read and take notes.

LISTING YOUR POINTS

<u>Tentative Thesis</u>: Not all Americans have equal access to the Internet, and this is a potentially serious problem.
- Give background about Internet; tell why it's important.
- Identify groups that don't have access to Internet.
- Explain problems this creates.
- Suggest possible solutions.

29e Doing Focused Research

Once you have decided on a tentative thesis and made a list of the points you plan to discuss in your paper, you are ready to begin your focused research. During **exploratory research,** you look at general reference works to get an overview of your topic. During **focused research,** however, you look for the specific information—facts, examples, statistics, definitions, quotations—you need to support your points.

1 Reading Sources

As you look for information, try to explore as many sources, and as many different viewpoints, as possible. It makes sense to examine more sources than you actually intend to use. This strategy will enable you to proceed even if one or more of your sources turns out to be biased, outdated, unreliable, superficial, or irrelevant—in other words, not suitable. Exploring different viewpoints is just as important. After all, if you read only those sources that agree on a particular issue, you will have difficulty understanding the full range of opinions about your topic.

As you explore various sources, try to evaluate each source's potential usefulness to you as quickly as possible. For example, if your source is a book, skim the table of contents and the index; if your source is a journal article, read the abstract. Then, if an article or a section of a book seems useful, photocopy it for future reference. Similarly, when you find an online source that looks promising, print it out (or send it to yourself as an email attachment) so that you can evaluate it further later on. (For information on evaluating library sources, see **30b**; for information on evaluating Internet sources, see **31c**.)

NOTE: Do not paste source material directly into your paper. This strategy can easily lead to unintentional **plagiarism**. See Ch. 33

2 Balancing Primary and Secondary Sources

In the course of your focused research, you will encounter both **primary sources** (original documents and observations) and **secondary sources** (interpretations of original documents and observations).

PRIMARY AND SECONDARY SOURCES	
Primary Source	**Secondary Source**
Novel, poem, play, film	Criticism
Diary, autobiography	Biography
Letter, historical document, speech, oral history	Historical analysis
Newspaper article	Editorial
Raw data from questionnaires or interviews	Social science article; case study
Observation/experiment	Scientific article

Primary sources are essential for many research projects, but secondary sources, which provide scholars' insights and interpretations, are also valuable. Remember, though, that the further you get from the primary source, the more likely you are to find inaccuracies introduced by researchers' inadvertent misinterpretations or distortions.

29f Taking Notes

As you locate information in the library and on the Internet, take notes (either by hand or on a computer) to create a record of exactly what you found and where you found it.

1 Recording Source Information

See
29f3 Each piece of information you record in your notes (whether **summarized**, **paraphrased**, or **quoted** from your sources) should be accompanied by a short descriptive heading that indicates its relevance to one of the points you will develop in your paper. Because you will use these descriptive headings to guide you as you organize your notes, you should make them as specific as possible. Labeling every note for a paper on the "digital divide" created by the Internet **Digital divide** or **Internet** will not prove very helpful later on. More focused headings—for instance, **Dangers of digital divide** or **Government's steps to narrow the gap**—will be much more useful.

Also include brief comments that make clear your reasons for recording the information. These comments (enclosed in brackets so you will know they express your own ideas, not those of your source) should establish the purpose of your note—what you think it can explain, support, clarify, describe, or contradict—and perhaps suggest its relationship to other notes or other sources. Any questions you have about the information or its source can also be included in your comments.

Finally, be sure each note accurately identifies the source of the information you are recording. You do not have to write out the complete citation, but you do have to include enough information to identify your source. For example, **Gates 499** would be enough to send you back to your working bibliography card or file, where you would be able to find the complete documentation for Henry Louis Gates's essay "One Internet, Two Nations." (If you use more than one source by the same author, you need a more complete reference.)

CLOSE-UP

TAKING NOTES

When you take notes, your goal is flexibility: you want to be able to arrange and rearrange information easily and efficiently as your paper takes shape.

- If you take notes **on your computer,** type each individual note (accompanied by source information) under a specific heading rather than listing all information from a single source under the same heading. (Later on, you can move notes around so notes on the same topic are grouped together.)

■ If you take notes **by hand,** use the time-tested index-card system, taking care to write on only one side of the card and to use a separate index card for each individual note rather than running several notes together on a single card.

Notes (in Computer File)

Short heading — *Problems of*   Dalton, *Knight Ridder/*
                digital divide   *Tribune,* 7/4/04

Source —

Note — "A recent report by the Pew Internet & American
(quotation)   Life Project revealed that minorities are slightly
more likely than whites to use the Internet at
places other than home or work, with 23 percent
of blacks and Hispanics using the Internet outside
home or work, compared with 19 percent of
whites."

Comment — [*Does this mean minorities are less likely to own
computers?*]

            Efforts to close   Dalton, *Knight Ridder/*
            gap   *Tribune,* 7/4/04

Note — 14 million Americans use the Internet at libraries,
(paraphrase)   and the availability of public-access computers
increased library visits by 17 percent between 1996
and 2001.

Comment — [*Are minorities more likely to use library computers
to access the Internet?*]

            Recommendations   Dalton, *Knight Ridder/*
            for the future   *Tribune,* 7/4/04

Note — In New York, many of the computer basics classes
(summary)   at libraries fill up quickly. Out of 40 classes, a
quarter of them were filled to capacity.
Consequently, libraries need more funding to
increase the availability of classes.

Comment — [*Who should provide this funding?*]

Notes (on Index Card)

Short heading | Source

Note ——

Comment ——

Initiatives questioned	Schwartz, "Lack"

As a result of the dot.com bust, organizations
like PowerUp, which created 1,000 community-based
technology centers, have disbanded. According to a
PowerUp spokesperson, ⁽"⁾The model that was launched
in late 1999. . . was a model that had its bloodlines
in different economic times. The model isn't
necessarily the best one for these economic times.⁽"⁾

[Is there a new model to replace these
organizations?]

CHECKLIST

TAKING NOTES

☐ **Identify the source of each piece of information.**

☐ **Include everything now that you will need later** to understand your note—names, dates, places, connections with other notes—and to remember why you recorded it.

☐ **Distinguish quotations from paraphrases and summaries and your own ideas from those of your sources.** If you copy a source's words, place them in quotation marks. (If you take notes by hand, circle the quotation marks; if you type your notes, put the quotation marks in boldface.) If you write down your own ideas, enclose them in brackets. These techniques will help you avoid accidental <u>plagiarism</u> in your paper.

☐ **Put a writer's comments into your own words whenever possible,** summarizing and paraphrasing material as well as adding your own observations and analyses.

☐ **Copy a writer's comments accurately if you quote a source,** using the exact words, spelling, punctuation marks, and capitalization.

See
Ch. 33

ESL TIP

If you take notes in English (rather than in your native language), you will probably find it easier to transfer the notes into a draft of your paper. However, you may find it faster and more efficient to use your native language when writing your own comments about each note.

2 Managing Photocopies and Printouts

Much of the information you gather will be in the form of photocopies (of articles, book sections, and so on) and material printed out from the Internet. Learning to manage this source information efficiently will save you a lot of time.

First, be careful not to allow the ease of copying to encourage you to postpone decisions about the usefulness of your sources. Remember, you can easily accumulate so many pages that it will be almost impossible for you to keep track of all your information.

Also keep in mind that photocopies and printouts are just raw information, not information that has already been interpreted and evaluated. Making copies of sources is only the first step in the process of taking thorough, careful notes. You still have to paraphrase and summarize your source's ideas and make connections among them.

Moreover, photocopies and printouts do not have much flexibility. For example, a single page of text may include information that should be earmarked for several different sections of your paper. This lack of flexibility makes it difficult for you to arrange source material into any meaningful order. Just as you would with any source, you have to transcribe your notes into your computer or onto index cards. These notes will give you the flexibility you need to write your paper.

Remember, you should approach photocopies and printouts just as you approach any other source: as material that you will read, highlight, annotate, and then take notes about.

See
Ch. 33

CLOSE-UP

AVOIDING PLAGIARISM

To avoid the possibility of accidental **plagiarism**, be sure to keep all downloaded material in a separate file—not in your Notes file. After you read this material and decide how to use it, you can move the notes you take into your Notes file (along with full source information).

CHECKLIST

WORKING WITH PHOTOCOPIES AND PRINTOUTS

To get the most out of photocopies and material printed out from the Internet, follow these guidelines:

☐ Record full and accurate source information— including the inclusive page numbers, electronic address (URL), and any other relevant information— on the first page of each copy.

☐ Clip or staple together consecutive pages of a single source.

☐ Do not copy a source without reminding yourself— *in writing*—why you are doing so. In pencil or on removable self-stick notes, record your initial responses to the source's ideas, jot down cross-references to other works or notes, and highlight important sections.

☐ Photocopying can be time-consuming and expensive, so try to avoid copying material that is only margin- ally relevant to your paper.

☐ Keep photocopies and printouts in a separate file so you will be able to find them when you need them.

3 Summarizing, Paraphrasing, and Quoting

Summarizing Sources. A **summary** is a brief restate- ment, *in your own words*, of the main idea of a passage or an article. A summary is always much shorter than the original because it omits the examples, asides, analogies, and rhetorical strategies that writers use to add emphasis and interest.

When you summarize, use your own words, not the exact language or phrasing of your source. If you think it is necessary to reproduce a distinctive word or phrase, place it in quotation marks; otherwise, you will be committing **plagiarism**. Remember that your summary should accurately represent the writer's ideas and should include only the ideas of your source, not your own interpretations or opinions. Finally, be sure to document all quoted words and paraphrases as well as the summary itself.

See Ch. 33

Original Source

Today, the First Amendment faces challenges from groups who seek to limit expressions of racism and bigotry. A growing number of legislatures have passed rules against "hate speech"—[speech] that is offensive on the basis of race, ethnicity, gender, or sexual orientation. The rules are intended to promote respect for all people and protect the targets of hurtful words, gestures, or actions.

Legal experts fear these rules may wind up diminishing the rights of all citizens. "The bedrock principle [of our society] is that government may never suppress free speech simply because it goes against what the community would like to hear," says Nadine Strossen, president of the American Civil Liberties Union and professor of constitutional law at New York University Law School. In recent years, for example, the courts have upheld the right of neo-Nazis to march in Jewish neighborhoods; protected cross-burning as a form of free expression; and allowed protesters to burn the American flag. The offensive, ugly, distasteful, or repugnant nature of expression is not reason enough to ban it, courts have said.

But advocates of limits on hate speech note that certain kinds of expression fall outside of First Amendment protection. Courts have ruled that "fighting words"—words intended to provoke immediate violence—or speech that creates a clear and present danger are not protected forms of expression. As the classic argument goes, freedom of speech does not give you the right to yell "Fire!" in a crowded theater. (Sudo, Phil. "Freedom of Hate Speech?" *Scholastic Update* 124.14 [1992]: 17–20.)

Summary

The right to freedom of speech, guaranteed by the First Amendment, is becoming more difficult to defend. Some people think stronger laws against the use of "hate speech" weaken the First Amendment, but others argue that some kinds of speech remain exempt from this protection (Sudo 17).

> ## CLOSE-UP
>
> ### SUMMARIES
>
> - **Summaries are original.** They should use your own language and phrasing, not the language and phrasing of your source.
> - **Summaries are concise.** They should always be much shorter than the original.
> - **Summaries are accurate.** They should express the main idea of your source.
> - **Summaries are objective.** They should not include your opinions.
> - **Summaries are complete.** They should reflect the entire passage, not just part of it.

Paraphrasing Sources. A summary conveys just the main idea of a source; a **paraphrase** is a *detailed* restatement, in your own words, of all a source's important ideas—but not your opinions or interpretations of those ideas. In a paraphrase, you indicate not only the source's main points but also its order, tone, and emphasis. Consequently, a paraphrase can sometimes be as long as the source itself.

Compare the following paraphrase with the summary of the same source on page 143.

Paraphrase

Many groups want to limit the right of free speech guaranteed by the First Amendment to the Constitution. They believe this is necessary to protect certain groups of people from "hate speech." Women, people of color, and gay men and lesbians, for example, may find that hate speech is used to intimidate them. Legal scholars are afraid that even though the rules against hate speech are well intentioned, such rules undermine our freedom of speech. As Nadine Strossen, president of the American Civil Liberties Union, says, "The bedrock principle [of our society] is that government may never suppress free speech simply because it goes against what the community would like to hear" (qtd. in Sudo 17). People who support speech codes point out, however, that certain types of speech are not protected by the First Amendment—for example, words that create a "clear and present danger" or that would lead directly to violence (Sudo 17).

CLOSE-UP

PARAPHRASES

- **Paraphrases are original.** They should use your own language and phrasing, not the language and phrasing of your source.
- **Paraphrases are accurate.** They should reflect both the ideas and the emphasis of your source.
- **Paraphrases are objective.** They should not include your own opinions or interpretations.
- **Paraphrases are complete.** They should include all the important ideas in your source.

ESL TIP

If you find yourself imitating a writer's sentence structure and vocabulary, try reading the passage you want to paraphrase and then putting it aside and thinking about it. Then, try to write down the ideas you remember without looking at the original text.

Quoting Sources. When you **quote,** you copy a writer's statements exactly as they appear in a source, word for word and punctuation mark for punctuation mark, enclosing the borrowed words in quotation marks. As a rule, you should not quote extensively in a research paper. Numerous quotations interrupt the flow of your discussion and give readers the impression that your paper is just an unassimilated collection of other people's ideas.

CHECKLIST

WHEN TO QUOTE

Quote a source only in the following situations:

☐ Quote when a source's wording or phrasing is so distinctive that a summary or paraphrase would diminish its impact.

☐ Quote when a source's words—particularly those of a recognized expert on your subject—will lend authority to your paper.

(continued)

> **WHEN TO QUOTE** (continued)
>
> ☐ Quote when paraphrasing would create a long, clumsy, or incoherent phrase or would change the meaning of the original.
>
> ☐ Quote when you plan to disagree with a source. Using a source's exact words helps to show readers that you are being fair.
>
> **NOTE:** Remember to document all quotations that you use in your paper.

29g Fine-Tuning Your Thesis

After you have finished your focused research and note-taking, you are ready to refine your tentative thesis into a carefully worded statement that expresses a conclusion that your research can support. This **thesis statement** should be more detailed than your tentative thesis, accurately conveying the direction, emphasis, and scope of your paper.

See 2b

FINE-TUNING YOUR THESIS

Tentative Thesis
Not all Americans have equal access to the Internet, and this is a potentially serious problem.

Thesis Statement
Although the Internet has changed our lives for the better, it has also left some people behind, creating two distinct classes—those who have access and those who do not.

29h Outlining, Drafting, and Revising

Keeping your thesis in mind, you are now ready to make an outline to guide you as you draft your paper.

1 Outlining

Before you can write your rough draft, you need to make some sense out of all the notes you have accumulated, and you do this by sorting and organizing them. By identifying categories and subcategories of information, you will begin to see your paper take shape and be able to construct an outline that reflects this shape. A **formal outline** indicates not only the exact order in which you will present your ideas but also the relationship between main ideas and supporting details.

CHECKLIST

CONSTRUCTING A FORMAL OUTLINE

When you construct a formal outline for your research paper, follow these guidelines:

☐ Write your thesis statement at the top of the page.

☐ Review your notes to make sure that each note expresses only one general idea. If this is not the case, recopy any unrelated information, creating a separate note.

☐ Check that the heading for each note specifically characterizes the note's information. If it does not, change the heading.

☐ Sort your notes by their headings, keeping a miscellaneous pile for notes that do not seem to fit into any category. Irrelevant notes—those unrelated to your paper's thesis—should be set aside (but not discarded).

☐ Check your categories for balance. If most of your notes fall into one or two categories, change some of your headings to create narrower, more focused categories. If you have only one or two notes in a category, you will need to do additional research or treat that topic only briefly (or not at all).

☐ Organize the individual notes within each group, adding more specific subheads as needed. Arrange your notes in an order that highlights the most important points and subordinates lesser ones.

☐ Decide on a logical order in which to discuss your paper's major points.

☐ Construct your formal outline, using divisions and subdivisions that correspond to your headings. (Outline only the body of your paper, not your introduction and conclusion.) Be sure each heading has at least two subheadings; if one does not, combine it with another heading. Follow outline format strictly:

(continued)

> **CONSTRUCTING A FORMAL OUTLINE** *(continued)*
>
>   I. First major point of your paper
>   A. First subpoint
>   1. First supporting example
>   2. Next supporting example
>   a. First specific detail
>   b. Next specific detail
>   B. Next subpoint
>   II. Second major point
>
> ☐ Entries in a **sentence outline** should be complete
> sentences, with all sentences in the same tense. Each
> entry should end with a period. Entries in a **topic
> outline** should be words or short phrases. In a topic
> outline, entries should not end with periods.
>
> ☐ Review your completed outline to make sure you
> have not placed too much emphasis on a relatively
> unimportant idea, ordered ideas illogically, or created
> sections that overlap with others.

The following is a formal outline for the model student research paper in **34c**.

Formal (Topic) Outline

<u>Thesis statement</u>: Although the Internet has changed our lives for the better, it has also left some people behind, creating two distinct classes—those who have access and those who do not.

    I. Development of the Internet
        A. Empowering tool
        B. Source of knowledge and prosperity
    II. Problems of digital divide
        A. Lack of access by many groups
        B. Educational and economic disadvantages
        C. Widening gap between haves and have-nots
    III. Efforts by government and others to close gap
        A. Community Technology Centers Program
        B. Commerce Department's Technology
            Opportunities Program
        C. Bill and Melinda Gates Foundation

   D. *The Digital Divide Network* and *The Civil Rights Forum*

IV. Need for initiatives questioned

   A. Increase in minority computer use

   B. Bush administration view

   C. Challenges by minority groups

V. Need for initiatives defended

   A. Benton Foundation report

   B. Popularity of public library programs

   C. Continued gap in schools

   D. Continued problems for minorities and the poor

VI. Recommendations for the future

   A. Improve access to technology, especially the Internet

   B. Redefine "digital divide" to make it more inclusive

   C. Continue federal funding

COMPUTER TIP   academic.cengage.com/eng/kirsznermandell

OUTLINING

Before you begin writing, create a separate file for each major section of your outline. Then, copy your notes into these files in the order in which you intend to use them. You can print out each file as you need it and use it as a guide as you write.

---

2 Drafting

When you write your **rough draft**, follow your outline, using your notes as needed. As you draft, jot down questions to yourself, and identify points that need further clarification (you can bracket those comments or print them in boldface on your draft, or you can write them on self-stick notes). Leave space for material you plan to add, and bracket phrases or whole sections that you think you may later decide to move or delete. In other words, lay the groundwork for revision.

See 2d1

   As your draft takes shape, you will need to supply transitions between sentences and paragraphs to show

how your points are related. Be careful to copy source information fully and accurately on this and every subsequent draft, placing documentation as close as possible to the material it identifies.

COMPUTER TIP | academic.cengage.com/eng/kirsznermandell

DRAFTING

You can use a split screen or multiple windows to view your notes as you draft your paper. You can also copy the material that you need from your notes and then insert it into the text of your paper. (As you copy, be especially careful that you do not unintentionally commit **plagiarism**.)

See 33b

Shaping the Parts of Your Paper. Like any other essay, a research paper has an introduction, a body, and a conclusion. In your rough draft, as in your outline, you focus on the body of your paper. You should not spend time planning an introduction or a conclusion at the drafting stage; your ideas will change as you write, and you will want to develop your opening and closing paragraphs later to reflect those changes.

See 3d1

In your **introduction,** you identify your topic and establish how you will approach it. Your **introduction** also includes your thesis statement, which expresses the position you will support in the rest of the paper.

See 3a

As you draft the **body** of your paper, indicate its direction with strong **topic sentences** that correspond to the divisions of your outline.

> In the late 1990s, many argued that the Internet had ushered in a new age, one in which instant communication would bring people closer together and eventually eliminate national boundaries.

See 40b

You can also use **headings** if they are a convention of the discipline in which you are writing.

<u>Responses to Digital Divide</u>

> In response, the government, corporations, nonprofit organizations, and public libraries made efforts to bridge the gap between the "haves" and the "have-nots."

Even in your rough draft, carefully worded topic sentences and headings will help you keep your discussion under control.

The **conclusion** of a research paper often restates the thesis. This is especially important in a long paper, because by the time your readers get to the end, they may have lost sight of your paper's main idea. Your **conclusion** can also include a summary of your key points, a call for action, or perhaps an apt quotation. Remember, however, that in your rough draft your concluding paragraph is usually very brief.

See 3d2

Working Source Material into Your Paper. In the body of your paper, you evaluate and interpret your sources, comparing different ideas and assessing various points of view. As a writer, your job is to draw your own conclusions, blending information from your sources into a paper that coherently and forcefully presents your own original viewpoint to your readers.

Be sure to **integrate source material** smoothly into your paper, clearly and accurately identifying the relationships among various sources (and between those sources' ideas and your own). If two sources present conflicting interpretations, you should be especially careful to use precise language and accurate transitions to make the contrast apparent (for instance, **Although the Bush administration remains optimistic, some studies suggest . . .**). When two sources agree, you should make this clear (for example, **Like Young, McPherson believes . . .** or **Department of Commerce statistics confirm Gates's point**). Such phrasing will provide a context for your own comments and conclusions. If different sources present complementary information about a subject, blend details from the sources carefully, keeping track of which ideas come from which source.

See Ch. 32

3 Revising

A good way to begin revising is to make an outline of your draft to check the logic of its organization and the relationships among sections of the paper. As you continue to revise, the checklists in **2d2** can help you assess your paper's overall structure and its individual paragraphs, sentences, and words.

Your instructor's revision suggestions, which can come in a conference or in handwritten comments on your paper, can also help you revise. Alternatively, your instructor may use *Microsoft Word*'s Comment tool to make comments electronically on a draft that you send by email. When you revise, you can incorporate these suggestions into your paper.

Rough Draft Incorporating Instructor's Suggestions (Excerpt)

|The|Bill and Melinda Gates Foundation has provided libraries across the country with funding that allows them to purchase computers

> **Comment:** You need a transition sentence before this one to show that this paragraph is about a new idea. See 3b.

and connect them to the Internet (Egan). Nonprofit organizations also sponsor Web sites, such as *The Digital Divide Network*, a site that posts stories about the digital divide from a variety of perspectives.|By posting information on the Web site that they created|, the site's sponsor hopes to raise awareness

> **Comment:** Wordy. See 12a.

of the problems that the digital divide causes.

Revision Incorporating Instructor's Suggestions

Nonprofit organizations also worked to bridge the digital divide. The Bill and Melinda Gates Foundation, for example, has provided libraries across the country with funding that allows them to purchase computers and connect to the Internet (Egan). Nonprofit organizations also sponsor Web sites, such as *The Digital Divide Network*, a site that posts stories about the digital divide from a variety of perspectives. By posting information, the site's sponsor hopes to raise awareness of the problems that the digital divide causes.

Feedback you get from **peer review**—other students' comments, handwritten or electronic—can also help you revise. As you incorporate your classmates' suggestions, as well as your own changes and any suggested by your instructor, you can use *Microsoft Word*'s Track Changes tool to help you keep track of the revisions you make on your draft.

Rough Draft with Three Peer Reviewers' Comments (Excerpt)

|||A recent article|observes that many African Americans and members of other minority groups argue that digital divide rhetoric might actually stereotype minorities. The article says that digital

> **Comment [TG 1]:** You need a transition sentence here!

> **Comment [DL 1]:** Ditto, this is really awk. ☺

> **Comment [RS 1]:** Tell us the name and where this came from.

divide rhetoric "could discourage businesses or academics from creating content or services tailored for minority communities—ultimately making the digital divide a self-fulfilling prophecy."|Many scholars and leaders in the African-American

> **Comment [DL 2]:** Do you need a p. #?

community fear that a focus on the digital divide will lead to its being seen as a fact to be accepted rather than as a problem to be solved. Tara L. McPherson|says|that "the idea of

> **Comment [TG 2]:** Use a stronger word—*asserts, claims,* etc. Wilson doesn't like us to keep using "says." ☺

challenging the digital divide is not about denying it's existence. But it is to ensure that the focus on the digital divide doesn't naturalize a kind of exclusion of investment.|"

> **Comment [DL 3]:** I think you're supposed to have the author's last name here.

Revision with Track Changes

In other cases, the groups targeted by digital divide programs argue that they might do more harm than good. A recent article in the *Chronicle of Higher Education* observes that many African Americans and members of other minority groups argue that digital divide rhetoric might actually stereotype minorities. The article says that digital divide rhetoric "could discourage businesses or academics from creating content or services tailored for minority communities—ultimately making the digital divide a self-fulfilling prophecy-." (Young). Many scholars and leaders in the African-American community fear that a focus on the digital divide will lead to its being seen as a fact to be accepted rather than as a problem to be solved. Tara L. McPherson says agrees, arguing that "the idea of challenging the digital divide is not about denying its existence. But it is to ensure that the focus on the digital divide doesn't naturalize a kind of exclusion of investment." (qtd. in Young).

NOTE: You will probably take your paper through several drafts, changing different parts of it each time or working on one part over and over again. After revising each draft thoroughly, print out a corrected version and make additional corrections by hand on that draft before typing in changes for the next version.

CHECKLIST

REVISING A RESEARCH PAPER

As you revise your research paper, keep the following questions in mind:

- [ ] Should you do more research to find support for certain points?
- [ ] Do you need to reorder the major sections of your paper?
- [ ] Should you rearrange the order in which you present your points within those sections?
- [ ] Do you need to add topic sentences? section headings? transitional paragraphs?

See Ch. 32

- [ ] Have you **integrated your notes** smoothly into your paper?

See 32a

- [ ] Do you introduce source material with **identifying tags**?
- [ ] Are quotations blended with paraphrase, summary, and your own observations and reactions?

See Ch. 33

- [ ] Have you avoided **plagiarism** by carefully documenting all borrowed ideas?
- [ ] Have you analyzed and interpreted the ideas of others rather than simply stringing those ideas together?
- [ ] Do your own ideas—not those of your sources—establish the focus of your discussion?

COMPUTER TIP   academic.cengage.com/eng/kirsznermandell

REVISING

When you finish revising your paper, copy the file that contains your working bibliography, and insert it at the end of your paper. Delete any irrelevant entries, and then compile your works-cited list. (Make sure that the format of the entries on your works-cited list conforms to the documentation style you are using.)

29i   Preparing a Final Draft

Before you print out the final version of your paper, <u>edit</u> <u>and proofread</u> a hard copy of your works-cited list as well as the paper itself. Next, consider (or reconsider) your paper's **title.** It should be descriptive enough to tell your readers what your paper is about, and it should create interest in your subject. Your title should also be consistent with the **purpose** and tone of your paper. (You would hardly want a humorous title for a paper about the death penalty or world hunger.) Finally, your title should be engaging and to the point—and perhaps even provocative. Often, a quotation from one of your sources will suggest a likely title.

See 2e

See 1a

When you are satisfied with your title, read your paper through one last time, proofreading for any grammar, spelling, or typing errors you may have missed. Pay particular attention to parenthetical documentation and works-cited entries. (Remember that every error undermines your credibility.) Finally, make sure your paper's format conforms to your instructor's guidelines. Once you are satisfied that your paper is as accurate as you can make it, print out a final copy. Then, fasten the pages with a paper clip (do not staple the pages or fold the corners together), and hand it in. (For a model MLA-style research paper, **see 34c.**)

30   Using and Evaluating Library Sources

30a   Using Library Sources

Even though the **Internet** has changed the nature of research, the library is still the best place to begin a research project. With its wide variety of print and electronic resources, the library gives you access to material that you cannot get anywhere else.

See Ch. 31

> ## CLOSE-UP
>
> ### ADVANTAGES OF USING THE LIBRARY
>
> - Many important and useful publications are available only in print or through the library's subscription databases and not on the Internet.
> - The information in your college library will almost always be more focused and more useful than much of what you will find on the Internet.
> - The information you see on an Internet site—unlike information in your library's subscription databases—may not be there when you try to access it at a later time. (For this reason, __MLA__ recommends that you print out all Internet documents you plan to use in your research.)
> - Anyone can publish on the Internet, so sites can vary greatly in quality. Because librarians screen the material in your college library, it will usually meet academic standards of reliability.
> - The authorship and affiliation of Internet documents can often be difficult or impossible to determine, but this is not usually the case with the sources in your college library.

See
Ch. 34

1 Using the Online Catalog

Most college and other libraries have replaced print catalog systems with **online catalogs**—computer databases that list the books, journals, and other materials held by the library. Figure 30.1 shows the home page of a university library's online catalog.

You access the online catalog (as well as the other electronic resources of the library) by using computer terminals located throughout the library. When you search an online catalog for information about a topic, you can conduct either a *keyword search* or a *subject search*.

Conducting a Keyword Search. When you carry out a **keyword search**, you enter into the online catalog a word or words associated with your topic. The screen then displays a list of catalog entries that contain those words. The more precise your keywords, the more specific and useful the information you will receive. (Combining search terms with AND, OR, and NOT enables you to narrow or broaden your search. This technique is called conducting a __Boolean search__.)

See
31a2

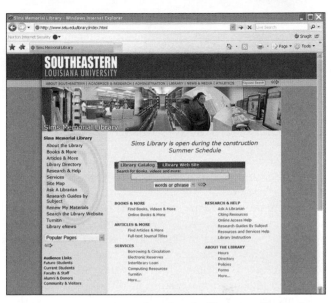

FIGURE 30.1 Home page of a university library's online catalog.

CHECKLIST

KEYWORD DOS AND DON'TS

When conducting a keyword search, remember the following hints:

☐ Use precise, specific keywords to distinguish your topic from similar topics.

☐ Enter both singular and plural keywords where appropriate—*printing press* and *printing presses*, for example.

☐ Enter both abbreviations and their full-word equivalents (for example, *US* and *United States*).

☐ Try variant spellings (for example, *color* and *colour*).

☐ Don't use too long a string of keywords. (If you do, you will retrieve large amounts of irrelevant material.)

Conducting a Subject Search. When you carry out a **subject search,** you enter specific subject headings into the online catalog. The subject headings in the library are most often arranged according to headings listed in the five-volume manual *Library of Congress Subject Headings*, which is held at the reference desk of your library. Although it may be possible to guess at a subject heading, your search will be more successful if you consult these volumes to identify the exact words you need.

2 Using Electronic Resources

The same computer terminals that enable you to access the online catalog also enable you to access a variety of electronic resources.

Online databases are collections of digital information—citations of books; reports; and journal, magazine, and newspaper articles (and sometimes the full text of articles)—arranged for easy access and retrieval by computer. Different libraries offer different databases and make them available in different ways. Most libraries have implemented Web-based systems that make it easy for users to access databases (from information providers such as DIALOG or Gale) that are not available on the free Internet. One of your first tasks should be to determine what your library has to offer. Visit your library's Web site, or ask a reference librarian for more information.

Once you have searched the databases and found useful information, you can print out or download bibliographic citations, **abstracts** (short summaries), or even full text.

General and Specialized Subscription Databases. The databases available in your college library are likely to be **subscription databases,** which means that the library must subscribe to them in order to make them available to students and faculty.

Some library databases cover many subject areas (*Expanded Academic ASAP* or *LexisNexis Academic Universe*, for example); others cover one subject area in great detail (*PsycINFO* or *Sociological Abstracts*, for example). Assuming that your library offers a variety of databases, how do you know which ones will be best for your research topic? One strategy is to begin by searching a general database that includes full-text articles and then move on to a more specialized database that covers your subject in more detail. The specialized databases are more likely to include scholarly and professional journal articles, but they are also less likely to include the full text.

Searching Databases. You can search library databases in two ways: by subject headings and by keyword(s). When you search by **subject headings,** you choose a heading (for example, *Arts, Business, Health,* and so on) from a list of terms recognized by that database.

The other option is **keyword searching,** which allows you to type in a term likely to be found in the title, subject headings, abstract, or (if the full text is available) text of an article. Keyword searching also allows you to link terms using **boolean operators** (AND, OR, NOT). For example, *elderly* AND *abuse* would retrieve only articles that mention both elderly people and abuse; *elderly* OR *aged* OR *senior citizens* would retrieve articles that mention any of these terms. Keyword searching is particularly helpful when you need to narrow or expand the focus of your search.

Both subject heading and keyword searches are useful ways to find articles on your topic. The most important thing is to be persistent. One good article often leads to another.

3 Consulting General Reference Works

During your **exploratory research,** general reference works can provide a broad overview of a particular subject. The following reference works, available in electronic form as well as in print, are useful for exploratory research.

General Encyclopedias. General multivolume encyclopedias are available both in electronic format and in print. For example, *The New Encyclopaedia Britannica* is available on CD-ROM and DVD, as well as on the World Wide Web at <http://www.britannica.com>.

Specialized Encyclopedias, Dictionaries, and Bibliographies. These specialized reference works contain in-depth articles focusing on a single subject area.

General Bibliographies. General bibliographies list books available in a wide variety of fields.

> *Books in Print.* An index of authors and titles of books in print in the United States. The *Subject Guide to Books in Print* indexes books according to subject area.
>
> *The Bibliographic Index.* A tool for locating bibliographies.

Biographical References. Biographical reference books provide information about people's lives as well as bibliographic listings.

> *Who's Who in America.* Gives concise biographical information about prominent Americans.
>
> *Who's Who.* Collects concise biographical facts about notable British men and women.
>
> *Current Biography.* Includes articles on people of many nationalities.

4 Consulting Specialized Reference Works

More specialized reference works can help you find the facts, examples, statistics, definitions, and quotations that you will need for your **focused research.** These specialized reference works—unabridged dictionaries, special dictionaries, yearbooks, almanacs, atlases, and so on—are available online as well as in print versions.

5 Finding Books

The online catalog gives you the call numbers you need for locating specific titles. A **call number** is like a book's address in the library: it tells you exactly where to find the book you are looking for.

CHECKLIST

TRACKING DOWN A MISSING BOOK

Problem	Possible Solution
1. Book has been checked out of library.	☐ Consult person at circulation desk. ☐ Check other nearby libraries.
2. Book is not in library's collection.	☐ Ask instructor if he or she owns a copy. ☐ Arrange for interlibrary loan (if time permits).
3. Journal is not in library's collection/ article is ripped out of journal.	☐ Arrange for interlibrary loan (if time permits). ☐ Check to see whether article is available in a full-text database. ☐ Ask librarian whether article has been reprinted as part of a collection.

6 Finding Periodical Articles

A **periodical** is a newspaper, magazine, scholarly journal, or other publication that is published at regular intervals (weekly, monthly, or quarterly). **Periodical indexes** list articles from a selected group of magazines, newspapers, or scholarly journals. Most college libraries offer these indexes online. Choosing the right index for your research saves you time and energy by allowing you to easily find articles written about your subject.

NOTE: Articles in scholarly journals provide current information and are written by experts in the field. Because these journals focus on a particular subject area, they can provide in-depth information.

CLOSE-UP

FREQUENTLY USED SUBSCRIPTION DATABASES

The following subscription databases are found in most academic libraries. (Be sure to check your library's Web site or ask a librarian about those available to you.)

General Indexes	Description
EBSCOhost	Database system for thousands of periodical articles on many subjects
Expanded Academic ASAP	A largely full-text database covering all subjects in thousands of magazines and scholarly journals
FirstSearch	Full-text articles from many popular and scholarly periodicals
LexisNexis Academic Universe	Includes full-text articles from national, international, and local newspapers; also includes large legal and business sections
Readers' Guide to Periodical Literature	Index to popular periodicals

Specialized Indexes	Description
Dow Jones Interactive	Full text of articles from US newspapers and trade journals

(continued)

FREQUENTLY USED SUBSCRIPTION
DATABASES *(continued)*

Specialized Indexes	Description
ERIC	Largest database of education-related journal articles and reports in the world
General BusinessFile ASAP	A full-text database covering business topics
PubMed (MEDLINE)	Covers articles in medical journals; some may be available in full text
PsycINFO	Covers psychology and related fields
Sociological Abstracts	Covers the social sciences

30b Evaluating Library Sources

Whenever you find information in the library (print or electronic), you should take the time to **evaluate** it—to assess its usefulness and its reliability. To determine the usefulness of a library source, ask the following questions:

- **Does the source treat your topic in enough detail?** To be useful, your source should treat your topic in detail. Skim the book's table of contents and index for references to your topic. To be of any real help, a book should include a section or chapter on your topic, not simply a footnote or a brief reference. For articles, read the abstract, or skim the entire article for key facts, looking closely at section headings, information set in boldface type, and topic sentences. An article should have your topic as its central subject, or at least one of its main concerns.
- **Is the source current?** The date of publication tells you whether the information in a book or article is up-to-date. A source's currency is particularly important for scientific and technological subjects, but even in the humanities, new discoveries and new ways of thinking lead scholars to reevaluate and modify their ideas.
- **Is the source respected?** A contemporary review of a source can help you make this assessment. *Book*

Review Digest, available in the reference section of your library, as well as online, lists popular books that have been reviewed in at least three newspapers or magazines and includes excerpts from representative reviews.

■ **Is the source reliable?** Is the source largely fact or unsubstantiated opinion? Does the writer support his or her conclusions? Does the writer include documentation? Is the supporting information balanced? Is the writer objective, or does he or she have a particular agenda to advance? Is the writer associated with a special interest group that may affect his or her view of the issue?

In general, **scholarly publications**—books and journals aimed at an audience of expert readers—are more respected and reliable than **popular publications**—books, magazines, and newspapers aimed at an audience of general readers. However (assuming they are current, written by reputable authors, and documented) articles from some popular publications (such as the *Atlantic* or *Harper's*) may be appropriate for your research. Check with your instructor to be sure.

SCHOLARLY VERSUS POPULAR PUBLICATIONS	
Scholarly Publications	**Popular Publications**
Report the results of research	Entertain and inform
Are often published by a university press or have some connection with a university or academic organization	Are published by commercial presses
Are usually **refereed;** that is, an editorial board or group of expert reviewers determines what will be published	Are usually not refereed
Are usually written by recognized authorities in the field about which they are writing	May be written by experts in a particular field, but more often they are written by staff or freelance writers

(continued)

Scholarly Publications	Popular Publications
Are written for a scholarly audience, so they often contain a highly technical vocabulary and challenging content	Are written for general readers, so they tend to use accessible language and do not have very challenging content
Nearly always contain extensive documentation as well as a bibliography of works consulted	Rarely cite sources or use documentation
Are published primarily because they make a contribution to a particular field of study	Are published primarily to make a profit

31 Using and Evaluating Internet Sources

The **Internet** is a vast system of networks that links millions of computers. Even with all its advantages, however, the Internet does not give you access to the high-quality print and electronic resources found in a typical college library. For this reason, you should consider the Internet to be a supplement to your library research, not a substitute for it.

31a Using the World Wide Web for Research

When most people refer to the Internet, they actually mean the **World Wide Web,** which is just a part of the Internet. (**See 31b** for other components of the Internet that you can use in your research.) The Web relies on **hypertext links,** key words highlighted in color. By clicking on these links, you can move easily from one part of a document to another or from one Web site to another.

To carry out a Web search, you need a **Web browser,** a tool that enables you to find information on the Web. Two of the most popular browsers—*Netscape Navigator* and *Microsoft Internet Explorer*—display the full range of text, photos, sound, and video available in Web documents.

Once you are connected to the Internet, you have to use your browser to connect to a **search engine,** a program that helps you retrieve information by searching the documents that are available on the Internet.

CLOSE-UP

POPULAR SEARCH ENGINES

AllTheWeb <www.alltheweb.com>: This excellent search engine provides comprehensive coverage of the Web. Many users think that this search engine is as good as *Google*.

AltaVista <www.altavista.com>: Good, precise engine for focused searches. Fast and easy to use.

Ask.com <www.ask.com>: Allows you to narrow your search by asking questions, such as *Are dogs smarter than pigs?*

Excite <www.excite.com>: Good for general topics. Because it searches over 250 million Web sites, you often get more information than you need.

Go <http://infoseek.go.com>: Enables you to access information in a directory of reviewed sites, news stories, and Usenet groups.

Google <www.google.com>: Arguably the best search engine available. Accesses a large database that enables you to carry out an image search as well as a Web page search. *Google* is easy to navigate, and searches usually yield a high percentage of useful hits.

HotBot <www.hotbot.com>: Excellent, fast search engine for locating specific information. Good search options allow you to fine-tune your searches.

Lycos <www.lycos.com>: Enables you to search for specific media (graphics, for example). A somewhat small index of Web pages.

Teoma <www.teoma.com>: Teoma is a search engine owned by *Ask.com*. Although it has a smaller index of the Web than *Google* and *AllTheWeb*, it is very effective when it comes to answering questions. It contains a Refine feature that offers suggested topics to explore after you do a search. It also has a Resources section of results that will point you to linked resources about various topics.

WebCrawler <www.webcrawler.com>: Good for beginners. Easy to use.

Yahoo! <www.yahoo.com>: Good for exploratory research. Enables you to search using either subject headings or keywords. Searches its own indexes as well as the Web.

COMPUTER TIP academic.cengage.com/eng/kirsznermandell

SPECIALIZED SEARCH ENGINES

Academic Index (academic search engine)

<http://www.academicindex.net/>

Voice of the Shuttle (humanities search engine)

<http://vos.ucsb.edu/>

Pilot-Search.com (literary search engine)

<http://www.pilot-search.com/>

FedWorld (US government database and report search engine)

<http://www.fedworld.gov/>

HealthFinder (health, nutrition, and diseases information for consumers)

<http://www.healthfinder.gov/default.htm>

The Internet Movie Database (search engine and database for film facts, reviews, and so on)

<http://www.imdb.com>

SportQuest (sports search engine)

<http://www.sportquest.com/>

FindLaw (legal search engine)

<http://www.findlaw.com/>

Because even the best search engines search only a fraction of what is on the Web, you should also carry out a metasearch using a **metacrawler,** a search engine that uses several search engines simultaneously. *Dogpile* <www.dogpile.com>, *Metacrawler* <www.metacrawler.com>, and *Zworks* <www.zworks.com> are useful tools for discovering the full range of online sources.

There are three ways to use search engines to find the information you want: *entering an electronic address, doing a keyword search,* and *using subject guides.*

1 Entering an Electronic Address

The most basic way to access information on the Web is to go directly to a specific electronic address, called a **URL.** Search engines and Web browsers enable you to enter a URL into the location field at the top of each page (see Figure 31.1). Once you type in an address and hit *enter* or

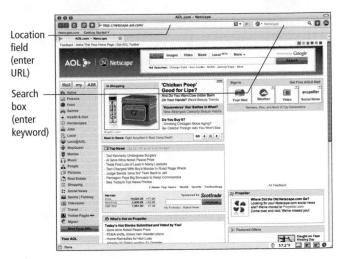

Location field (enter URL)

Search box (enter keyword)

FIGURE 31.1 Entering an address in *Netscape Navigator*.

the return key, you will be connected to the Web site you want. Make sure that you type the electronic address exactly as it appears, without adding spaces or adding or deleting punctuation marks. Omitting just a single letter or punctuation mark will send you to the wrong site—or to no site at all.

2 Doing a Keyword Search

Search engines also enable you to do a keyword search. On the first page (home page) of the search engine that you have chosen, you will find a box in which you can enter a keyword or keywords (see Figure 31.1). When you hit *enter* or the return key, the search engine retrieves and displays all the Web pages that contain your keywords.

Keep in mind that a search engine identifies any site in which the keyword or keywords that you have typed appear. (These sites are called **hits.**) Thus, a general keyword such as *Baltimore* could result in over a million hits. Because examining all these sites would be impossible, you need to focus your search. By carrying out a **Boolean search,** combining keywords with AND, OR, or NOT (typed in capital letters), you can eliminate irrelevant hits from your search. For example, to find Web pages that have to do with Baltimore's economy, type *Baltimore* AND *economy*. Some search engines allow you to search using three or four keywords—*Baltimore* AND *economy* NOT *agriculture*, for example.

3 Using Subject Guides

Some search engines, such as *Yahoo!*, *About.com*, and *Google*, contain a **subject guide** (or **search directory**)—a list of general categories (*Arts & Humanities, Education, Entertainment, Business,* and so on) from which you can choose (see Figure 31.2). Each of these categories will lead you to more specific lists of categories and subcategories, until eventually you get to the topic you want. For example, clicking on *Humanities* would lead you to *History,* which in turn would lead you to *American History* and eventually to *Vietnam War.* Although this is a time-consuming strategy for finding specific information, it can be an excellent tool for finding or narrowing a topic.

FIGURE 31.2 *Yahoo!* directory.

CHECKLIST

TIPS FOR EFFECTIVE WEB SEARCHES

☐ **Choose the right search engine.** No one all-purpose search engine exists. Make sure you review the lists of search engines in the boxes on pages 165 and 166.

☐ **Choose your keywords carefully.** A search engine is only as good as the keywords you use.

☐ **Narrow your search.** Carry out a Boolean search to make your searches more productive.

☐ **Check your spelling.** If your search does not yield the results you expect, check to make sure you have spelled your search terms correctly.

☐ **Include enough terms.** If you are looking for information on housing, for example, search for several variations of your keyword: *housing, houses, home buyer, buying houses, residential real estate,* and so on.

☐ **Consult the Help screen.** Most search engines have a help screen. If you have trouble with your search, do not hesitate to consult it.

☐ **Add useful sites to your Bookmark or Favorites list.** Whenever you find a particularly useful Web site, **bookmark** it by selecting this option on the menu bar of your browser (with some browsers, such as *Microsoft Explorer,* this option is called Favorites).

31b Using Other Internet Tools

In addition to the World Wide Web, the Internet contains a number of other components that you can use for your research.

1 Using Email

Email can be very useful as you do research because it enables you to exchange ideas with classmates, ask questions of your instructors, and even conduct long-distance interviews. You can follow email links in Web documents, and you can transfer word-processing documents or other files (as email attachments) from one computer to another.

2 Using Listservs

Listservs, (sometimes called **discussion lists**), electronic mailing lists to which you must subscribe, enable you to communicate with groups of people interested in particular topics. (Many schools, and many individual courses, have their own listservs.) Individuals in a listserv send emails to a main email address, and these messages are routed to all members in the group. Some listserv subscribers may be experts who can answer your queries. Keep in mind, however,

See
31c that anyone can join a listserv, so make sure you **evaluate** the information you get before you use it in your research.

3 Using Newsgroups

Like listservs, **newsgroups** are discussion groups. Unlike listserv messages, which are sent to you as email, newsgroup messages are collected on the **Usenet** system, a global collection of news servers, where anyone who subscribes can access them. In a sense, newsgroups function as gigantic bulletin boards where users post messages that others can read and respond to. Thus, newsgroups can be a source of specific information as well as suggestions about where to look for further information. Just as you would with a listserv, you should evaluate information you get from a newsgroup before you use it.

4 Using MUDS, MOOS, IRCS, and Instant Messaging

With emails and listservs, there is a delay between the time a message is sent and the time it is received. **MUDS, MOOS, IRCS,** and **instant messaging** enable you to send and receive messages in real time. Communication is **synchronous;** that is, messages are sent and received as they are typed. Synchronous communication programs are being used more and more in college settings—for class discussions, online workshops, and collaborative projects.

31c Evaluating Internet Sites

Web sites vary greatly in reliability. Because anyone can operate a Web site and thereby publish anything, regardless of quality, critical evaluation of Web-based material is even more important than evaluation of more traditional sources of information, such as books and journal articles.

Determining the quality of a Web site is crucial if you plan to use it as a source for your research. For this reason, you should evaluate the content of any Web site for *accuracy, credibility, objectivity* or *reasonableness, currency,* and *scope of coverage.*

Accuracy. **Accuracy** refers to the reliability of the material itself and to the use of proper documentation. Factual errors—especially errors in facts that are central to the main point of the source—should cause you to question the reliability of the material you are reading. To evaluate a site's accuracy, ask these questions:

- Is the text free of basic grammatical and mechanical errors?
- Does the site contain factual errors?
- Does the site provide a list of references?
- Are links available to other references?
- Can information be verified with print or other resources?

Credibility. **Credibility** refers to the credentials of the person or organization responsible for the site. Web sites operated by well-known institutions (the Smithsonian or the U.S. Department of Health and Human Services, for example) have a high degree of credibility. Those operated by individuals (private Web pages or blogs, for example) are often less reliable. To evaluate a site's credibility, ask these questions:

- Does the site list an author? Are credentials (for example, professional or academic affiliations) provided for the author or authors?
- Is the author a recognized authority in his or her field?
- Is the site **refereed**? That is, does an editorial board or a group of experts determine what material appears on the Web site?
- Does the organization sponsoring the site exist apart from its Web presence?
- Can you determine how long the site has existed?

CHECKLIST

DETERMINING THE LEGITIMACY OF AN ANONYMOUS OR QUESTIONABLE WEB SOURCE

When a Web source is anonymous (or has an author whose name is not familiar to you), you can take these steps to determine its legitimacy:

☐ **Post a query.** If you subscribe to a newsgroup or listserv, ask others in the group what they know about the source and its author.

(continued)

DETERMINING THE LEGITIMACY OF AN ANONYMOUS OR QUESTIONABLE WEB SOURCE *(continued)*

☐ **Follow the links.** Follow the hypertext links in a document to other documents. If the links take you to legitimate sources, you know that the author is aware of these sources of information.

☐ **Do a keyword search.** Do a search using the name of the sponsoring organization or the author as keywords. Other documents (or citations in other works) may identify the author.

☐ **Look at the URL.** The last part of a Web site's URL can tell you whether the site is sponsored by a business (*.com*), a nonprofit organization (*.org*), an educational institution (*.edu*), the military (*.mil*), or a government agency (*.gov*). Knowing this information can tell you whether an organization is trying to sell you something (*.com*) or just providing information (*.edu* or *.org*).

Objectivity or Reasonableness. **Objectivity** or **reasonableness** refers to the degree of bias that a Web site exhibits. Some Web sites make no secret of their biases. They openly advocate a particular point of view or action, or they are clearly trying to sell something. Other sites may hide their biases. For example, a site may present itself as a source of factual information when it is actually advocating a political point of view. To evaluate a site's objectivity, ask these questions:

- Does advertising appear in the text?
- Does a business, a political organization, or a special interest group sponsor the site?
- Does the site express a particular viewpoint?
- Does the site contain links to other sites that express a particular viewpoint?

Currency. **Currency** refers to how up-to-date the Web site is. The easiest way to assess a site's currency is to determine when it was last updated. Keep in mind, however, that even if the date on the site is current, the information that the site contains may not be. To evaluate a site's currency, ask these questions:

- Is the most recent update displayed?
- Are all the links to other sites still functioning?
- Is the actual information on the page up-to-date?
- Does the site clearly identify the date it was created?

Scope of Coverage. **Scope of coverage** refers to the comprehensiveness of the information on a Web site. More is not necessarily better, but some sites may be incomplete. Others may provide information that is no more than common knowledge. Still others may present discussions that may not be suitable for college-level research. To evaluate a site's scope of coverage, ask these questions:

- Does the site provide in-depth coverage?
- Does the site provide information that is not available elsewhere?
- Does the site identify a target audience? Does this target audience suggest the site is appropriate for your research needs?

32 Integrating Source Material into Your Writing

When you write a research paper, you need to weave quotations, paraphrases, and summaries of source material smoothly into your text. Add your own analysis or explanation to increase coherence and to show the relevance of your sources to the points you are making.

32a Integrating Quotations

Quotations should never be awkwardly dropped into your paper, leaving the exact relationship between the quotation and your point unclear. Instead, use a brief introductory remark to provide a context for the quotation.

Unacceptable: For the Amish, the public school system represents a problem. "A serious problem confronting Amish society from the viewpoint of the Amish themselves is the threat of absorption into mass society through the values promoted in the public school system" (Hostetler 193).

Improved: For the Amish, the public school system is a problem because it represents "the threat of absorption into mass society" (Hostetler 193).

Whenever possible, use an **identifying tag** (a phrase that identifies the source) to introduce the quotation.

As John Hostetler points out, the Amish see the public school system as a problem because it represents "the threat of absorption into mass society" (193).

CLOSE-UP

INTEGRATING SOURCE MATERIAL INTO YOUR WRITING

To make sure all your sentences do not sound the same, experiment with different methods of integrating source material into your paper.

- Vary the verbs you use to introduce a source's words or ideas (instead of repeating *says*).

acknowledges	discloses	observes
admits	explains	predicts
affirms	finds	proposes
believes	illustrates	reports
claims	implies	speculates
comments	indicates	suggests
concludes	insists	summarizes
concurs	notes	warns

- Vary the placement of the identifying tag, putting it sometimes in the middle or at the end of the quoted material instead of always at the beginning.

    Quotation with Identifying Tag in Middle: "A serious problem confronting Amish society from the viewpoint of the Amish themselves," observes Hostetler, "is the threat of absorption into mass society through the values promoted in the public school system" (193).

    Paraphrase with Identifying Tag at End: The Amish are also concerned about their children's exposure to the public school system's values, notes Hostetler (193).

CLOSE-UP

PUNCTUATING IDENTIFYING TAGS

Whether or not you use a comma with an identifying tag depends on where you place it in the sentence. If the identifying tag immediately precedes a quotation, use a comma.

> As Hostetler points out, "The Amish are successful
> in maintaining group identity" (56).

If the identifying tag does not immediately precede a quotation, do not use a comma.

> Hostetler points out that the Amish frequently "use
> severe sanctions to preserve their values" (56).

NOTE: Never use a comma after *that:* Hostetler says that,
Amish society is "defined by religion" (76).

Substitutions or Additions within Quotations. Indicate changes or additions that you make to a quotation by enclosing them in brackets.

Original Quotation: "Immediately after her wedding, she and her husband followed tradition and went to visit almost everyone who attended the wedding" (Hostetler 122).

Quotation Revised to Make Verb Tenses Consistent: Nowhere is the Amish dedication to tradition more obvious than in the events surrounding marriage. Right after the wedding celebration, the Amish bride and groom "visit almost everyone who [has] attended the wedding" (Hostetler 122).

Quotation Revised to Supply an Antecedent for a Pronoun: "Immediately after her wedding, [Sarah] and her husband followed tradition and went to visit almost everyone who attended the wedding" (Hostetler 122).

Quotation Revised to Change a Capital to a Lowercase Letter: The strength of the Amish community is illustrated by the fact that "[i]mmediately after her wedding, she and her husband followed tradition and went to visit almost everyone who attended the wedding" (Hostetler 122).

Omissions within Quotations. When you delete words from a quotation, substitute an **ellipsis** (three spaced periods) for the deleted words.

See
22f

Original: "Not only have the Amish built and staffed their own elementary and vocational schools, but they have gradually organized on local, state, and national levels to cope with the task of educating their children" (Hostetler 206).

Quotation Revised to Eliminate Unnecessary Words: "Not only have the Amish built and staffed their own elementary and vocational schools, but they have gradually organized . . . to cope with the task of educating their children" (Hostetler 206).

NOTE: If the passage you are quoting already contains ellipses, place brackets around any ellipses you add.

CLOSE-UP

OMISSIONS WITHIN QUOTATIONS

Be sure that you do not misrepresent quoted material when you delete words. For example, do not say, "the Amish have managed to maintain . . . their culture" when the original quotation is "the Amish have managed to maintain *parts of* their culture."

NOTE: For information on integrating long quotations into your papers, **see 21a.**

32b Integrating Paraphrases and Summaries

Introduce paraphrases and summaries with identifying tags, and end them with appropriate documentation. By doing so, you enable readers to differentiate your ideas from those of your sources.

Misleading (Ideas of Source Blend with Ideas of Writer): Art can be used to uncover many problems that children have at home, in school, or with their friends. For this reason, many therapists use art therapy extensively. Children's views of themselves in society are often reflected by their art style. For example, a cramped, crowded art style using only a portion of the paper shows their limited role (Alschuler 260).

Correct (Identifying Tag Differentiates Ideas of Source from Ideas of Writer): Art can be used to uncover many problems that children have at home, in school, or with their friends. For this reason, many therapists use art therapy extensively. According to William Alschuler in *Art and Self-Image,* children's views of themselves in society are often reflected by their art style. For example, a cramped, crowded art style using only a portion of the paper shows their limited role (260).

33 Avoiding Plagiarism

33a Defining Plagiarism

Plagiarism is presenting another person's ideas or words as if they were your own. Most plagiarism that occurs is **unintentional plagiarism**—for example, inadvertently pasting a quoted passage from a downloaded file directly into a paper and forgetting to include the quotation marks and documentation.

There is a difference, however, between an honest mistake and **intentional plagiarism**—for example, copying sentences from a journal article or submitting a paper that someone else has written. The penalties for unintentional plagiarism may sometimes be severe, but intentional plagiarism is almost always dealt with harshly: students who intentionally plagiarize can receive a failing grade for the paper (or the course) or even be expelled from school.

33b Avoiding Unintentional Plagiarism

The most common cause of unintentional plagiarism is sloppy research habits. To avoid this problem, do not cut and paste text from a Web site or full-text database directly into your paper. Never use sources that you have not actually read or invent sources that do not exist. If you paraphrase, do so correctly by following the examples in **29f3;** changing a few words here and there is copying, not paraphrasing.

ESL TIP

Because writing in a second language can be difficult, you may be tempted to closely follow the syntax and word choice of your sources. Be aware, however, that this constitutes plagiarism.

Another cause of unintentional plasiarism is failure to use proper **documentation**. In general, you must document any words, ideas, and images that you borrow from your sources (whether print or electronic). Of course, certain items need not be documented: **common knowledge** (information most readers probably know), facts available from a variety of reference sources, familiar sayings and

See Pts. 7–8

well-known quotations, and your own original research (interviews and surveys, for example). Information that is another writer's original contribution, however, must be acknowledged. So, although you do not have to document the fact that John F. Kennedy graduated from Harvard in 1940 or that he was elected president in 1960, you do have to document a historian's evaluation of his presidency.

The availability on the Web of information that can be downloaded and copied has also increased the likelihood of unintentional plagiarism. In fact, the freewheeling appropriation and circulation of information that routinely takes place on the Web may give the false impression that this material does not need to be documented. Whether they appear in print or in electronic form, however, the words, ideas, and images of others (including photographs, graphs, charts, and statistics) must be properly documented.

33c Revising to Eliminate Plagiarism

You can avoid plagiarism by using documentation wherever it is required and by following these guidelines.

1 Enclose Borrowed Words in Quotation Marks

Original: DNA profiling begins with the established theory that no two people, except identical twins, have the same genetic makeup. Each cell in the body contains a complete set of genes. (Tucker, William. "DNA in Court." *The American Spectator* Nov. 1994: 26)

Plagiarism: William Tucker points out that DNA profiling is based on the premise that genetic makeup differs from person to person and that each cell in the body contains a complete set of genes (26).

Even though the student writer documents the source of his information, he uses the source's exact words without placing them in quotation marks.

Correct (Borrowed Words in Quotation Marks): William Tucker points out that DNA profiling is based on the premise that genetic makeup differs from person to person and that "[e]ach cell in the body contains a complete set of genes" (26).

Correct (Paraphrase): William Tucker points out that DNA profiling is based on the premise that genetic makeup differs from person to person and that every cell includes a full set of an individual's genes (26).

COMPUTER TIP   academic.cengage.com/eng/kirsznermandell

PLAGIARISM AND INTERNET SOURCES

Any time you download text from the Internet, you risk committing plagiarism. To avoid the possibility of unintentional plagiarism, follow these guidelines:

- Download information into individual files so that you can keep track of your sources.
- Do not simply cut and paste blocks of downloaded text into your paper; summarize or paraphrase this material first.
- If you do record the exact words of your source, enclose them in quotation marks.
- Whether your information is from emails, online discussion groups, listservs, or World Wide Web sites, give proper credit by providing appropriate documentation.

---

2 Do Not Imitate a Source's Syntax and Phrasing

Original: If there is a garbage crisis, it is that we are treating garbage as an environmental threat and not what it is: a manageable—though admittedly complex—civic issue. (Poore, Patricia. "America's 'Garbage Crisis.'" *Harper's* Mar. 1994: 39)

Plagiarism: If a garbage crisis does exist, it is that people see garbage as a menace to the environment and not what it actually is: a controllable—if obviously complicated—public problem (Poore 39).

Although this student does not use the exact words of her source, she closely imitates the original's syntax and phrasing, simply substituting synonyms for the author's words.

Correct (Paraphrase in Writer's Own Words; One Distinctive Phrase Placed in Quotation Marks): Patricia Poore argues that America's "garbage crisis" is exaggerated; rather than viewing garbage as a serious environmental hazard, she says, we should look at garbage as a public problem that may be complicated but that can be solved (39).

3 Document Statistics Obtained from a Source

Although many people assume that statistics are common knowledge, they are usually the result of original research and must be documented.

Correct (Documentation Provided): According to one study of 303 accidents recorded, almost one-half took place before the drivers were legally allowed to drive at eighteen (Schuman et al. 1027).

4 Differentiate Your Words and Ideas from Those of Your Source

Original: At some colleges and universities traditional survey courses of world and English literature . . . have been scrapped or diluted. . . . What replaces them is sometimes a mere option of electives, sometimes "multicultural" courses introducing material from Third World cultures and thinning out an already thin sampling of Western writings, and sometimes courses geared especially to issues of class, race, and gender. (Howe, Irving. "The Value of the Canon." *New Republic* 2 Feb. 1991: 40–47).

Plagiarism: At many universities the Western literature survey courses have been edged out by courses that emphasize minority concerns. These courses are "thinning out an already thin sampling of Western writings" in favor of courses geared especially to issues of "class, race, and gender" (Howe 40).

Because the student writer does not differentiate his ideas from those of his source, it appears that only the quotation in the last sentence is borrowed when, in fact, the first sentence also owes a debt to the original. The writer should have clearly identified the boundaries of the borrowed material by introducing it with an identifying tag and ending with documentation. (Note that a quotation *always* requires its own documentation.)

Correct: According to critic Irving Howe, at many universities the Western literature survey courses have been edged out by courses that emphasize minority concerns (41). These courses, says Howe, are "thinning out an already thin sampling of Western writings" in favor of "courses geared especially to issues of class, race, and gender" (40).

CHECKLIST

AVOIDING PLAGIARISM

☐ **Take careful notes.** Be sure you have recorded information from your sources carefully and accurately.

☐ **In your notes, clearly identify borrowed material.** In handwritten notes, put all words borrowed from your sources inside *circled* quotation marks, and enclose your own comments within brackets. If you are taking notes on a computer, boldface all quotation marks.

☐ **In your paper, differentiate your ideas from those of your sources** by clearly introducing borrowed material with an identifying tag and by following it with documentation.

☐ **Enclose all direct quotations** used in your paper within quotation marks.

☐ **Review all paraphrases and summaries** in your paper to make certain they are in your own words and that any distinctive words and phrases from a source are quoted.

☐ **Document all quoted material and all paraphrases and summaries** of your sources.

☐ **Document all information** that is open to dispute or that is not common knowledge.

☐ **Document all opinions, conclusions, figures, tables, statistics, graphs, and charts** taken from a source.

☐ **Never submit the work of another person as your own.** Do not buy a paper online or use a paper given to you by a friend. In addition, never include in your paper passages that have been written by a friend, relative, or writing tutor.

☐ **Never use sources that you have not actually read** (or invent sources that do not exist).

WRITING IN THE DISCIPLINES: AN OVERVIEW

Humanities

Disciplines	Assignments	Style and Format
Languages	Response essay	*Style*
Literature	Summary essay	Specialized
Philosophy	Annotated	vocabulary
History	bibliography	Direct quotations
Linguistics	Bibliographic	from sources
Religion	essay	
Art history	Analysis essay	*Format*
Music		Little use of internal
		headings or visuals

Social Sciences

Disciplines	Assignments	Style and Format
Anthropology	Personal	*Style*
Psychology	experience essay	Specialized vocabu-
Economics	Book review	lary including
Business	Case study	statistical
Education	Annotated	terminology
Sociology	bibliography	
Political science	Review of research	*Format*
Social work	essay	Internal headings
Criminal justice	Proposal	Visuals (graphs,
		maps, flowcharts,
		photographs)
		Numerical data (in
		tables)

Natural and Applied Sciences

Disciplines	Assignments	Style and Format
Natural Sciences	Laboratory report	*Style*
Biology	Observation/essay	Frequent use of
Chemistry	Literature survey	passive voice
Physics	Abstract	Few direct
Astronomy	Biographical essay	quotations
Geology		
Mathematics		*Format*
		Internal headings
Applied Sciences		Tables, graphs, and
Engineering		illustrations (exact
Computer science		formats vary)
Nursing		
Pharmacy		

Documentation	Research Methods and Sources	
English, languages, philosophy: **MLA**	Library sources (print and electronic)	See Ch. 34
History, art history: **Chicago**	Interviews	See Ch. 36
	Observations (museums, concerts)	
	Oral history	

Documentation	Research Methods and Sources	
APA	Library sources (print and electronic)	See Ch. 35
	Surveys	
	Observations (behavior of groups and individuals)	

Documentation	Research Methods and Sources	
Biological sciences: **CSE**	Library sources (print and electronic)	See Ch. 37
Other scientific disciplines use a variety of different documentation styles; **see 37d**	Observations	
	Experiments	
	Surveys	

183

PART 7

Documenting Sources: MLA Style

Works-Cited Entry for a Book

Author's last name | First name | Period followed by one space | Italicized title (all major words and first word of subtitle capitalized)

Kilbourne, Jean. *Can't Buy My Love: How Advertising Changes the Way We Think and Feel.* New York: Simon, 1999. Print.

City (first city on title page) | Publisher's name (abbreviated) | Year of publication | Publication medium

Works-Cited Entry for an Article

Author's last name | First name | Title of article (in quotation marks)

Harkin, Patricia. "The Reception of Reader-Response Theory." *College Composition and Communication* 56.3 (2005): 410-25. Print.

Inclusive page numbers | Publication medium | Title of periodical (italicized) | Volume and issue numbers | Year of publication

Works-Cited Entry for an Article in an Online Magazine

Author's last name | First name | Title of article (in quotation marks) | Name of site (italicized)

Baard, Mark. "Will Genetic Engineering Kill Us?" *Wired News.* Lycos, 16 Apr. 2003. Web. 12 Feb. 2004. <www.wired.com/news/medtech/0,1286,58467,00.html>.

Sponsor of site | Date of publication | Publication medium | Date of access | URL (in angle brackets)

PRINT SOURCES: *Entries for Articles*

ENTRIES FOR MISCELLANEOUS PRINT AND NONPRINT SOURCES

Letters

36. A personal letter (p. 206)
37. A letter published in a collection (p. 206)
38. A letter in a library's archives (p. 207)

Films, Videotapes, Radio and Television Programs, and Recordings

39. A film (p. 207)
40. A videotape, DVD, or laser disc (p. 207)
41. A radio or television program (p. 207)
42. A recording (p. 207)

Paintings, Photographs, Cartoons, and Advertisements

43. A painting (p. 208)
44. A photograph (p. 208)
45. A cartoon or comic strip (p. 208)
46. An advertisement (p. 208)

ELECTRONIC SOURCES: *Entries for Sources from Internet Sites*

Internet-Specific Sources

47. An entire Web site (p. 209)
48. A document within a Web site (p. 209)
49. A home page for a course (p. 209)
50. A personal home page (p. 209)
51. A radio program accessed from an Internet archive (p. 209)
52. An email (p. 209)
53. An online posting (p. 210)

Books, Articles, Reviews, Letters, and Reference Works on the Internet

54. A book (p. 210)
55. An article in a scholarly journal (p. 210)
56. An article in a magazine (p. 210)
57. An article in a newspaper (p. 210)
58. An article in a newsletter (p. 210)
59. A review (p. 211)
60. A letter to the editor (p. 211)
61. An article in an encyclopedia (p. 211)
62. A government publication (p. 211)

34 MLA Documentation Style

Documentation is the formal acknowledgment of the sources you use in your paper. This chapter explains and illustrates the documentation style recommended by the Modern Language Association (MLA). Chapter 35 discusses the documentation style of the American Psychological Association (APA), Chapter 36 gives an overview of the format recommended by *The Chicago Manual of Style*, and Chapter 37 presents the formats recommended by the Council of Science Editors (CSE) and organizations in other disciplines.

34a Using MLA Style

MLA style* is required by instructors of English and other languages as well as by many instructors in other humanities disciplines. MLA documentation has three parts: *parenthetical references in the body of the paper (also known as in-text citations), a works-cited list, and content notes.*

1 Parenthetical References

MLA documentation uses parenthetical references in the body of the paper keyed to a works-cited list at the end of the paper. A typical parenthetical reference consists of the author's last name and a page number.

The colony appealed to many idealists in Europe (Kelley 132).

If you state the author's name or the title of the work in your discussion, do not include it in the parenthetical reference.

Penn's political motivation is discussed by Joseph J. Kelley

in *Pennsylvania, The Colonial Years, 1681-1776* (44).

To distinguish two or more sources by the same author, include a shortened title after the author's name. When you shorten a title, begin with the word by which the work is alphabetized in the list of works cited.

Penn emphasized his religious motivation (Kelley,

Pennsylvania 116).

---

*MLA documentation style follows the guidelines set in the *MLA Handbook for Writers of Research Papers*, 7th ed. (New York: MLA, 2009).

> ## CLOSE-UP
>
> ### PUNCTUATING WITH MLA PARENTHETICAL REFERENCES
>
> **Paraphrases and Summaries** Parenthetical references are placed *before* the sentence's end punctuation.
>
> Penn's writings epitomize seventeenth-century religious
>
> thought (Dengler and Curtis 72).
>
> **Quotations Run In with the Text** Parenthetical references are placed *after* the quotation but *before* the end punctuation.
>
> As Ross says, "Penn followed his conscience in all
>
> matters" (127).
>
> According to Williams, "Penn's utopian vision was
>
> informed by his Quaker beliefs . . ." (72).
>
> **Quotations Set Off from the Text** When you quote more than four lines of **prose** or more than three lines of **poetry**, parenthetical references are placed one space *after* the end punctuation.
>
> According to Arthur Smith, William Penn envisioned a
>
> state based on his religious principles:
>
>> Pennsylvania would be a commonwealth in
>> which all individuals would follow God's
>> truth and develop according to God's law.
>> For Penn, this concept of government was
>> self-evident. It would be a mistake to see
>> Pennsylvania as anything but an expression
>> of Penn's religious beliefs. (314)

See 21a

SAMPLE MLA PARENTHETICAL REFERENCES

1. A Work by a Single Author

Fairy tales reflect the emotions and fears of children (Bettelheim 23).

2. A Work by Two or Three Authors

The historian's main job is to search for clues and solve mysteries (Davidson and Lytle 6).

With the advent of behaviorism, psychology began a new

phase of inquiry (Cowen, Barbo, and Crum 31-34).

3. A Work by More Than Three Authors

List only the first author, followed by **et al.** ("and others").

Helping each family reach its goals for healthy child

development and overall family well-being was the primary

approach of Project EAGLE (Bartle et al. 35).

Or, list the last names of all authors in the order in which
they appear on the work's title page.

Helping each family reach its goals for healthy child

development and overall family well-being was the primary

approach of Project EAGLE (Bartle, Couchonnal, Canda, and

Staker 35).

4. A Work in Multiple Volumes

If you list more than one volume of a multivolume work in
your works-cited list, include the appropriate volume and
page number (separated by a colon followed by a space).

Gurney is incorrect when he says that a twelve-hour limit is

negotiable (6: 128).

5. A Work without a Listed Author

Use the full title (if brief) or a shortened version of the
title (if long), beginning with the word by which it is alphabetized in the works-cited list.

The group issued an apology a short time later ("Satire

Lost" 22).

6. A Work That Is One Page Long

Do not include a page reference for a one-page article.

Sixty percent of Arab Americans work in white-collar jobs

(El-Badru).

7. An Indirect Source

If you use a statement by one author that is quoted in the
work of another author, indicate that the material is from an
indirect source with the abbreviation **qtd. in** ("quoted in").

According to Valli and Lucas, "the form of the symbol is an

icon or picture of some aspect of the thing or activity being

symbolized" (qtd. in Wilcox 120).

8. More Than One Work

Cite each work as you normally would, separating one citation from another with a semicolon.

> The Brooklyn Bridge has been used as a subject by many
>
> American artists (McCullough 144; Tashjian 58).

See
34a3 **NOTE:** Long parenthetical references can distract readers. Whenever possible, present them as **content notes**.

9. A Literary Work

When citing a work of **fiction,** it is often helpful to include more than the author's name and the page number in the parenthetical citation. Follow the page number with a semicolon, and then add any additional information that might be helpful.

> In *Moby-Dick,* Melville refers to a whaling expedition funded
>
> by Louis XIV of France (151; ch. 24).

Parenthetical references to **poetry** do not include page numbers. In parenthetical references to *long poems,* cite division and line numbers, separating them with a period.

> In the *Aeneid,* Virgil describes the ships as cleaving the
>
> "green woods reflected in the calm water" (8.124).

(In this citation, the reference is to book 8, line 124 of the *Aeneid.*)

When citing *short poems,* identify the poet and the poem in the text of the paper, and use line numbers in the citation.

> In "A Song in the Front Yard," Brooks's speaker says, "I've
>
> stayed in the front yard all my life / I want a peek at the
>
> back" (lines 1-2).

NOTE: When citing lines of a poem, include the word **line** (or **lines**) in the first parenthetical reference; use just the line numbers in subsequent references.

When citing a **play,** include the act, scene, and line numbers (in arabic numerals), separated by periods. Titles of well-known literary works (such as Shakespeare's plays) are often abbreviated (*Mac.* **2.2.14-16**).

10. The Bible

MLA style requires that a biblical citation include the version of the Bible (italicized) and the book (abbreviated if longer than four letters, but not italicized or enclosed in quotation marks), followed by the chapter and verse numbers (separated by a period).

> The cynicism of the speaker is apparent when he says, "All
>
> things are wearisome; no man can speak of them all"
>
> (*New English Bible,* Eccles. 1.8).

NOTE: The first time you use a biblical citation, include the version in your parenthetical reference; after that, only include the book. If you are using more than one version of the Bible, however, include the version in each in-text citation.

11. An Entire Work
When citing an entire work, include the author's name and the work's title in the text of your paper rather than in a parenthetical reference.

> Lois Lowry's *Gathering Blue* is set in a technologically
>
> backward village.

12. Two or More Authors with the Same Last Name
To distinguish authors with the same last name, include their initials in your parenthetical references.

> Recent increases in crime have caused thousands of urban
>
> homeowners to install alarms (L. Cooper 115). Some of these
>
> alarms use sophisticated sensors that were developed by the
>
> army (D. Cooper 76).

13. A Government Document or a Corporate Author
Cite such works using the organization's name (usually abbreviated) followed by the page number (**Amer. Automobile Assn.** 34). You can avoid long parenthetical references by working the organization's name (not abbreviated) into your discussion.

> According to the President's Commission for the Study of Ethical
>
> Problems in Medicine and Biomedical and Behavioral Research,
>
> the issues relating to euthanasia are complicated (76).

14. A Legal Source
Titles of acts or laws that appear in the text of your paper or in the works-cited list should not be italicized or enclosed in quotation marks. In the parenthetical reference, titles are usually abbreviated, and the act or law is referred to by sections. Include the USC (United States Code) and the year the act or law was passed (if relevant).

Such research should include investigations into the cause, diagnosis, early detection, prevention, control, and treatment of autism (42 USC 284q, 2000).

Names of legal cases are usually abbreviated (**Roe v. Wade**). They are italicized in the text of your paper but not in the works-cited list.

In *Goodridge v. Department of Public Health,* the court ruled that the Commonwealth of Massachusetts had not adequately provided a reasonable constitutional cause for barring homosexual couples from civil marriages (2003).

15. An Electronic Source

If a reference to an electronic source includes paragraph numbers rather than page numbers, use the abbreviation **par.** or **pars.** followed by the paragraph number or numbers.

The earliest type of movie censorship came in the form of licensing fees, and in Deer River, Minnesota, "a licensing fee of $200 was deemed not excessive for a town of 1000" (Ernst, par. 20).

If the electronic source has no page or paragraph numbers, try to cite the work in your discussion rather than in a parenthetical reference. By consulting your works-cited list, readers will be able to determine that the source is electronic and may therefore not have page numbers.

In her article "Limited Horizons," Lynne Cheney observes that schools do best when students read literature not for practical information but for its insights into the human condition.

2 Works-Cited List

The **works-cited list,** which appears at the end of your paper, is an alphabetical listing of all the research materials you cite. Double-space within and between entries on the list, and indent the second and subsequent lines of each entry one-half inch. (**See 34b** for full manuscript guidelines.)

Book citations include the author's name; book title (underlined); and publication information (place, publisher, date). Capitalize all major words of the book's title except articles, coordinating conjunctions, prepositions, and the *to* of an infinitive (unless such a word is the first or last word of the title or subtitle). Do not italicize the period that follows a book's title.

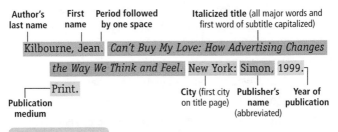

Author's last name | First name | Period followed by one space | Italicized title (all major words and first word of subtitle capitalized)

Kilbourne, Jean. *Can't Buy My Love: How Advertising Changes the Way We Think and Feel.* New York: Simon, 1999. Print.

Publication medium | City (first city on title page) | Publisher's name (abbreviated) | Year of publication

CLOSE-UP

PUBLISHERS' NAMES

MLA requires abbreviated forms of publishers' names in the list of works cited. In general, omit articles; abbreviations, such as *Inc.* and *Corp.*; and words such as *Publishers*, *Books*, and *Press*. If the publisher's name includes a person's name, use the last name only. Finally, use standard abbreviations whenever you can—*UP* for University Press and *P* for Press, for example.

Authors

1. A Book by One Author

Bettelheim, Bruno. *The Uses of Enchantment: The Meaning and Importance of Fairy Tales.* New York: Knopf, 1976. Print.

2. A Book by Two or Three Authors

List the first author with last name first. List subsequent authors with first name first in the order in which they appear on the title page.

Peters, Michael A., and Nicholas C. Burbules. *Poststructuralism and Educational Research.* Lanham: Rowman, 2004. Print.

3. A Book by More Than Three Authors

List the first author only, followed by **et al.** ("and others").

> Badawi, El Said, et al. *Modern Written Arabic*. London:
>
> Routledge, 2004. Print.

Or, include all the authors in the order in which they appear on the title page.

> Badawi, El Said, Daud A. Abdu, Mike Carfter, and Adrian
>
> Gully. *Modern Written Arabic*. London: Routledge,
>
> 2004. Print.

4. Two or More Books by the Same Author

List books by the same author in alphabetical order by title. After the first entry, use three unspaced hyphens followed by a period in place of the author's name.

> Ede, Lisa. *Situating Composition: Composition Studies and the*
>
> *Politics of Location*. Carbondale: Southern Illinois UP,
>
> 2004. Print.
>
> ---. *Work in Progress*. 6th ed. Boston: Bedford, 2004. Print.

NOTE: If the author is the editor or translator of the second entry, place a comma and the appropriate abbreviation after the hyphens (**---, ed.**). See entry 6 for more on edited books and entry 13 for more on translated books.

5. A Book by a Corporate Author

A book is cited by its corporate author when individual members of the association, commission, or committee that produced it are not identified on the title page.

> American Automobile Association. *Western Canada and*
>
> *Alaska*. Heathrow: AAA, 2004. Print.

6. An Edited Book

An edited book is a work prepared for publication by a person other than the author. If your focus is on the *author's* work, begin your citation with the author's name. After the title, include the abbreviation **Ed.** ("Edited by"), followed by the editor or editors.

> Twain, Mark. *Adventures of Huckleberry Finn*. Ed. Michael
>
> Patrick Hearn. New York: Norton, 2001. Print.

If your focus is on the *editor's* work, begin your citation with the editor's name followed by the abbreviation **ed.**

("editor") if there is one editor or **eds.** ("editors") if there are more than one. After the title, give the author's name, preceded by the word **By**.

> Hearn, Michael Patrick, ed. *Adventures of Huckleberry Finn*.
>
> > By Mark Twain. New York: Norton, 2001. Print.

Editions, Multivolume Works, Forewords, Translations, and Sacred Works

7. A Subsequent Edition of a Book

When citing an edition other than the first, include the edition number that appears on the work's title page.

> Wilson, Charles Banks. *Search for the Native American*
>
> > *Purebloods*. 3rd ed. Norman: U of Oklahoma P, 2000.
> >
> > Print.

8. A Republished Book

Include the original publication date after the title of a republished book—for example, a paperback version of a hardcover book.

> Wharton, Edith. *The House of Mirth*. 1905. New York:
>
> > Scribner's, 1975. Print.

9. A Book in a Series

If the title page indicates that the book is a part of a series, include the series name, neither italicized nor enclosed in quotation marks, and the series number at the end of the entry after the publication medium.

> Davis, Bertram H. *Thomas Percy*. Boston: Twayne, 1981.
>
> > Print. Twayne's English Authors Ser. 313.

10. A Multivolume Work

When all volumes of a multivolume work have the same title, include the number of the volume you are using.

> Fisch, Max H., ed. *Writings of Charles S. Peirce: A*
>
> > *Chronological Edition*. Vol. 4. Bloomington: Indiana UP,
> >
> > 2000. Print.

If you use two or more volumes that have the same title, cite the entire work.

> Fisch, Max H., ed. *Writings of Charles S. Peirce: A*
>
> > *Chronological Edition*. 6 vols. Bloomington: Indiana UP,
> >
> > 2000. Print.

When the volume you are using has an individual title, you may cite the title without mentioning any other volumes.

> Mareš, Milan. *Fuzzy Cooperative Games: Cooperation with Vague*
>
> *Expectations*. New York: Physica-Verlag, 2001. Print.

If you wish, however, you may include supplemental information, such as the number of the volume, the title of the entire work, the total number of volumes, or the inclusive publication dates.

11. The Foreword, Preface, or Afterword of a Book

> Campbell, Richard. Preface. *Media and Culture: An*
>
> *Introduction to Mass Communication*. By Bettina
>
> Fabos. Boston: Bedford, 2005. vi-xi. Print.

12. A Book with a Title within Its Title

If the book you are citing contains a title that is normally italicized (a novel, play, or long poem, for example), do not italicize the interior title.

> Fulton, Joe B. *Mark Twain in the Margins: The Quarry Farm*
>
> *Marginalia and* A Connecticut Yankee in King Arthur's
>
> Court. Tuscaloosa: U of Alabama P, 2000. Print.

If the book you are citing contains a title that is normally enclosed in quotation marks, keep the quotation marks.

> Hawkins, Hunt, and Brian W. Shaffer, eds. *Approaches to*
>
> *Teaching Conrad's "Heart of Darkness" and "The Secret*
>
> *Sharer."* New York: MLA, 2002. Print.

13. A Translation

> García Márquez, Gabriel. *One Hundred Years of Solitude*.
>
> Trans. Gregory Rabassa. New York: Avon, 1991. Print.

14. The Bible

Italicize the title, and give full publication information.

> *The New English Bible with the Apocrypha*. Oxford Study ed.
>
> New York: Oxford UP, 1976. Print.

Parts of Books

15. A Short Story, Play, or Poem in an Anthology

Chopin, Kate. "The Storm." *Literature: Reading, Reacting,*
    Writing. Ed. Laurie G. Kirszner and Stephen R. Mandell.
    6th ed. Boston: Wadsworth, 2007. 281-85. Print.

Shakespeare, William. *Othello, the Moor of Venice*.
    Shakespeare: Six Plays and the Sonnets. Ed. Thomas
    Marc Parrott and Edward Hubler. New York: Scribner's,
    1956. 145-91. Print.

See entry 18 for information on how to cite more than one
work from the same anthology.

16. A Short Story, Play, Poem, or Essay in a Collection of an Author's Work

Bukowski, Charles. "lonely hearts." *The Flash of Lightning*
    behind the Mountain: New Poems. New York: Ecco,
    2004. 115-16. Print.

NOTE: The title of the poem is not capitalized because it
appears in lowercase letters in the original.

17. An Essay in an Anthology

Even if you cite only one page of an essay in your paper,
supply inclusive page numbers for the entire essay.

Crevel, René. "From *Babylon*." *Surrealist Painters and Poets:*
    An Anthology. Ed. Mary Ann Caws. Cambridge: MIT P,
    2001. 175-77. Print.

18. More Than One Work from the Same Anthology

List each work from the same anthology separately, followed by a cross-reference to the entire anthology. Also
list complete publication information for the anthology
itself.

Agar, Eileen. "Am I a Surrealist?" Caws 3-7.

Caws, Mary Ann, ed. *Surrealist Painters and Poets: An*
    Anthology. Cambridge: MIT P, 2001. Print.

Crevel, René. "From *Babylon*." Caws 175-77.

19. An Article in a Reference Book (Signed/Unsigned)
For a signed article, begin with the author's name. For unfamiliar reference books, include full publication information.

> Drabble, Margaret. "Expressionism." *The Oxford Companion to*
>
> *English Literature*. 6th ed. New York: Oxford UP, 2000.
>
> Print.

If the article is unsigned, begin with the title. For familiar reference books, do not include full publication information.

> "Cubism." *The Encyclopedia Americana*. 2004 ed. Print.

NOTE: Omit page numbers when the reference book lists entries alphabetically. If you are listing one definition among several from a dictionary, include the abbreviation **Def.** ("Definition") along with the letter and/or number that corresponds to the definition.

> "Justice." Def. 2b. *The Concise Oxford Dictionary*. 10th ed.
>
> 1999. Print.

Dissertations, Pamphlets, Government Publications, and Legal Sources

20. A Dissertation (Published/Unpublished)
Cite a published dissertation the same way you would cite a book, but add relevant dissertation information before the publication information.

> Rodriguez, Jason Anthony. *Bureaucracy and Altruism:*
>
> *Managing the Contradictions of Teaching*. Diss. U of
>
> Texas at Arlington, 2003. Ann Arbor: UMI, 2004.
>
> Print.

NOTE: University Microfilms International (UMI), which publishes most of the dissertations in the United States, is also available online by subscription. For the proper format for citing online databases, see entries 67–71.

Use quotation marks for the title of an unpublished dissertation.

> Bon Tempo, Carl Joseph. "Americans at the Gate: The Politics
>
> of American Refugee Policy." Diss. U of Virginia, 2004.
>
> Print.

21. A Pamphlet

Cite a pamphlet as you would a book. If no author is listed, begin with the title (italicized).

> *Choosing the Right Digital Camera*. Rochester: Kodak, 2004. Print.

22. A Government Publication

If the publication has no listed author, begin with the name of the government, followed by the name of the agency. You may use an abbreviation if its meaning is clear: **United States. Cong. Senate**.

> United States. Office of Consumer Affairs. *2003 Consumer's*
>
> *Resource Handbook*. Washington: GPO, 2003. Print.

When citing two or more publications by the same government, use three unspaced hyphens (followed by a period) in place of the name for the second and subsequent entries. When you cite more than one work from the same agency of that government, use an additional set of unspaced hyphens in place of the agency name.

> United States. FAA. *Passenger Airline Safety in the Twenty-*
>
> *First Century*. Washington: GPO, 2003. Print.
>
> ---. ---. *Recycled Air in Passenger Airline Cabins*. Washington:
>
> GPO, 2002. Print.

23. A Legal Source

In general, you do not need a works-cited entry for familiar historical documents. Parenthetical references in the text are sufficient—for example, **(US Const., art. 3, sec. 2)**. If you cite an act in the works-cited list, include the name of the act, its Public Law (Pub. L.) number, its Statutes at Large (Stat.) cataloging number, its enactment date, and the medium consulted.

> Children's Health Act. Pub. L. 106-310. 114 Stat. 1101.
>
> 17 Oct. 2000. Print.

In works-cited entries for legal cases, abbreviate names of cases, but spell out the first important word of each party's name. Include the volume number, abbreviated name (not italicized), and inclusive page numbers of the law report; the name of the deciding court; the decision year; and publication information for the source. Do not italicize the case name in the works-cited list.

> Abbott v. Blades. 544 US 929. Supreme Court of the US. 2005.
>
> *United States Reports*. Washington: GPO, 2007. Print.

Article citations include the author's name; the title of the article (in quotation marks); the title of the periodical (italicized); the volume and issue numbers (when applicable; see below); the year or date of publication; the pages on which the full article appears, without the abbreviations *p.* or *pp.*; and the publication medium.

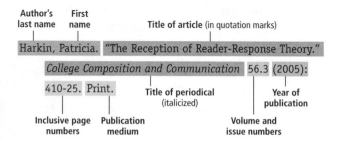

Author's last name — **Harkin, Patricia.**
First name — **Patricia.**
Title of article (in quotation marks) — **"The Reception of Reader-Response Theory."**

College Composition and Communication **56.3 (2005):**

410-25. Print.

Inclusive page numbers — **410-25.**
Publication medium — **Print.**
Title of periodical (italicized) — *College Composition and Communication*
Year of publication — **(2005)**
Volume and issue numbers — **56.3**

Articles in Scholarly Journals

24. An Article in a Scholarly Journal
MLA guidelines now recommend that you include both the volume number and the issue number (separated by a period) for all scholarly journal articles that you cite, regardless of whether they are paginated continuously through an annual volume or separately in each issue. Follow the volume and issue numbers with the year of publication (in parentheses), the inclusive page numbers, and the publication medium.

> Siderits, Mark. "Perceiving Particulars: A Buddhist Defense."
>
> *Philosophy East and West* 54.3 (2004): 367-83. Print.

Articles in Magazines and Newspapers

25. An Article in a Weekly Magazine (Signed/Unsigned)
For signed articles, start with the author, last name first. In dates, the day precedes the month (abbreviated except for May, June, and July).

Corliss, Richard. "His Days in Hollywood." *Time* 14 June

2004: 56-62. Print.

For unsigned articles, start with the title of the article.

"Ronald Reagan." *National Review* 28 June 2004: 14-17.

Print.

26. An Article in a Monthly Magazine

Thomas, Evan. "John Paul Jones." *American History* Aug.

2003: 22-25. Print.

27. An Article That Does Not Appear on Consecutive Pages

When, for example, an article begins on page 120 and then skips to page 186, include only the first page number, followed by a plus sign.

Di Giovanni, Janine. "The Shiites of Iraq." *National*

Geographic June 2004: 62+. Print.

28. An Article in a Newspaper (Signed/Unsigned)

Krantz, Matt. "Stock Success Not Exactly Unparalleled." *Wall*

Street Journal 11 June 2004: B1+. Print.

"A Steadfast Friend on 9/11 Is Buried." *New York Times*

6 June 2002: B8. Print.

NOTE: Omit the article *the* from the title of a newspaper even if the newspaper's actual title includes the article.

29. An Editorial in a Newspaper

Brooks, David. "Living in the Age of Political Segregation."

Editorial. *Dayton Daily News* 1 July 2004, final ed.: A12.

Print.

30. A Letter to the Editor of a Newspaper

Chang, Paula. Letter. *Philadelphia Inquirer* 10 Dec. 2006,

suburban ed.: A17. Print.

31. A Book Review in a Newspaper

Straw, Deborah. "Thinking about Tomorrow." Rev. of *Planning*

for the 21st Century: A Guide for Community Colleges, by

William A. Wojciechowski and Dedra Manes. *Community*

College Week 7 June 2004: 15. Print.

32. An Article with a Title within Its Title

If the article you are citing contains a title that is normally enclosed in quotation marks, use single quotation marks for the interior title.

> Zimmerman, Brett. "Frantic Forensic Oratory: Poe's 'The Tell-
>
> Tale Heart.'" *Style* 35 (2001): 34-50. Print.

If the article you are citing contains a title that is normally italicized, use italics for the title in your works-cited entry.

> Lingo, Marci. "Forbidden Fruit: The Banning of *The Grapes of*
>
> *Wrath* in the Kern County Free Library." *Libraries and*
>
> *Culture* 38 (2003): 351-78. Print.

MLA ENTRIES FOR MISCELLANEOUS PRINT AND NONPRINT SOURCES

Lectures and Interviews

33. A Lecture

> Grimm, Mary. "An Afternoon with Mary Grimm." Visiting
>
> Writers Program. Dept. of English, Wright State U,
>
> Dayton. 16 Apr. 2004. Lecture.

34. A Personal Interview

> West, Cornel. Personal interview. 28 Dec. 2005.
>
> Tannen, Deborah. Telephone interview. 8 June 2005.

35. A Published Interview

> Huston, John. "The Outlook for Raising Money: An Investment
>
> Banker's Viewpoint." *NJBIZ* 30 Sept. 2002: 2-3. Print.

Letters

36. A Personal Letter

> Tan, Amy. Letter to the author. 7 Apr. 2006. TS.

37. A Letter Published in a Collection

> Joyce, James. "Letter to Louis Gillet." 20 Aug. 1931. *James*
>
> *Joyce*. By Richard Ellmann. New York: Oxford UP,
>
> 1965. 631. Print.

38. A Letter in a Library's Archives

Stieglitz, Alfred. Letter to Paul Rosenberg. 5 Sept. 1923. MS.

Stieglitz Archive. Yale U Arts Lib., New Haven.

Films, Videotapes, Radio and Television Programs, and Recordings

39. A Film

Include the title of the film (italicized), the distributor, and the date, along with other information that may be useful to readers, such as the names of the performers, the director, and the screen writer. Conclude with the publication medium.

Citizen Kane. Dir. Orson Welles. Perf. Welles, Joseph Cotten,

Dorothy Comingore, and Agnes Moorehead. RKO, 1941.

Film.

If you are focusing on the contribution of a particular person, begin with that person's name.

Welles, Orson, dir. *Citizen Kane*. Perf. Welles, Joseph Cotten,

Dorothy Comingore, and Agnes Moorehead. RKO, 1941.

Film.

40. A Videotape, DVD, or Laser Disc

Cite a videotape, DVD, or laser disc as you would cite a film, but include the original release date (when available).

Bowling for Columbine. Dir. Michael Moore. 2002. United

Artists and Alliance Atlantis, 2003. DVD.

41. A Radio or Television Program

"War Feels Like War." *P.O.V.* Dir. Esteban Uyarra. PBS. WPTD,

Dayton. 6 July 2004. Television.

42. A Recording

List the composer, conductor, or performer (whomever you are focusing on), followed by the title, publisher, year of issue, and publication medium.

Boubill, Alain, and Claude-Michel Schönberg. *Miss Saigon*. Perf.

Lea Salonga, Claire Moore, and Jonathan Pryce. Cond.

Martin Koch. Geffen, 1989. Audiocassette.

Marley, Bob. "Crisis." *Kaya*. Kava Island, 1978. LP.

Paintings, Photographs, Cartoons, and Advertisements

43. A Painting

> Hopper, Edward. *Railroad Sunset*. 1929. Oil on canvas.
>
> Whitney Museum of American Art, New York.

44. A Photograph

Cite a photograph in a museum's collection in the same way you cite a painting.

> Stieglitz, Alfred. *The Steerage*. 1907. Photograph. Los
>
> Angeles County Museum of Art, Los Angeles.

45. A Cartoon or Comic Strip

> Trudeau, Garry. "Doonesbury." Comic strip. *Philadelphia*
>
> *Inquirer* 15 Sept. 2003, late ed.: E13. Print.

46. An Advertisement

> Microsoft. Advertisement. *National Review* 8 June 2004: 17.
>
> Print.

MLA ELECTRONIC SOURCES: *Entries for Sources from Internet Sites*

MLA style* recognizes that full source information for Internet sources is not always available. Include in your citation whatever information you can reasonably obtain: the author or editor of the site (if available); the name of the site (italicized); the version number of the source (if applicable); the name of any institution or sponsor (if unavailable, include the abbreviation **N.p.** for "no publisher"); the date of electronic publication or update (if unavailable, include the abbreviation **n.d.** for "no date of publication"); the publication medium (**Web**); the date you accessed the source; and the URL. (MLA style recommends omitting the URL from the citation unless it is necessary to find the source. Although the URL in the labeled citation that follows is not needed to locate the source, it is included in the example to illustrate proper format.)

---

*The documentation style for Internet sources presented here conforms to the most recent guidelines published in the *MLA Handbook for Writers of Research Papers* (7th ed.) and found online at <http://www.mlahandbook.org>.

If an electronic address (URL) is necessary, MLA requires that you enclose the URL within angle brackets to distinguish the address from the punctuation in the rest of the citation. If a URL will not fit on a line, the computer will carry the entire URL over to the next line. If you prefer to divide the URL, divide it after a slash. (Do not insert a hyphen.)

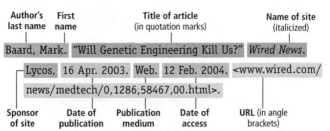

Internet-Specific Sources

47. An Entire Web Site

Nelson, Cary, ed. *Modern American Poetry*. Dept. of English, U
of Illinois, Urbana-Champaign, 2002. Web. 26 May 2008.

48. A Document within a Web Site

"D Day: June 7th, 1944." *History.com*. History Channel, 1999.
Web. 7 June 2002.

49. A Home Page for a Course

Walker, Janice R. Home page. Georgia Southern University.
Dept. of Writing and Linguistics, Georgia Southern U,
5 June 2008. Web. 30 Mar. 2009.

50. A Personal Home Page

Gainor, Charles. Home page. U of Toronto, 22 July 2005. Web.
10 Nov. 2005. <http://www.chass.utoronto.ca:9094/
~char>.

51. A Radio Program Accessed from an Internet Archive

"Teenage Skeptic Takes on Climate Scientists." Narr. David
Kestenbaum. *Morning Edition*. Natl. Public Radio.
WNYC, New York, 15 Apr. 2008. Transcript. *NPR*. Web.
30 Apr. 2008.

52. An Email

Mauk, Karen R. Message to the author. 28 June 2005. E-mail.

53. An Online Posting

Schiller, Stephen. "Paper Cost and Publishing Costs."

> Online posting. *New York Times*. New York Times,
> 11 May 2002. Web. 17 May 2002.webin/webx?13A^41356.ee765e/0>.

Books, Articles, Reviews, Letters, and Reference Works on the Internet

54. A Book

Douglass, Frederick. *My Bondage and My Freedom*. Boston,

> 1855. *Google Book Search*. Web. 8 June 2005.

55. An Article in a Scholarly Journal

When you cite information from an electronic source that has a print version, include the publication information for the print source, the inclusive page numbers if available (if unavailable, include the abbreviation **n. pag.** for "no pagination"), the publication medium, and the date you accessed it.

DeKoven, Marianne. "Utopias Limited: Post-Sixties and

> Postmodern American Fiction." *Modern Fiction Studies*
> 41.1 (1995): 75-97. Web. 20 Jan. 2005.

56. An Article in a Magazine

Weiser, Jay. "The Tyranny of Informality." *Time*. Time,

> 26 Feb. 1996. Web. 1 Mar. 2002.

57. An Article in a Newspaper

Wyatt, Edward. "Electronic Device Stirs Unease at Book Fair."

> *New York Times*. New York Times, 2 June 2008. Web.
> 12 June 2008.

58. An Article in a Newsletter

Sullivan, Jennifer S., comp. "Documentation Preserved, New

> Collections." *AIP Center for History of Physics* 39.2
> (2007): n. pag. Web. 26 Feb. 2008.

59. A Review

Ebert, Roger. Rev. of *Star Wars: Episode I—The Phantom*
  Menace, dir. George Lucas. *Chicago Sun-Times.* Digital
  Chicago, 8 June 2000. Web. 22 June 2000.

60. A Letter to the Editor

Chen-Cheng, Henry H. Letter. *New York Times.* New York Times,
  19 July 1999. Web. 1 Jan. 2009.

61. An Article in an Encyclopedia

Include the article's title, the title of the database (italicized), the version number (if available), the sponsor, the date of electronic publication, the publication medium, and the date of access.

"Hawthorne, Nathaniel." *Encyclopaedia Britannica Online.*
  Encyclopaedia Britannica, 2008. Web. 16 May 2008.

62. A Government Publication

Cite an online government publication as you would cite a print version; end with the information required for an electronic source.

United States. Dept. of Justice. Office of Justice Programs.
  Violence against Women: Estimates from the Redesigned
  National Crime Victimization Survey. By Ronet Bachman
  and Linda E. Saltzman. Aug. 1995. *Bureau of Justice*
  Statistics. Web. 10 Jan. 2008.

Paintings, Photographs, Cartoons, and Maps on the Internet

63. A Painting

Seurat, Georges-Pierre. *Evening, Honfleur.* 1886. Museum
  of Mod. Art, New York. *MoMA.org.* Web. 8 Jan. 2004.

64. A Photograph

Brady, Mathew. *Ulysses S. Grant 1822-1885.*
  Mathew Brady's National Portrait Gallery. Web.
  2 Oct. 2002.

65. A Cartoon

Stossel, Sage. "Star Wars: The Next Generation." Cartoon.
Atlantic Unbound. Atlantic Monthly Group, 2 Oct. 2002.
Web. 14 Nov. 2002.

66. A Map

"Philadelphia, Pennsylvania." Map. *U.S. Gazetteer*.
US Census Bureau, n.d. Web. 17 July 2000.

MLA **ELECTRONIC SOURCES:**
Entries for Sources from Online Databases

To cite information from an online database, supply the
publication information (including page numbers, if available; if unavailable, use **n. pag.**) followed by the name of
the database (italicized), the publication medium (**Web**),
and the date of access.

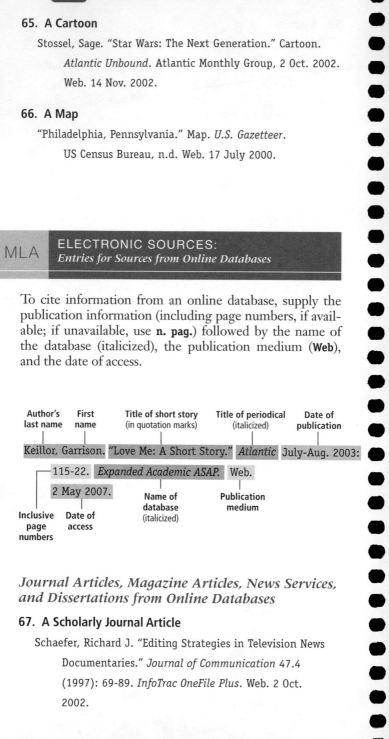

Keillor, Garrison. "Love Me: A Short Story." *Atlantic* July-Aug. 2003:
115-22. *Expanded Academic ASAP.* Web. 2 May 2007.

Author's last name — First name — Title of short story (in quotation marks) — Title of periodical (italicized) — Date of publication — Inclusive page numbers — Date of access — Name of database (italicized) — Publication medium

*Journal Articles, Magazine Articles, News Services,
and Dissertations from Online Databases*

67. A Scholarly Journal Article

Schaefer, Richard J. "Editing Strategies in Television News
Documentaries." *Journal of Communication* 47.4
(1997): 69-89. *InfoTrac OneFile Plus*. Web. 2 Oct.
2002.

68. A Monthly Magazine Article

Livermore, Beth. "Meteorites on Ice." *Astronomy* July 1993:
54-58. *Expanded Academic ASAP Plus*. Web. 12 Nov.
2003.

Wright, Karen. "The Clot Thickens." *Discover* Dec. 1999.
MasterFILE Premier. Web. 10 Oct. 2003.

69. A News Service

Ryan, Desmond. "Some Background on the Battle of
Gettysburg." *Knight Ridder/Tribune News Service* 7 Oct.
1993: n. pag. *InfoTrac OneFile Plus*. Web. 16 Nov. 2003.

70. A Newspaper Article

Meyer, Greg. "Answering Questions about the West Nile
Virus." *Dayton Daily News* 11 July 2002: Z3-7.
LexisNexis. Web. 17 Feb. 2003.

71. A Published Dissertation

Rodriguez, Jason Anthony. *Bureaucracy and Altruism:
Managing the Contradictions of Teaching*. Diss. U of
Texas at Arlington, 2003. *ProQuest*. Web. 4 Mar.
2006.

OTHER ELECTRONIC SOURCES   MLA

DVD-ROMs and CD-ROMs

72. A Nonperiodical Publication on DVD-ROM or CD-ROM

Cite a nonperiodical publication on DVD-ROM or CD-
ROM the same way you would cite a book, but include
the appropriate medium of publication.

"Windhover." *The Oxford English Dictionary*. 2nd ed.
Oxford: Oxford UP, 2001. DVD-ROM.

"Whitman, Walt." *DiskLit: American Authors*. Boston: Hall,
2000. CD-ROM.

73. A Periodical Publication on DVD-ROM or CD-ROM

Zurbach, Kate. "The Linguistic Roots of Three Terms." *Linguistic*
  Quarterly 37 (1994): 12-47. CD-ROM. *InfoTrac: Magazine*
  Index Plus. Information Access. Jan. 2001.

3 Content Notes

Content notes—multiple bibliographical citations or
other material that does not fit smoothly into your
paper—are indicated by a **superscript** (raised numeral)
in the text. Notes can appear either as footnotes at the
bottom of the page or as endnotes on a separate sheet
entitled **Notes**, placed after the last page of the paper
and before the works-cited list. Content notes are double-spaced within and between entries. The first line is
indented one-half inch, and subsequent lines are typed
flush left.

For Multiple Citations

In the Paper

Many researchers emphasize the necessity of having dying
patients share their experiences.[1]

In the Note

   1. Kübler-Ross 27; Stinnette 43; Poston 70; Cohen and
Cohen 31-34; Burke 1: 91-95.

For Other Material

In the Paper

The massacre during World War I is an event the survivors
could not easily forget.[2]

In the Note

   2. For a firsthand account of these events, see
Bedoukian 178-81.

34b MLA-Style Manuscript Guidelines

Although MLA papers do not usually include abstracts or internal headings, this situation is changing. Be sure you know what your instructor expects.

The following guidelines are based on the latest version of the *MLA Handbook for Writers of Research Papers*.

CHECKLIST

TYPING YOUR PAPER

When typing your paper, use the student paper in **34c** as your model.

☐ Leave a one-inch margin at the top and bottom and on both sides of the page. Double-space your paper throughout.

☐ Your first page should follow the format shown on page 219.

☐ Capitalize all important words in your title, but not prepositions, articles, coordinating conjunctions, or the *to* in infinitives (unless they begin or end the title or subtitle). Do not underline your title or enclose it in quotation marks. Never put a period after the title, even if it is a sentence.

☐ Number all pages of your paper consecutively— including the first—in the upper right-hand corner, one-half inch from the top, flush right. Type your last name followed by a space before the page number on every page.

☐ Set off quotations of more than four lines of prose or more than three lines of poetry by indenting the whole quotation one inch. If you quote a single paragraph or part of a paragraph, do not indent the first line beyond one inch. If you quote two or more paragraphs, however, indent the first line of each paragraph an additional quarter inch. (If the first sentence does not begin a paragraph, do not indent it. Indent the first line only in successive paragraphs.)

☐ If you use source material in your paper, follow **MLA documentation style**.

See 34a

CHECKLIST

USING VISUALS

See
40d

☐ Insert <u>visuals</u> into the text as close as possible to where they are discussed.

☐ *Above the table*, label each table with the word **Table** followed by an arabic numeral (for instance, **Table 1**). Double-space, and type a descriptive caption, with the first line flush with the left-hand margin; indent subsequent lines one-quarter inch. Capitalize the caption as if it were a title. *Below the table*, type the word **Source**, followed by a colon and all source information. Type the first line of the source information flush with the left-hand margin; indent subsequent lines one-quarter inch.

☐ Label other types of visual material—graphs, charts, photographs, clip art, drawings, and so on—**Fig.** (Figure) followed by an arabic numeral (for example, **Fig. 2**). Type each label and a title or caption on the same line, followed by source information, directly below the visual. Type all lines flush with the left-hand margin.

☐ Do not include the source of the visual in the works-cited list unless you use other material from that source elsewhere in the paper.

CHECKLIST

PREPARING THE MLA WORKS-CITED LIST

When typing your works-cited list, follow these guidelines:

☐ Begin the works-cited list on a new page after the last
page of text or <u>content notes</u>, numbered as the next
page of the paper.

See
34a3

☐ Center the title **Works Cited** one inch from the top of the
page. Double-space between the title and the first entry.

☐ Each entry on the works-cited list has three divisions:
author, title, and publication information. Separate
divisions with a period and one space.

☐ List entries alphabetically, with last name first. Use the
author's full name as it appears on the title page. If a
source has no listed author, alphabetize it by the first
word of the title (not counting the article).

☐ Type the first line of each entry flush with the left-
hand margin; indent subsequent lines one-half inch.

☐ Double-space within and between entries.

34c Model MLA-Style Research Paper

The following student paper, "The Great Digital Divide," uses MLA documentation style. It includes MLA-style in-text citations, a bar graph, a notes page, and a works-cited list.

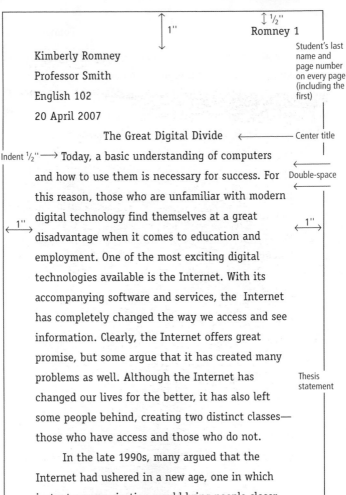

Romney 1

Student's last name and page number on every page (including the first)

Kimberly Romney
Professor Smith
English 102
20 April 2007

The Great Digital Divide ← Center title

Indent ½" → Today, a basic understanding of computers

← Double-space

and how to use them is necessary for success. For
this reason, those who are unfamiliar with modern
digital technology find themselves at a great
disadvantage when it comes to education and
employment. One of the most exciting digital
technologies available is the Internet. With its
accompanying software and services, the Internet
has completely changed the way we access and see
information. Clearly, the Internet offers great
promise, but some argue that it has created many
problems as well. Although the Internet has

Thesis statement

changed our lives for the better, it has also left
some people behind, creating two distinct classes—
those who have access and those who do not.

In the late 1990s, many argued that the
Internet had ushered in a new age, one in which
instant communication would bring people closer
together and eventually eliminate national
boundaries. In his speech "Building a Global
Community," former Vice President Al Gore took this
optimistic view, seeing the Internet as a means "to
deepen and extend our oldest and most cherished
global values: rising standards of living and literacy,
an ever-widening circle of freedom, and individual
empowerment." Gore went on to say that he could

Romney 2

imagine the day when we would "extend our
knowledge and our prosperity to our most isolated
inner cities, to the barrios, the favelas, the
colonias, and our most remote rural villages."

Others, however, argued that for many people,
the benefits of the Internet were not nearly this
obvious or far-reaching. They maintained that the
Internet was creating what many have called a
"digital divide," which excludes a large percentage
of the poor, elderly, disabled, and members of many
minority groups from current technological
advancements (*Digital Divide Network*).

A survey conducted by the United States
Department of Commerce in 2002 showed that
white people and those with higher annual
incomes were more likely to own computers than
minorities and people from low-income households.
In households where the average income was
$75,000 and over, 89% had access to a computer.
In households earning $10,000-$14,999, only 25%
had access to a computer. Moreover, although 61%
of white households had access to a computer,
only 37.1% of African-American and 40% of
Hispanic households had home computers.

While the Department of Commerce study
suggested that financial circumstances were
largely responsible for the "digital divide,"
some believed that other factors might also be
contributing to the disparity. For example, in a
1999 *New York Times* op-ed article, Henry Louis
Gates, Jr., argued that bridging the digital divide

Parenthetical
documentation
refers to
material
accessed from
a Web site

Paragraph
synthesizes
information
from a
Commerce
Department
study and a
newspaper
article

Romney 3

would "require more than cheap PC's"; it would "involve content" (500).[1] African Americans were not interested in the Internet, Gates wrote, because the content rarely appealed to them. Gates compared the lack of interest in the Internet with the history of African Americans' relationship to the recording industry. According to Gates, blacks began to buy records "only when mainstream companies . . . introduced so-called race records, blues and jazz discs aimed at a nascent African-American market" (501). Gates suggested that Web sites that address the needs of African Americans could play the same role that race records did for the music industry. Ignoring the race problem, Gates warned, would lead to a form of "cybersegregation" that would devastate the African-American community (501).

It was clear to many that people without Internet access had difficulty at school, trouble obtaining jobs, and fewer opportunities to save money and time as consumers. They also lacked access to educational materials and to jobs posted on the Internet. With access to only a portion of available goods and services, people who were not connected did not have the advantages that people who were online could routinely get. Thus, instead of bringing people together, the Internet seemed to be widening the economic and social divide that already separated people in this country.

In response to this situation, the government, corporations, nonprofit organizations, and public

Margin annotations:

Superscript number identifies content note

Ellipsis indicates that the student has deleted words from the quotation

Student's original conclusions; no documentation necessary

Romney 4

libraries made efforts to bridge the gap between the "haves" and "have-nots." For example, the Education Department's Community Technology Centers Program helped finance computer activity centers for students and adults. Also, the Department of Commerce's Technology Opportunities Program (TOP) provided money and services to organizations that needed more technology to operate efficiently. One recipient was America's Second Harvest, which used the funds to track donations to its national network of food banks (Schwartz, "Report").

Nonprofit organizations also worked to bridge the digital divide. The Bill and Melinda Gates Foundation, for example, provided libraries across the country with funding that allowed them to purchase computers and connect to the Internet (Egan). Nonprofit organizations also began to sponsor Web sites, such as *The Digital Divide Network,* a site that posted stories about the digital divide from a variety of perspectives. By posting information, the site's sponsor hoped to raise awareness of the problems that the digital divide causes.

Recently, however, some people have begun to question the need for many of these initiatives. In fact, as illustrated in fig. 1, computer use by young people between the ages of three and twenty-four rose dramatically between 1998 and 2001.

Several recent studies seem to support this view. For example, a 2004 study by the Pew Research Center found that nearly 66% of whites

Parenthetical documentation includes abbreviated title when two or more works by the same author are cited in the paper

Romney 5

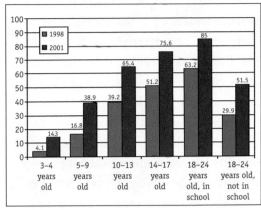

Graph summarizes relevant data; source information is typed directly below the figure

Fig. 1. United States, Dept. of Commerce, Economics and Statistics Admin., Natl. Telecommunications and Information Admin.; *A Nation Online: How Americans Are Expanding Their Use of the Internet;* 2002; *National Telecommunications and Information Administration;* Web; 20 Jan. 2007.

and Hispanics and 61% of African Americans used the Internet (Nelson). Another study, conducted by the University of Texas at Dallas, also found that the digital divide seemed to be closing. According to Professor Donald Hicks, research showed that "broadband Internet [was] more readily available in minority neighborhoods than in areas that [were] home to more whites" (Nelson). Even earlier, a 2002 report by the United States Department of Commerce, using the most recent census data then available, concluded that Internet access in homes had increased significantly between

Romney 6

1999 and 2001, even among minorities. A more recent national study by the Pew Foundation, conducted in 2006, reported that "74 percent of whites go online, 61 percent of African Americans do and 80 percent of English-speaking Hispanic Americans report using the Internet" (Marriott).

Arguing that significant strides have been made to bridge the digital divide, the Bush administration has questioned whether programs like the Community Technology Centers Program are still needed (Pekow). At the same time, private industry has withdrawn some support for efforts to bridge the digital divide. One organization, called PowerUp, worked with corporations to create community-based technology centers. In places like Austin, Texas, PowerUp established a computer center in the city's impoverished neighborhoods by collaborating with AOL Time Warner and the Austin Urban League (Doggett). Despite its initial success, the organization was hard hit by an economic downturn. According to a PowerUp spokesperson, "The model that was launched in late 1999 . . . was a model that had its bloodlines in different economic times. The model isn't necessarily the best one for these economic times" (Schwartz, "Lack"). In 2002, PowerUp closed its offices, leaving the community centers they created to find funding on their own.

In other cases, the groups targeted by digital divide programs argued that such programs might do more harm than good. A 2001 article in the

Romney 7

Chronicle of Higher Education observed that many African Americans and members of other minority groups argue that digital divide rhetoric actually stereotypes minorities. The article pointed out that digital divide rhetoric "could discourage businesses or academics from creating content or services tailored for minority communities—ultimately making the digital divide a self-fulfilling prophecy" (Young). Many scholars and leaders in the African-American community feared that a focus on the digital divide would lead to its being seen as a fact to be accepted rather than as a problem to be solved. Tara L. McPherson agreed, arguing that "the idea of challenging the digital divide is not about denying its existence. But it is to ensure that the focus on the digital divide doesn't naturalize a kind of exclusion of investment" (qtd. in Young).

Qtd. in indicates that McPherson's comments were quoted in Young's article

However, despite the appearance that the digital divide is closing and the claims that digital divide rhetoric may actually be harmful, many public officials and private interest groups continued to voice their concerns that gaps in technological literacy and availability remained a problem among many populations and communities. In fact, a 2002 report published by the Benton Foundation disagreed with the United States Department of Commerce's optimistic findings. This report contended that federal funding should be key in continuing to bring more people into the digital age (Dickard et al.).

Romney 8

While the Department of Commerce report maintained that most people had access to computers in their homes, the Benton Foundation's report used the same statistics to argue that many people continued to have difficulty accessing the Internet. The Benton report found that 75% of people with household incomes of less than $15,000 and 66% with incomes between $15,000 and $35,000 were not yet using the Internet (Dickard et al.). Wealthier Americans, however, had significantly greater access to the Internet. Of the Americans with incomes of $50,000-$75,000 a year, 67.3% used the Internet (Dickard et al.). As a result, the Benton Foundation strongly disagreed with the Bush administration's recommendation to cut programs like the Department of Commerce's Technology Opportunities Program (TOP) and the Community Technology Centers Program (CTC):

> TOP and CTC are important engines of digital opportunity. . . . A federal retreat from that leadership role would undermine innovative efforts to bring digital opportunity to underserved communities and jeopardize many successful community programs. Rather than walking away from the investment, the federal government should build upon the success of these programs to bring digital opportunity to the entire nation (Dickard et al.).

Quotation of more than four lines is typed as a block, indented 1", and double-spaced, with no quotation marks

Romney 9

The popularity of programs offered by the public library system also challenges the wisdom of the federal government's desire to cut funding for programs that increase computer literacy. According to an article published in the *Knight Ridder/Tribune Business News,* the New York public library system's computer literacy courses drew over eighteen thousand people in 2003. The demand for these classes was so high that many classes filled up, leaving people frustrated and disappointed (Dalton). The clear conclusion is that although the gap between the haves and have-nots may be closing, continued success depends on continued financial support of successful programs.[2]

> Superscript number identifies content note

Evidence suggests that although progress has been made in closing the digital divide, the gap still exists. As Michel Marriott points out, some groups that study Internet use or work to introduce young people to computers continue to believe that "[d]espite the dissolving gap . . . the digital divide is still vast in more subtle ways." For example, a coordinator for the Digital Divide Network notes that minorities and low-income Internet users are still less likely to own computers and therefore more likely to rely on school or office computers, which are not always available to them. As a result, their computer skills may not be as sophisticated as those of people who have unlimited Internet access (Marriott).

Romney 10

It is not only minorities and the impoverished who are affected by the digital divide. Many people know that children in inner-city schools lack access to computer technology and to the Internet, but few know that children attending schools in rural areas are also at risk. Vicky Wellborn, a high school English teacher in a small town, reports that her school only recently instituted a computer literacy program. As they ordered computers, the instructors realized that one of their biggest challenges would be training themselves. Certainly the computer literacy program has been helpful to many students, but the difficulties of teaching an unfamiliar subject continue to challenge teachers at the school (Wellborn).

Conclusion recommends solutions for problem of "digital divide"

Although many strides have been made in closing the gap between those who have access to the Internet and those who do not, problems and new challenges remain. Steps must be taken to solve these problems. First, we must continue efforts to make the Internet available to the widest possible audience. We must also ensure that the rhetoric surrounding the term *digital divide* is used to close this gap, not to create a new one by establishing or reinforcing stereotypes about minorities. A broader definition of what the digital divide is might help us to see that it has the potential to marginalize many groups of people—the poor, the elderly, the disabled, and rural schoolchildren, for example—not just members of

Romney 11

minority groups. On a practical level, the federal government should continue to fund programs that increase access to computer technology in general, and to the Internet in particular. Unless we take steps to make sure these resources are available to all, we are still in danger of becoming two separate and unequal societies: one "plugged-in" and privileged and one "unplugged" and marginalized.

Because concluding paragraph summarizes material already discussed and presents student's original conclusions, no documentation is necessary

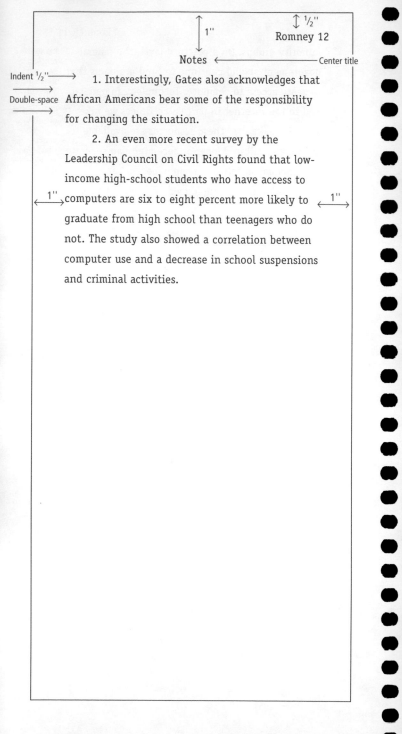

↕ ½"
Romney 12

↑ 1"

Notes ← ———————— Center title

Indent ½" →

Double-space →

1. Interestingly, Gates also acknowledges that African Americans bear some of the responsibility for changing the situation.

2. An even more recent survey by the Leadership Council on Civil Rights found that low-income high-school students who have access to computers are six to eight percent more likely to graduate from high school than teenagers who do not. The study also showed a correlation between computer use and a decrease in school suspensions and criminal activities.

←1" →   ←1" →

Romney 13

Works Cited ← Center title

"Civil Rights Groups Urge Congress to Close 'Digital
Divide.'" *Communications Daily* 28 Sept.
2005: n. pag. *LexisNexis*. Web. 23 Jan. 2007.

Dalton, Richard J., Jr. "New York Libraries Try to
Close Minorities' Digital Divide." *Knight
Ridder/Tribune Business News* 4 July 2004.
Expanded Academic ASAP. Web. 20 Jan. 2007.

Dickard, Norris, et al. *Bringing a Nation Online:
The Importance of Federal Leadership*. Benton
Foundation, July 2002. Web. 7 Feb. 2007.

The Digital Divide Network. TakingItGlobal, 2007.
Web. 2 Feb. 2007.

Doggett, Shelley. "'E-Team' Provides Local Youth
with Lessons in Technology." *The Daily Texan
Online*. Texas Student Media, U of Texas at
Austin, 14 Feb. 2001. Web. 3 Jan. 2007.

Egan, Timothy. "Bill Gates Views What He's Sown in
Libraries." *New York Times* 6 Nov. 2002: A18.
Print.

Gates, Henry Louis, Jr. "One Internet, Two Nations."
The Blair Reader. 4th ed. Ed. Laurie G.
Kirszner and Stephen R. Mandell. Upper
Saddle River: Prentice, 2002. 499-501. Print.

Gore, Al. "Building a Global Community."
International ITU Conference. Minneapolis.
12 Oct. 1998. Speech.

Annotations (margin labels):
- Newspaper article accessed from an online database
- Double-space
- Entry for an entire Web site
- Article from a newspaper
- Essay in an anthology
- Speech

Romney 14

Marriott, Michel. "Blacks Turn to Internet Highway,
    and Digital Divide Starts to Close." *New York
    Times* 31 Mar. 2006: A1+. Print.

Nelson, Colleen McCain. "Ethnic Gap on Internet
    Narrowing, Study Says." *Knight Ridder/Tribune
    Business News* 10 June 2004: n. pag.
    Expanded Academic ASAP. Web. 20 Jan. 2007.

Pekow, Charles. "Community Technology Program in
    Crosshairs of Congress." *Community College Week*
    15 Aug. 2005: n. pag. *Academic Search Premier*.
    Web. 30 Jan. 2007.

Schwartz, John. "A Lack of Money Forces Computer
    Initiative to Close." *New York Times* 30 Oct.
    2002: n. pag. *Expanded Academic ASAP*. Web.
    20 Jan. 2007.

---. "Report Disputes Bush Approach to Bridging
    'Digital Divide.'" *New York Times* 11 July
    2002: n. pag. *Expanded Academic ASAP*. Web.
    19 Jan. 2007.

United States. Dept. of Commerce. Economics and
    Statistics Admin. Natl. Telecommunications
    and Information Admin. *A Nation Online:
    How Americans Are Expanding Their Use
    of the Internet*. 2002. *National
    Telecommunications and Information
    Administration*. Web. 20 Jan. 2007.

Three unspaced hyphens used instead of repeating author's name

Government document accessed from the Internet

Romney 15

Wellborn, Vicky. "Re: Computer Literacy." Message
    to the author. 23 Jan. 2007. E-mail.
Young, Jeffrey R. "Does 'Digital Divide' Rhetoric Do
    More Harm than Good?" *The Chronicle of
    Higher Education*. Chronicle of Higher Educ.,
    9 Nov. 2001. Web. 10 Jan. 2007.

PART 8

Documenting Sources: APA and Other Styles

35 APA Documentation Style

35a Using APA Style

APA style* is used extensively in the social sciences. APA documentation has three parts: *parenthetical references in the body of the paper, a reference list,* and optional *content footnotes.*

1 Parenthetical References

APA documentation uses short parenthetical references in the body of the paper keyed to an alphabetical list of references that follows the paper. A typical parenthetical reference consists of the author's last name (followed by a comma) and the year of publication.

> Many people exhibit symptoms of depression after the death
> of a pet (Russo, 2000).

If the author's name appears in an introductory phrase, include the year of publication there as well.

> According to Russo (2000), many people exhibit symptoms
> of depression after the death of a pet.

Note that you may include the author's name and the date either in the introductory phrase or in parentheses at the end of the borrowed material.

When quoting directly, include the page number in parentheses after the quotation.

> According to Weston (1996), children from one-parent
> homes read at "a significantly lower level than those from
> two-parent homes" (p. 58).

NOTE: A long quotation (forty words or more) is not set in quotation marks. It is set as a block, and the entire quotation is double-spaced and indented one-half inch from the left margin. Parenthetical documentation is placed one space after the final punctuation.

---

*APA documentation format follows the guidelines set in the *Publication Manual of the American Psychological Association*, 5th ed. Washington, DC: APA, 2001.

SAMPLE APA IN-TEXT CITATIONS

1. A Work by a Single Author

Many college students suffer from sleep deprivation (Anton, 1999).

2. A Work by Two Authors

There is growing concern over the use of psychological testing in elementary schools (Albright & Glennon, 1982).

3. A Work by Three to Five Authors

If a work has more than two but fewer than six authors, mention all names in the first reference; in subsequent references in the same paragraph, cite only the first author followed by **et al.** ("and others"). When the reference appears in later paragraphs, include the year.

First Reference

(Sparks, Wilson, & Hewitt, 2001)

Subsequent References in the Same Paragraph

(Sparks et al.)

References in Later Paragraphs

(Sparks et al., 2001)

4. A Work by Six or More Authors

When a work has six or more authors, cite the name of the first author followed by **et al.** and the year in all references.

(Miller et al., 1995)

CLOSE-UP

CITING WORKS BY MULTIPLE AUTHORS

When referring to multiple authors in the text of your paper, join the last two names with **and**.

According to Rosen, Wolfe, and Ziff (1988). . . .

In-text citations (as well as reference list entries) require an **ampersand (&)**.

(Rosen, Wolfe, & Ziff, 1988)

5. Works by Authors with the Same Last Name

If your reference list includes works by two or more authors with the same last name, use each author's initials in all in-text citations.

F. Bor (2001) and S. D. Bor (2000) concluded that no further study was needed.

6. A Work by a Corporate Author

If the name of a corporate author is long, abbreviate it after the first citation.

First Reference

(National Institute of Mental Health [NIMH], 2001)

Subsequent Reference

(NIMH, 2001)

7. A Work with No Listed Author

If a work has no listed author, cite the first two or three words of the title (followed by a comma) and the year. Use quotation marks around titles of periodical articles and chapters of books; use italics for titles of books, periodicals, brochures, reports, and the like.

("New Immigration," 2000)

8. A Personal Communication

Cite letters, memos, telephone conversations, personal interviews, emails, messages from electronic bulletin boards, and so on only in the text—*not* in the reference list.

(R. Takaki, personal communication, October 17, 2001)

9. An Indirect Source

Cogan and Howe offer very different interpretations of the problem (cited in Swenson, 2000).

10. A Specific Part of a Source

Use abbreviations for the words *page* **(p.)**, *pages* **(pp.)**, *chapter* **(chap.)**, and *section* **(sec.)**.

These theories have an interesting history (Lee, 1966, chap. 2).

11. An Electronic Source

For an electronic source that does not show page numbers, use the paragraph number preceded by a ¶ symbol or the abbreviation **para.**

Conversation at the dinner table is an example of a family

ritual (Kulp, 2001, ¶ 3).

In the case of an electronic source that has neither page nor paragraph numbers, cite both the heading in the source and the number of the paragraph following the heading in which the material is located.

Healthy eating is a never-ending series of free choices

(Shapiro, 2001, Introduction section, para. 2).

If the source has no headings, you may not be able to specify an exact location.

12. Two or More Works within the Same Parenthetical Reference

List works by different authors in alphabetical order, separated by semicolons.

This theory is supported by several studies (Barson & Roth,

1995; Rose, 2001; Tedesco, 2002).

List two or more works by the same author or authors in order of date of publication (separated by commas), with the earliest date first.

This theory is supported by several studies (Rhodes &

Dollek, 2000, 2002, 2003).

For two or more works by the same author published in the same year, designate the work whose title comes first alphabetically *a*, the one whose title comes next *b*, and so on; repeat the year in each citation.

This theory is supported by several studies (Shapiro, 2003a,

2003b).

13. A Table

If you use a table from a source, give credit to the author in a note at the bottom of the table. Do not include this information in the reference list.

Note. From "Predictors of Employment and Earnings Among

JOBS Participants," by P. A. Neenan and D. K. Orthner, 1996,

Social Work Research, 20(4), p. 233.

2 Reference List

The **reference list** gives the publication information for all the sources you cite. It should appear at the end of your paper on a new numbered page titled **References**. Entries in the reference list should be arranged alphabetically. Double-space within and between reference list entries. The first line of each entry should start at the left margin, with the second and subsequent lines indented one-half inch. (**See 35b** for full manuscript guidelines.)

APA	PRINT SOURCES: *Entries for Books*

Book citations include the author's name (last name first); the year of publication (in parentheses); the book title (italicized); and publication information.

Capitalize only the first word of the title and subtitle and any proper nouns. Include any additional necessary information—edition, report number, or volume number, for example—in parentheses after the title. In the publication information, write out in full the names of associations, corporations, and university presses. Include the words **Book** and **Press**, but do not include terms such as **Publishers**, **Co.**, or **Inc.**

Author's last name | Initials | Year of publication (in parentheses) | Title (italicized, with only first word of title and subtitle capitalized)

Levine, R. V. (2003). *The power of persuasion: How we're bought and sold.* Hoboken, NJ: John Wiley & Sons.

City | State (to clarify unfamiliar or ambiguous city) | Publisher (not including terms Publisher, Co., or Inc.)

Authors

1. A Book with One Author

Maslow, A. H. (1974). *Toward a psychology of being.* Princeton: Van Nostrand.

2. A Book with More Than One Author

List up to six authors by last name and initials, using an ampersand (&) to connect the last two names. For more than six authors, add **et al.** after the sixth name.

Wolfinger, D., Knable, P., Richards, H. L., & Silberger, R. (1990).

The chronically unemployed. New York: Berman Press.

3. A Book with No Listed Author or Editor

Writing with a computer. (2006). Philadelphia: Drexel Press.

4. A Book with a Corporate Author

When the author and the publisher are the same, include the word **Author** at the end of the citation instead of repeating the publisher's name.

League of Women Voters of the United States. (2005). *Local*

league handbook. Washington, DC: Author.

5. An Edited Book

Lewin, K., Lippitt, R., & White, R. K. (Eds.). (1985). *Social*

learning and imitation. New York: Basic Books.

Editions, Multivolume Works, Forewords

6. A Work in Several Volumes

Jones, P. R., & Williams, T. C. (Eds.). (1990–1993). *Handbook*

of therapy (Vols. 1–2). Princeton: Princeton University

Press.

7. The Foreword, Preface, or Afterword of a Book

Taylor, T. (1979). Preface. In B. B. Ferencz, *Less than slaves*

(pp. ii–ix). Cambridge: Harvard University Press.

Parts of Books

8. A Selection from an Anthology

Give inclusive page numbers preceded by **pp.** (in parentheses) after the title of the anthology. The title of the selection is not enclosed in quotation marks.

Lorde, A. (1984). Age, race, and class. In P. S. Rothenberg

(Ed.), *Racism and sexism: An integrated study* (pp.

352–360). New York: St. Martin's Press.

NOTE: If you cite two or more selections from the same anthology, give the full citation for the anthology in each entry.

9. An Article in a Reference Book

Edwards, P. (Ed.). (1987). Determinism. In *The encyclopedia of philosophy* (Vol. 2, pp. 359–373). New York: Macmillan.

Government Reports

10. A Government Report

National Institute of Mental Health. (1987). *Motion pictures and violence: A summary report of research* (DHHS Publication No. ADM 91-22187). Washington, DC: U.S. Government Printing Office.

APA PRINT SOURCES:
Entries for Articles

Article citations include the author's name (last name first); the date of publication (in parentheses); the title of the article; the title of the periodical (italicized); the volume number (italicized); the issue number, if any (in parentheses); and the inclusive page numbers (including all digits).

Capitalize the first word of the article's title and subtitle as well as any proper nouns. Do not underline or italicize the title of the article or enclose it in quotation marks. Give the periodical title in full, and capitalize all words except articles, prepositions, and conjunctions of fewer than four letters. Use **p.** or **pp.** when referring to page numbers in newspapers, but omit this abbreviation when referring to page numbers in journals and popular magazines.

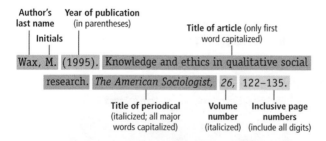

Author's last name | Year of publication (in parentheses)
Initials | Title of article (only first word capitalized)

Wax, M. (1995). Knowledge and ethics in qualitative social research. *The American Sociologist,* 26, 122–135.

Title of periodical (italicized; all major words capitalized) | Volume number (italicized) | Inclusive page numbers (include all digits)

Articles in Scholarly Journals

11. An Article in a Scholarly Journal with Continuous Pagination through an Annual Volume

Miller, W. (1969). Violent crimes in city gangs. *Journal of Social Issues, 27,* 581–593.

12. An Article in a Scholarly Journal with Separate Pagination in Each Issue

Williams, S., & Cohen, L. R. (1984). Child stress in early learning situations. *American Psychologist, 21*(10), 1–28.

NOTE: Do not leave a space between the volume and issue numbers.

Articles in Magazines and Newspapers

13. A Magazine Article

McCurdy, H. G. (1983, June). Brain mechanisms and intelligence. *Psychology Today, 46,* 61–63.

14. A Newspaper Article

If an article appears on nonconsecutive pages, give all page numbers, separated by commas (for example, **A1, A14**). If the article appears on consecutive pages, indicate the full range of pages (for example, **A7–A9**).

James, W. R. (1993, November 16). The uninsured and health care. *Wall Street Journal*, pp. A1, A14.

15. A Letter to the Editor of a Newspaper

Williams, P. (2000, July 19). Self-fulfilling stereotypes [Letter to the editor]. *Los Angeles Times*, p. A22.

ENTRIES FOR MISCELLANEOUS PRINT SOURCES

APA

Letters

16. A Personal Letter

References to unpublished personal letters, like references to all other personal communications, should be included only in the text of the paper, not in the reference list.

17. A Published Letter

Joyce, J. (1931). Letter to Louis Gillet. In Richard Ellmann,
James Joyce (p. 631). New York: Oxford University
Press.

*Television Broadcasts, Films, CDs, Audiocassette
Recordings, Computer Software*

18. A Television Broadcast

Murphy, J. (Executive Producer). (2002, March 4). *The CBS
evening news* [Television broadcast]. New York:
Columbia Broadcasting Service.

19. A Television Series

Sorkin, A., Schlamme, T., & Wells, J. (Executive Producers).
(2002). *The west wing* [Television series]. Los Angeles:
Warner Bros. Television.

20. A Film

Spielberg, S. (Director). (1994). *Schindler's list* [Motion
picture]. United States: Universal.

21. A CD Recording

Marley, B. (1977). Waiting in vain. On *Exodus* [CD]. New
York: Island Records.

22. An Audiocassette Recording

Skinner, B. F. (Speaker). (1972). *Skinner on Skinnerism*
[Cassette recording]. Hollywood, CA: Center for
Cassette Studies.

23. Computer Software

Sharp, S. (1995). *Career Selection Tests* (Version 5.0)
[Computer software]. Chico, CA: Avocation Software.

APA guidelines for documenting electronic sources focus on Web sources, which often do not include all the bibliographic information that print sources do. For example, Web sources may not include page numbers or a place of publication. At a minimum, a Web citation should have a title, a date (the date of publication, update, or retrieval), and an electronic address (URL). If possible, also include the author(s) of a source. When you need to divide a URL at the end of a line, break it after a slash or before a period (do not add a hyphen). Do not add a period at the end of the URL. (Current guidelines for citing electronic sources can be found on the APA Web site at <www.apa.org>.)

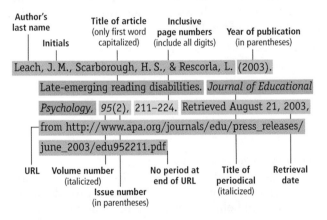

Internet-Specific Sources

24. An Internet Article Based on a Print Source

If you have seen the article only in electronic format, include the phrase **Electronic version** in brackets after the title.

Winston, E. L. (2000). The role of art therapy in treating

chronically depressed patients [Electronic version].

Journal of Bibliographic Research, 5, 54–72.

NOTE: If you think the article you retrieved may be different from the print version, add the date you retrieved it and the URL.

25. An Article in an Internet-Only Journal

Hornaday, J., & Bunker, C. (2001). The nature of the

entrepreneur. *Personal Psychology, 23*, Article 2353b.

Retrieved November 21, 2001, from http://journals

.apa.org/volume23/pre002353b.html

26. A Document from a University Web Site

Beck, E. (1997, July). *The good, the bad & the ugly: Or, why*

it's a good idea to evaluate web sources. Retrieved

January 7, 2002, from New Mexico State University

Library Web site: http://lib.nmsu.edu/instruction/

evalcrit.html

27. A Web Document (No Author Identified, No Date)

A document with no author or date should be listed by
title, followed by the abbreviation **n.d.** (for "no date"), the
retrieval date, and the URL.

The stratocaster appreciation page. (n.d.). Retrieved July 27,

2002, from http://members.tripod.com/~AFH/

28. An Email

As with all other personal communications, references to
personal email should be included only in the text of your
paper, not in the reference list.

29. A Message Posted to a Newsgroup

List the author's full name—or, if that is not available,
the screen name. In brackets after the title, provide information that will help readers access the message.

Shapiro, R. (2001, April 4). Chat rooms and interpersonal

communication [Msg 7]. Message posted to news://

sci.psychology.communication

30. A Searchable Database

Nowroozi, C. (1992). What you lose when you miss sleep.

Nation's Business, 80(9), 73–77. Retrieved April 22,

2001, from Expanded Academic ASAP database.

Abstracts, Newspaper Articles

31. An Abstract

Guinot, A., & Peterson, B. R. (1995). *Forgetfulness and partial*

cognition (Drexel University Cognitive Research Report

No. 21). Abstract retrieved December 4, 2001, from

http://www.Drexel.edu/~guinot/deltarule-abstract

.html

32. An Article in a Daily Newspaper

Farrell, P. D. (1997, March 23). New high-tech stresses hit

traders and investors on the information superhighway.

Wall Street Journal. Retrieved April 4, 2007, from

http://wall-street.news.com/forecasts/stress/

stress.html

3 Content Footnotes

APA format permits content notes, indicated by **super-scripts** (raised numerals) in the text. The notes are listed on a separate numbered page, titled **Footnotes**, following the appendixes (or after the reference list if there are no appendixes). Double-space all notes, indenting the first line of each note one-half inch and beginning subsequent lines flush left. Number the notes with superscripts that correspond to the numbers in your text.

35b APA-Style Manuscript Guidelines

Social science papers label sections with headings. Sections may include an introduction (untitled), followed by headings like **Background**, **Method**, **Results**, and **Discussion**. Each section of a social science paper is a complete unit with a beginning and an end so that it can be read separately and still make sense out of context. The body of the paper may include charts, graphs, maps, photographs, flowcharts, or tables.

The following guidelines are based on the latest version of the *Publication Manual of the American Psychological Association*.

CHECKLIST

TYPING YOUR PAPER

When typing your paper, use the student paper in **35c** as your model.

(continued)

TYPING YOUR PAPER (continued)

☐ Leave one-inch margins at the top and bottom and on both sides. Double-space your paper throughout.

☐ Indent the first line of every paragraph and the first line of every content footnote one-half inch from the left-hand margin.

☐ Set off a **long quotation** (more than forty words) in a block format by indenting the entire quotation one-half inch from the left-hand margin. Do not indent the first line further.

☐ Number all pages consecutively. Each page should include a **page header** (an abbreviated title) and a page number typed one-half inch from the top and one inch from the right-hand edge of the page. Leave one-half inch between the page header and the page number.

See 40b
☐ Center major <u>headings</u>, and type them with uppercase and lowercase letters. Place minor headings flush left, typed with uppercase and lowercase letters and italicized.

See 40c
☐ Format items in a series as a numbered <u>list</u>.

☐ Arrange the pages of the paper in the following order:

■ Title page (page 1) with a page header, running head, title, byline (your name), and the name of your school. (Your instructor may require additional information.)

■ Abstract (page 2)

■ Text of paper (beginning on page 3)

■ Reference list (new page)

■ Appendixes (start each on a new page)

■ Content footnotes (new page)

See 35a
☐ If you use source material in your paper, citations should be consistent with **APA documentation style**.

CHECKLIST

USING VISUALS

APA style distinguishes between two types of visuals: **tables** and **figures** (charts, graphs, photographs, and diagrams). In manuscripts not intended for publication, tables and figures are included in the text. A short table or figure should appear on the page where it is discussed; a long table or figure should be placed on a separate page just after the page where it is discussed.

Tables

Number all **tables** consecutively. Each table should have a *label* and a *title*.

☐ The **label** consists of the word **Table** (not in italics), along with an arabic numeral, typed flush left above the table.

☐ Double-space and type a brief explanatory **title** for each table (in italics) flush left below the label. Capitalize the first letters of principal words of the title.

Table 7

Frequency of Negative Responses of Dorm Students to Questions Concerning Alcohol Consumption

Figures

Number all **figures** consecutively. Each figure should have a *label* and a *caption*.

☐ The **label** consists of the word **Figure** (typed flush left below the figure) followed by the figure number (both in italics).

☐ The **caption** explains the figure and serves as a title. Double-space the caption, but do not italicize it. Capitalize only the first word, and end the caption with a period. The caption follows the label (on the same line).

Figure 1. Duration of responses measured in seconds.

NOTE: If you use a table or figure from an outside source, include full source information in a note at the bottom of the table or figure. This information does not appear in your reference list.

CHECKLIST

PREPARING THE APA REFERENCE LIST

When typing your reference list, follow these guidelines:

☐ Begin the reference list on a new page after the last page of text, numbered as the next page of the paper.

☐ Center the title **References** at the top of the page.

☐ List the items in the reference list alphabetically (with author's last name first).

☐ Type the first line of each entry at the left margin. Indent subsequent lines one-half inch.

☐ Separate the major divisions of each entry with a period and one space.

☐ Double-space the reference list within and between entries.

CLOSE-UP

ARRANGING ENTRIES IN THE APA REFERENCE LIST

■ Single-author entries precede multiple-author entries that begin with the same name.

Field, S. (1987)

Field, S., & Levitt, M. P. (1984)

■ Entries by the same author or authors are arranged according to date of publication, starting with the earliest date.

Ruthenberg, H., & Rubin, R. (1985)

Ruthenberg, H., & Rubin, R. (1987)

■ Entries with the same author or authors and date of publication are arranged alphabetically according to title. Lowercase letters (*a*, *b*, *c*, and so on) that indicate the order of publication are placed within parentheses.

Wolk, E. M. (1996a). Analysis . . .

Wolk, E. M. (1996b). Hormonal . . .

35c Model APA-Style Research Paper

The following student paper, "Sleep Deprivation in College Students," uses APA documentation style. It includes a title page, an abstract, a reference list, a table, and a bar graph.

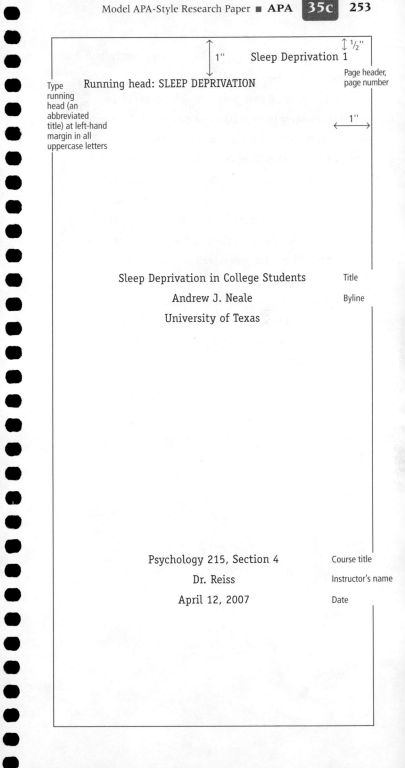

1"

Sleep Deprivation 1

↕ ½"

Page header, page number

Type running head (an abbreviated title) at left-hand margin in all uppercase letters

Running head: SLEEP DEPRIVATION

1"

Sleep Deprivation in College Students

Title

Andrew J. Neale

Byline

University of Texas

Psychology 215, Section 4

Course title

Dr. Reiss

Instructor's name

April 12, 2007

Date

1" Sleep Deprivation 2

Center heading ─────────────→ Abstract

A survey of 50 first-year college students in an introductory biology class was conducted. The survey consisted of 5 questions regarding the causes and results of sleep deprivation and specifically addressed the students' study methods and the grades they received on the fall midterm. The study's hypothesis was that although students believe that forgoing sleep to study will yield better grades, sleep deprivation may actually cause a decrease in performance. The study concluded that while only 43% of the students who received either an A or a B on the fall midterm deprived themselves of sleep in order to cram for the test, 90% of those who received a C or a D were sleep deprived.

Abstract typed as a single paragraph in block format (not indented)

Sleep Deprivation 3

Full title
(centered) ——→ Sleep Deprivation in College Students

Indent ½" ——→ For many college students, sleep is a luxury
they feel they cannot afford. Bombarded with tests
and assignments and limited by a 24-hour day,
students often attempt to make up time by doing
without sleep. Ironically, however, students may
actually hurt their academic performance by
failing to get enough sleep. According to several
psychological and medical studies, sleep
deprivation can lead to memory loss and health
problems, both of which are likely to harm a
student's academic performance.

Background

Sleep is often overlooked as an essential part
of a healthy lifestyle. Millions of Americans wake
up daily to alarm clocks because their bodies have
not gotten enough sleep. This indicates that for
many people, sleep is viewed as a luxury rather than
a necessity. As National Sleep Foundation Executive
Director Richard L. Gelula observes, "Some of the
problems we face as a society—from road rage to
obesity—may be linked to lack of sleep or poor
sleep" (National Sleep Foundation, 2002, ¶ 3). In
fact, according to the National Sleep Foundation,
"excessive sleepiness is associated with reduced
short-term memory and learning ability, negative
mood, inconsistent performance, poor productivity
and loss of some forms of behavioral control"
(2000, ¶ 2).

Sleep deprivation is particularly common
among college students, many of whom have busy

Annotations:
1" Double-space
Introduction
Thesis statement
Heading (centered)
Literature review (¶s 2–7)
Quotation requires its own documentation and a page number (or a paragraph number for Internet sources)
1"
1"

Sleep Deprivation 4

lifestyles and are required to memorize a great deal of material before their exams. It is common for college students to take a quick nap between classes or fall asleep while studying in the library because they are sleep deprived. Approximately 44% of young adults experience daytime sleepiness at least a few days a month (National Sleep Foundation, 2002, ¶ 6). Many students face daytime sleepiness on the day of an exam because they stayed up all night studying. These students believe that if they read and review immediately before taking a test—even though this usually means losing sleep—they will remember more information and thus get better grades. However, this is not the case.

A study conducted by professors Mary Carskadon at Brown University in Providence, Rhode Island, and Amy Wolfson at the College of the Holy Cross in Worcester, Massachusetts, showed that high school students who got adequate sleep were more likely to do well in their classes (Carpenter, 2001). According to their study of the correlation between grades and sleep, students who went to bed earlier on both weeknights and weekends earned mainly A's and B's. The students who received D's and F's averaged about 35 minutes less sleep per day than the high achievers (cited in Carpenter). Apparently, then, sleep is essential to high academic achievement.

Once students reach college and have the freedom to set their own schedules, however, many

---

Student uses past tense when discussing other researchers' studies

Cited in indicates an indirect source

Sleep Deprivation 5

believe that sleep is a luxury they can do without. For example, students believe that if they use the time they would normally sleep to study, they will do better on exams. A recent survey of 144 undergraduate students in introductory psychology classes contradicted this assumption. According to this study, "long sleepers," those individuals who slept 9 or more hours out of a 24-hour day, had significantly higher grade point averages (GPAs) than "short sleepers," individuals who slept less than 7 hours out of a 24-hour day. Therefore, contrary to the belief of many college students, more sleep is often required to achieve a high GPA (Kelly, Kelly, & Clanton, 2001).

Many students believe that sleep deprivation is not the cause of their poor performance, but rather that a host of other factors might be to blame. A study in the *Journal of American College Health* tested the effect that several factors have on a student's performance in school, as measured by students' GPAs. Some of the factors considered included exercise, sleep, nutritional habits, social support, time management techniques, stress management techniques, and spiritual health (Trockel, Barnes, & Egget, 2000). The most significant correlation discovered in the study was between GPA and the sleep habits of students. Sleep deprivation had a more negative impact on GPAs than any other factor did (Trockel et al.).

First reference includes all three authors; *et al.* replaces second and third authors in subsequent reference in same paragraph

Despite these findings, many students continue to believe that they will be able to remember more material if they do not sleep at all before an exam. They fear that sleeping will interfere with their ability to retain information. Pilcher and Walters (1997), however, showed that sleep deprivation actually impaired learning skills. In this study, one group of students was sleep-deprived, while the other got 8 hours of sleep before the exam. Each group estimated how well it had performed on the exam. The students who were sleep-deprived believed their performance on the test was better than did those who were not sleep-deprived, but actually the performance of the sleep-deprived students was significantly worse than that of those who got 8 hours of sleep prior to the test (Pilcher & Walters, 1997, cited in Bubolz, Brown, & Soper, 2001). This study confirms that sleep deprivation harms cognitive performance even though many students believe that the less sleep they get, the better they will do.

A survey of students in an introductory biology class at the University of Texas demonstrated the effects of sleep deprivation on academic performance and supported the hypothesis that despite students' beliefs, forgoing sleep does not lead to better test scores.

Student uses past tense when discussing his own research study

Method

To determine the causes and results of sleep deprivation, a study of the relationship between sleep and test performance was conducted. A survey of 50 first-year college students in an introductory biology class was completed, and

Sleep Deprivation 7

their performance on the fall midterm was analyzed.

Each student was asked to complete a survey consisting of the following five questions about their sleep patterns and their performance on the fall midterm:

1. Do you regularly deprive yourself of sleep when studying for an exam?
2. Did you deprive yourself of sleep when studying for the fall midterm?
3. What was your grade on the exam?
4. Do you feel your performance was helped or harmed by the amount of sleep you had?
5. Will you deprive yourself of sleep when you study for the final exam?

List is indented ½'' and set in block format

To maintain confidentiality, the students were asked not to put their names on the survey. Also, to determine whether the students answered question 3 truthfully, the group grade distribution from the surveys was compared to the number of A's, B's, C's, and D's shown in the instructor's record of the test results. The two frequency distributions were identical.

Results

Analysis of the survey data indicated a significant difference between the grades of students who were sleep-deprived and the grades of those who were not. The results of the survey are presented in Table 1.

Table 1 introduced

The grades in the class were curved so that out of 50 students, 10 received A's, 20 received B's,

Sleep Deprivation 8

10 received C's, and 10 received D's. For the purposes of this survey, an A or B on the exam indicates that the student performed well. A grade of C or D on the exam is considered a poor grade.

Table 1

Results of Survey of Students in University of Texas Introduction to Biology Class Examining the Relationship between Sleep Deprivation and Academic Performance

Grade Totals	Sleep-Deprived	Not Sleep-Deprived	Usually Sleep-Deprived	Improved	Harmed	Continue Sleep Deprivation?
A = 10	4	6	1	4	0	4
B = 20	9	11	8	8	1	8
C = 10	10	0	6	5	4	7
D = 10	8	2	2	1	3	2
Total	31	19	17	18	8	21

Of the 50 students in the class, 31 (or 62%) said they deprived themselves of sleep when studying for the fall midterm. Of these students, 17 (or 34% of the class) answered yes to the second question, reporting they regularly deprive themselves of sleep before an exam.

Of the 31 students who said they deprived themselves of sleep when studying for the fall midterm, only 4 earned A's, and the majority of the A's in the class were received by those students who were not sleep-deprived. Even more significant was the fact that of the 4 students who were sleep-deprived and got A's, only one student claimed to usually be sleep-deprived on the day of an exam. Thus, assuming the students who earn A's in a class do well in general, it is possible that sleep deprivation did not help or harm these students' grades. Not surprisingly, of the 4 students who received A's and were sleep-deprived, all said they would continue to use sleep deprivation to enable them to study for longer hours.

The majority of those who used sleep deprivation in an effort to obtain a higher grade received B's and C's on the exam. A total of 20 students earned a grade of B on the exam. Of those students, only 9, or 18% of the class, said they were deprived of sleep when they took the test.

Students who said they were sleep-deprived when they took the exam received the majority of the poor grades. Ten students got C's on the midterm, and of these 10 students, 100% said they were sleep-deprived when they took the test. Of the 10 students (20% of the class) who got D's, 8 said they were sleep-deprived. Figure 1 shows the significant relationship that was found between poor grades on the exam and sleep deprivation.

Figure 1 introduced

Discussion

For many students, sleep is viewed as a luxury rather than as a necessity. Particularly during the exam period, students use the hours in which they would normally sleep to study. However, this method does not seem to be effective. The survey discussed here reveals a clear

Sleep Deprivation 10

Figure placed
as close as
possible to
discussion in
paper

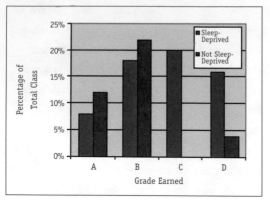

Label and
caption

(No source
information
needed for
graph based
on student's
original data)

Fig. 1. Results of survey of students in University of
Texas introduction to biology class examining the
relationship between sleep deprivation and academic
performance.

correlation between sleep deprivation and lower
exam scores. In fact, the majority of students who
performed well on the exam, earning either an A
or a B, were not deprived of sleep. Therefore,
students who choose studying over sleep should
rethink their approach and consider that sleep
deprivation may actually lead to impaired academic
performance.

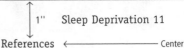

1'' Sleep Deprivation 11

References ← Center heading

Bubolz, W., Brown, F., & Soper, B. (2001). Sleep

Indent ½'' ⟶ habits and patterns of college students:

A preliminary study. *Journal of American*

College Health, 50, 131–135.

← Double-space

Carpenter, S. (2001). Sleep deprivation may be

underminimg teen health. *Monitor on*

Psychology, 32(9). Retrieved March 9, 2007,

from http://www. apa.org/monitor/oct01/

sleepteen.html

Kelly, W. E., Kelly, K. E., & Clanton, R. C. (2001).

The relationship between sleep length and

grade-point average among college students.

College Student Journal, 35(1), 84–90.

National Sleep Foundation. (2000). *Adolescent*

sleep needs and patterns: Research report and

resource guide. Retrieved March 16, 2007,

from http://www. sleepfoundation.org/

publications/sleep_and_teens_report1.pdf

National Sleep Foundation. (2002, April). *Epidemic*

of daytime sleepiness linked to increased

feelings of anger, stress, and pessimism.

Retrieved March 14, 2007, from http://www

.sleepfoundation.org/nsaw/pk_pollresultsmood

.html

Trockel, M., Barnes, M., & Egget, D. (2000).

Health-related variables and academic

performance among first-year college

students: Implications for sleep and other

behaviors. *Journal of American College Health,*

49, 125–131.

Entries listed in alphabetical order

36 Chicago Documentation Style

36a Using Chicago Style

The Chicago Manual of Style is used in history and in some social science and humanities disciplines. **Chicago style**[*]

---

[*]Chicago-style documentation follows the guidelines set in *The Chicago Manual of Style*, 15th ed. Chicago: University of Chicago Press, 2003. The manuscript guidelines and sample research paper at the end of this chapter follow guidelines set in Kate L. Turabian's *A Manual for Writers of Research Papers, Theses, and Dissertations*, 7th ed. Chicago: University of Chicago Press, 2007. Turabian style, which is based on Chicago style, addresses formatting concerns specific to college writers.

has two parts: *notes at the end of the paper* (**endnotes**) and *a list of bibliographic citations.* (Chicago style encourages the use of endnotes, but it allows the use of footnotes at the bottom of the page.)

1 Endnotes and Footnotes

The notes format calls for a **superscript** (raised numeral) in the text after source material you have either quoted or referred to. This numeral, placed after all punctuation marks except dashes, corresponds to the numeral that accompanies the note.

Endnote and Footnote Format: Chicago Style

In the Text

By November of 1942, the Allies had proof that the Nazis were engaged in the systematic killing of Jews.[1]

In the Note

1. David S. Wyman, *The Abandonment of the Jews: America and the Holocaust 1941–1945* (New York: Pantheon Books, 1984), 65.

CLOSE-UP

SUBSEQUENT REFERENCES TO THE SAME WORK

In the first reference to a work, use the full citation; in subsequent references to the same work, list only the author's last name, followed by a comma, an abbreviated title, another comma, and a page number.

First Note on Espinoza

1. J. M. Espinoza, *The First Expedition of Vargas in New Mexico, 1692* (Albuquerque: University of New Mexico Press, 1949), 10–12.

Subsequent Note

5. Espinoza, *First Expedition,* 29.

NOTE: *The Chicago Manual of Style* allows the use of the abbreviation *ibid.* ("in the same place") for subsequent references to the same work as long as there are no intervening references. *Ibid.* takes the place of the author's name and the work's title—but not the page number.

First Note on Espinoza

    1. J. M. Espinoza, *The First Expedition of Vargas in New Mexico, 1692* (Albuquerque: University of New Mexico Press, 1949), 10–12.

Subsequent Note

    2. Ibid., 23.

2 Bibliography

In addition to the heading **Bibliography**, Chicago style allows **Selected Bibliography**, **Works Cited**, and **References**. Bibliography entries are arranged alphabetically. Double-space within and between entries.

SAMPLE CHICAGO-STYLE ENDNOTES AND BIBLIOGRAPHY ENTRIES

PRINT SOURCES:
Entries for Books

Chicago

Capitalize the first, last, and all major words of titles and subtitles. Chicago style recommends the use of italics for titles, but underlining to indicate italics is also acceptable.

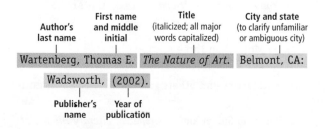

Authors

1. A Book by One Author

Endnote

> 1. Robert Dallek, *An Unfinished Life: John F. Kennedy 1917–1963* (New York: Little Brown, 2003), 213.

Bibliography

> Dallek, Robert. *An Unfinished Life: John F. Kennedy 1917–1963*. New York: Little Brown, 2003.

2. A Book by Two or Three Authors

Endnote

Two Authors

> 2. Jack Watson and Grant McKerney, *A Cultural History of the Theater* (New York: Longman, 1993), 137.

Three Authors

> 2. Nathan Caplan, John K. Whitmore, and Marcella H. Choy, *The Boat People and Achievement in America: A Study of Economic and Educational Success* (Ann Arbor: University of Michigan Press, 1990), 51.

Bibliography

Two Authors

> Watson, Jack, and Grant McKerney. *A Cultural History of the Theater*. New York: Longman, 1993.

Three Authors

> Caplan, Nathan, John K. Whitmore, and Marcella H. Choy. *The Boat People and Achievement in America: A Study of Economic and Educational Success*. Ann Arbor: University of Michigan Press, 1990.

3. A Book by More Than Three Authors

Endnote

Chicago style favors **and others** rather than **et al.** in endnotes.

> 3. Robert E. Spiller and others, eds., *Literary History of the United States* (New York: Macmillan, 1953), 24.

Bibliography

All authors' names are listed in the bibliography.

> Spiller, Robert E., Willard Thorp, Thomas H. Johnson, and
>> Henry Seidel Canby, eds. *Literary History of the United*
>> *States.* New York: Macmillan, 1953.

4. A Book by a Corporate Author

If a publication issued by an organization does not identify a person as the author, the organization is listed as the author, even if its name is repeated in the title, in the series title, or as the publisher.

Endnote

> 4. National Geographic Society, *National Parks of the*
> *United States,* 3rd ed. (Washington, DC: National Geographic
> Society, 1997), 77.

Bibliography

> National Geographic Society. *National Parks of the United*
>> *States.* 3rd ed. Washington, DC: National Geographic
>> Society, 1997.

5. An Edited Book

Endnote

> 5. William Bartram, *The Travels of William Bartram,* ed.
> Mark Van Doren (New York: Dover Press, 1955), 85.

Bibliography

> Bartram, William. *The Travels of William Bartram.* Edited by
>> Mark Van Doren. New York: Dover Press, 1955.

Editions, Multivolume Works

6. A Subsequent Edition of a Book

Endnote

> 6. Laurie G. Kirszner and Stephen R. Mandell, *The*
> *Wadsworth Handbook,* 8th ed. (Boston: Wadsworth, 2008), 52.

Bibliography

> Kirszner, Laurie G., and Stephen R. Mandell. *The Wadsworth*
>> *Handbook.* 8th ed. Boston: Wadsworth, 2008.

7. A Multivolume Work

Endnote

> 7. Kathleen Raine, *Blake and Tradition* (Princeton, NJ: Princeton University Press, 1968), 1:143.

Bibliography

> Raine, Kathleen. *Blake and Tradition*. Vol. 1. Princeton, NJ: Princeton University Press, 1968.

Parts of Books

8. A Chapter in a Book

Endnote

> 8. Roy Porter, "Health, Disease, and Cure," in *Quacks: Fakers and Charlatans in Medicine* (Gloucestershire, UK: Tempus Publishing, 2003), 182–205.

Bibliography

> Porter, Roy. "Health, Disease, and Cure." Chap. 5 in *Quacks: Fakers and Charlatans in Medicine*. Gloucestershire, UK: Tempus Publishing, 2003.

9. An Essay in an Anthology

Endnote

> 9. G. E. R. Lloyd, "Science and Mathematics," in *The Legacy of Greece,* ed. Moses Finley (New York: Oxford University Press, 1981), 270.

Bibliography

> Lloyd, G. E. R. "Science and Mathematics." In *The Legacy of Greece,* edited by Moses Finley, 256–300. New York: Oxford University Press, 1981.

Religious Works

10. A Religious Work

References to religious works (such as the Bible) are usually confined to the text or notes and not listed in the bibliography. In citing the Bible, include the book (abbreviated), the chapter (followed by a colon), and the verse numbers. Identify the version, but do not include a page number.

Endnote

> 10. Phil. 1:9–11 (King James Version).

PRINT SOURCES:
Entries for Articles

Chicago

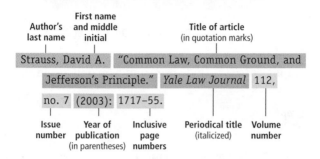

Author's last name | First name and middle initial | Title of article (in quotation marks)

Strauss, David A. "Common Law, Common Ground, and Jefferson's Principle." *Yale Law Journal* 112, no. 7 (2003): 1717–55.

Issue number | Year of publication (in parentheses) | Inclusive page numbers | Periodical title (italicized) | Volume number

Articles in Scholarly Journals

11. An Article in a Scholarly Journal with Continuous Pagination through an Annual Volume

Endnote

> 11. John Huntington, "Science Fiction and the Future," *College English* 37 (Fall 1975): 341.

Bibliography

Huntington, John. "Science Fiction and the Future." *College English* 37 (Fall 1975): 340–58.

12. An Article in a Scholarly Journal with Separate Pagination in Each Issue

Endnote

> 12. R. G. Sipes, "War, Sports, and Aggression: An Empirical Test of Two Rival Theories," *American Anthropologist* 4, no. 2 (1973): 80.

Bibliography

Sipes, R. G. "War, Sports, and Aggression: An Empirical Test of Two Rival Theories." *American Anthropologist* 4, no. 2 (1973): 65–84.

Articles in Magazines and Newspapers

13. An Article in a Weekly Magazine (Signed/Unsigned)

Endnote

Signed

> 13. Pico Iyer, "A Mum for All Seasons," *Time,* April 8, 2002, 51.

Unsigned

> 13. "Burst Bubble," *NewScientist,* July 27, 2002, 24.

Although both endnotes above specify page numbers, the bibliography entries include page numbers only when the pages are consecutive.

Bibliography

Signed

> Iyer, Pico. "A Mum for All Seasons." *Time,* April 8, 2002.

Unsigned

> "Burst Bubble." *NewScientist,* July 27, 2002, 24–25.

14. An Article in a Monthly Magazine (Signed/Unsigned)

Endnote

Signed

> 14. Tad Suzuki, "Reflecting Light on Photo Realism," *American Artist,* March 2002, 47.

Unsigned

> 14. "Repowering the U.S. with Clean Energy Development." *BioCycle,* July 2002, 14.

Bibliography

Signed

> Suzuki, Tad. "Reflecting Light on Photo Realism." *American Artist,* March 2002, 46–51.

Unsigned

> "Repowering the U.S. with Clean Energy Development." *BioCycle,* July 2002, 14.

15. An Article in a Newspaper (Signed/Unsigned)

Endnote

Because the pagination of newspapers can change from edition to edition, Chicago style recommends not giving page numbers for newspaper articles.

Signed

> 15. Francis X. Clines, "Civil War Relics Draw Visitors, and Con Artists," *New York Times,* August 4, 2002, national edition, sec. A.

Unsigned

> 15. "Feds Lead Way in Long-Term Care," *Atlanta Journal-Constitution,* July 21, 2002, sec. E.

Bibliography

Signed

> Clines, Francis X. "Civil War Relics Draw Visitors, and Con Artists." *New York Times,* August 4, 2002, national edition, sec. A.

Unsigned

> "Feds Lead Way in Long-Term Care." *Atlanta Journal-Constitution,* July 21, 2002, sec. E.

NOTE: Omit the article *the* from the newspaper's title, but include a city name in the title, even if it is not part of the actual title.

ENTRIES FOR MISCELLANEOUS PRINT AND NONPRINT SOURCES   Chicago

---

Interviews

16. A Personal Interview

Endnote

> 16. Cornel West, interview by author, tape recording, June 8, 2006.

Bibliography

Personal interviews are not listed in the bibliography.

17. A Published Interview

Endnote

17. Gwendolyn Brooks, interview by George Stavros, *Contemporary Literature* 11, no. 1 (Winter 1970): 12.

Bibliography

Brooks, Gwendolyn. Interview by George Stavros. *Contemporary Literature* 11, no. 1 (Winter 1970): 1–20.

Letters, Government Documents

18. A Personal Letter

Endnote

18. Julia Alvarez, letter to the author, April 10, 2006.

Bibliography

Personal letters are not listed in the bibliography.

19. A Government Document

Endnote

19. U.S. Department of Transportation, *The Future of High-Speed Trains in the United States: Special Study, 2001* (Washington, DC: GPO, 2002), 203.

Bibliography

U.S. Department of Transportation. *The Future of High-Speed Trains in the United States: Special Study, 2001.* Washington, DC: GPO, 2002.

Videotapes, DVDs, and Recordings

20. A Videotape or DVD

Endnote

20. *Interview with Arthur Miller,* dir. William Schiff, 17 min., The Mosaic Group, 1987, videocassette.

Bibliography

Interview with Arthur Miller. Directed by William Schiff. 17 min. The Mosaic Group, 1987. Videocassette.

21. A Recording

Endnote

21. Bob Marley, "Crisis," *Bob Marley and the Wailers,* Kava Island Records 423 095-3, compact disc.

Bibliography

> Marley, Bob. "Crisis." *Bob Marley and the Wailers.* Kava Island
>
> > Records 423 095-3. Compact disc.

ELECTRONIC SOURCES:
Entries for Sources from Internet Sites

Chicago

Internet citations for electronic sources include the author's name; the title of the document (enclosed in quotation marks); the title of the Internet site (italicized); the publication date (or, if no date is available, the abbreviation **n.d.**); the URL; and the date of access (in parentheses).

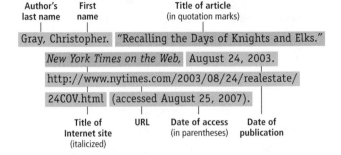

Author's last name | First name | Title of article (in quotation marks)
Gray, Christopher. "Recalling the Days of Knights and Elks."
New York Times on the Web, August 24, 2003.
http://www.nytimes.com/2003/08/24/realestate/
24COV.html (accessed August 25, 2007).

Title of Internet site (italicized) | URL | Date of access (in parentheses) | Date of publication

Internet-Specific Sources

22. An Article in an Online Journal

Endnote

> 22. Robert F. Brooks, "Communication as the Foundation
> of Distance Education," *Kairos: A Journal of Rhetoric, Technology,
> and Pedagogy* 7, no. 2 (2002), http://english.ttu.edu/
> kairos/index.html (accessed March 20, 2006).

Bibliography

> Brooks, Robert F. "Communication as the Foundation of
>
> > Distance Education." *Kairos: A Journal of Rhetoric,
> > Technology, and Pedagogy* 7, no. 2 (2002). http://
> > english.ttu.edu/kairos/index.html (accessed March 20,
> > 2006).

23. An Article in an Online Magazine

Endnote

    23. Steven Levy, "I Was a Wi-Fi Freeloader," *Newsweek,* October 9, 2002, http://www.msnbc.com/news/816606.asp (accessed January 9, 2007).

Bibliography

Levy, Steven. "I Was a Wi-Fi Freeloader." *Newsweek,* October 9, 2002. http://www.msnbc.com/news/816606.asp (accessed January 9, 2007).

24. An Article in an Online Newspaper

Endnote

    24. William J. Broad, "Piece by Piece, the Civil War *Monitor* Is Pulled from the Atlantic's Depths," *New York Times on the Web,* July 18, 2002, http://query.nytimes.com/search/advanced (accessed June 15, 2006).

Bibliography

Broad, William J. "Piece by Piece, the Civil War *Monitor* Is Pulled from the Atlantic's Depths." *New York Times on the Web,* July 18, 2002. http://query.nytimes.com/search/advanced (accessed June 15, 2006).

25. A Web Site or Home Page

Endnote

    25. David Perdue, "Dickens's Journalistic Career," *David Perdue's Charles Dickens Page,* September 24, 2002, http://www.fidnet.com/~dap1955/dickens (accessed September 10, 2007).

Bibliography

Perdue, David. "Dickens's Journalistic Career." *David Perdue's Charles Dickens Page.* September 24, 2002. http://www.fidnet.com/~dap1955/dickens (accessed September 10, 2007).

26. An Email Message

Endnote

     26. Meg Halverson, "Scuba Report," email message to author, April 2, 2007.

Bibliography

Email messages are not listed in the bibliography.

27. A Listserv Message

Include the name of the list and the date of the individual posting. Include the listserv address after the date of publication.

Endnote

     27. Dave Shirlaw, email to Underwater Archeology discussion list, September 6, 2002, http://lists.asu.edu/ archives/sub-arch.html (accessed May 12, 2006).

Bibliography

Listserv messages are not listed in the bibliography.

ELECTRONIC SOURCES:
Entries for Sources from Subscription Services   Chicago

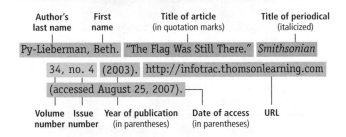

| Author's last name | First name | Title of article (in quotation marks) | Title of periodical (italicized) |

Py-Lieberman, Beth. "The Flag Was Still There." *Smithsonian*

34, no. 4 (2003). http://infotrac.thomsonlearning.com

(accessed August 25, 2007).

| Volume number | Issue number | Year of publication (in parentheses) | Date of access (in parentheses) | URL |

Sources from a Subscription Service

28. A Scholarly Journal Article

Include as much publication information as you can. Always give the URL of the service's main entrance; the date of access (in parentheses) is optional.

Endnote

     28. Richard J. Schaefer, "Editing Strategies in Television Documentaries," *Journal of Communication* 47, no. 4 (1997): 80, http://www.galegroup.com/onefile (accessed October 2, 2007).

Bibliography

> Schaefer, Richard J. "Editing Strategies in Television
> Documentaries." *Journal of Communication* 47, no. 4
> (1997): 80. http://www.galegroup.com/onefile
> (accessed October 2, 2007).

36b Chicago-Style Manuscript Guidelines

CHECKLIST

TYPING YOUR PAPER

When you type your paper, use the student paper in **36c** as your model.

☐ On the title page, include the full title of your paper. Also include your name, the course title, and the date. The title of your paper should appear entirely in capitals.

☐ Leave a one-inch margin at the top, at the bottom, and on both sides of the page.

☐ Double-space your paper throughout.

☐ Indent the first line of each paragraph one-half inch. Set off a long prose quotation (ten or more typed lines or more than one paragraph) from the text by indenting the entire quotation one-half inch from the left-hand margin. Do not use quotation marks. If the quotation is a full paragraph, include the paragraph indentation.

☐ Number all pages consecutively at the top of the page, with the number either centered or flush right. Page numbers should appear at a consistent distance (at least three-fourths of an inch) from the top edge. The title page is not numbered; the first full page of the paper is numbered page 1.

☐ Use superscript numbers to indicate in-text citations. Type superscript numbers at the end of cited material (quotations, paraphrases, or summaries). Leave no space between the superscript number and the preceding letter or punctuation mark. The note number should be placed at the end of a sentence (or at the end of a clause). The number should come after any punctuation mark except for a dash, which it precedes.

See 36a ☐ When you cite source material in your paper, use **Chicago documentation style**.

CHECKLIST

USING VISUALS

According to *The Chicago Manual of Style*, there are two types of visuals: **tables** and **figures** (or **illustrations**), including charts, graphs, photographs, maps, and diagrams.

Tables

☐ Give each **table** a label and an arabic number (**TABLE 1**, **TABLE 2**, and so on).

☐ Give each table a descriptive title in the form of a sentence. Place the title after the table number.

☐ Place both the label and title above the table.

☐ Place source information below the table, introduced by the word **Source**. (If there is more than one source, begin with **Sources**.)

Source: David E. Fisher and Marshall Jon Fisher, *Tube: The*

Invention of Television (Washington, DC: Counterpoint Press,

1996), 185.

If the sources are listed in the bibliography, use a shortened form below the table.

Source: Fisher and Fisher 1996.

Figures

☐ Give each **figure** a label, an arabic number, and a caption. The label **Figure** may be abbreviated **Fig.** (**Figure 1**, **Fig- 1**).

☐ Place both the label and caption below the figure, on the same line.

☐ Place source information in parentheses at the end of the title or caption.

Fig. 1. Television and its influence on young children.

(Photograph from ABC Photos.)

CHECKLIST

PREPARING CHICAGO-STYLE ENDNOTES

When typing your endnotes, follow these guidelines:

☐ Begin the endnotes on a new page after the last page of the paper and preceding the bibliography.

(continued)

PREPARING CHICAGO-STYLE ENDNOTES
(continued)

☐ Type the title **NOTES** entirely in capitals and center it two inches from the top of the page.

☐ Number the page on which the endnotes appear as the next page of the paper.

☐ Type and number notes in the order in which they appear in the paper, beginning with number 1.

☐ Type the note number on (not above) the line, followed by a period and one space.

☐ Indent the first line of each note one-half inch; type subsequent lines flush with the left-hand margin.

☐ Double-space within and between entries.

☐ Break URLs after slashes, before punctuation marks, or before or after the symbols = and &.

CHECKLIST

PREPARING A CHICAGO-STYLE BIBLIOGRAPHY

When typing your bibliography, follow these guidelines:

☐ Type entries on a separate page after the endnotes.

☐ Type the title **BIBLIOGRAPHY** entirely in capitals, and center it two inches from the top of the page.

☐ List entries alphabetically according to the author's last name.

☐ Type the first line of each entry flush with the left-hand margin. Indent subsequent lines one-half inch.

☐ Double-space within and between entries.

36c Model Chicago-Style Research Paper (Excerpts)

The following pages are from a student paper, "The Flu of 1918 and the Potential for Future Pandemics," that was written for a history course. It uses Chicago-style documentation and includes a title page, a notes page, and a bibliography.

Title page is not numbered

THE FLU OF 1918 AND THE POTENTIAL FOR
FUTURE PANDEMICS

Title (all capitals)
centered

Rita Lin
American History 301
May 3, 2007

Course title
Date

Title (centered)

Indent ½" →

Introduction

Superscript numbers refer to endnotes

The Flu of 1918 and the Potential for
Future Pandemics

Double-space

In November 2002, a mysterious new
illness surfaced in China. By May 2003, what
became known as SARS (Severe Acute Respiratory
Syndrome) had been transported by air travelers to
Europe, South America, South Africa, Australia,
and North America, and the worldwide death toll
had grown to 250.[1] By June 2003, there were more
than 8,200 suspected cases of SARS in 30 countries
and 750 deaths related to the outbreak, including
30 in Toronto. Just when SARS appeared to be
waning in Asia, a second outbreak in Toronto, the
hardest hit of all cities outside of Asia, reminded
everyone that SARS remained a deadly threat.[2]
As SARS continued to claim more victims and
expand its reach, fears of a new pandemic spread
throughout the world.

The belief that a pandemic could occur in the
future is not a far-fetched idea. During the
twentieth century, there were three, and the most
deadly one, in 1918, has several significant
similarities to the SARS outbreak. As David Brown
points out, in many ways, the 1918 influenza
pandemic is a mirror reflecting the causes and
symptoms, as well as the future potential, of SARS.
Both are caused by a virus, lead to respiratory
illness, and spread through casual contact and
coughing. Outbreaks for both are often traced to
one individual, quarantine is the major weapon
against the spread of both, and both likely arose

2

from mutated animal viruses. Moreover, as Brown observes, the greatest fear regarding SARS is that it will become so widespread that transmission chains will be undetectable, and health officials will be helpless to restrain outbreaks. Such was the case with the 1918 influenza, which also began mysteriously in China and was transported around the globe (at that time by World War I military ships). By the time the flu lost its power in the spring of 1919, in a year's time it had killed more than 50 million people worldwide,[3] more than twice as many as those who died during the four and a half years of World War I. Thus, if SARS is a reflection of the potential for a future flu pandemic—and experts believe it is—the international community needs to acknowledge the danger, accelerate its research, and develop an extensive virus-surveillance system.

Thesis statement

Clearly, the 1918 flu was different from anything previously known to Americans. Among the peculiarities of the pandemic was its origin and cause. In the spring of 1918, the virus, in

History of 1918 pandemic

2''

10

Center ————————→ NOTES

Indent ½'' ——→ 1. Nancy Shute, "SARS Hits Home," *U.S.* ← Double-space

News & World Report, May 5, 2003, 42.

Endnotes listed in order in which they appear in the paper

2. "Canada Waits for SARS News as Asia Under Control," *Sydney Morning Herald on the Web,* June 2, 2003, http://www.smh.com.au/text/articles/ 2003/06/01/1054406076596.htm (accessed April 2, 2007).

3. David Brown, "A Grim Reminder in SARS Fight: In 1918, Spanish Flu Swept the Globe, Killing Millions," *MSNBC News Online,* June 4, 2003, http://www.msnbc.com/news/921901.asp (accessed April 2, 2007).

4. Doug Rekenthaler, "The Flu Pandemic of 1918: Is a Repeat Performance Likely?—Part 1 of 2," *Disaster Relief: New Stories,* February 22, 1999, http://www.disasterrelief.org/Disasters/990219Flu/ (accessed March 9, 2007).

Subsequent references to the same source include author's last name, shortened title, and page number(s)

5. Lynette Iezzoni, *Influenza 1918: The Worst Epidemic in American History* (New York: TV Books, 1999), 40.

6. "1918 Influenza Timeline," *Influenza 1918,* 1999, http://www.pbs.org/wgbh/amex/influenza/ timeline/index.html (accessed March 9, 2007).

Ibid. is used for a subsequent reference to the same source when there are no intervening references

7. Iezonni, *Influenza 1918,* 131–32.

8. Brown, "Grim Reminder."

9. Iezonni, *Influenza 1918,* 88–89.

10. Ibid., 204.

13

BIBLIOGRAPHY

"1918 Influenza Timeline." *Influenza 1918,* 1999.
http://www.pbs.org/wgbh/amex/influenza/
timeline/index.html (accessed March 9, 2007).

Billings, Molly. "The Influenza Pandemic of 1918."
*Human Virology at Stanford: Interesting Viral
Web Pages,* June 1997. http://www.stanford
.edu/group/virus/uda/index.html (accessed
March 17, 2007).

Brown, David. "A Grim Reminder in SARS Fight: In
1918, Spanish Flu Swept the Globe, Killing
Millions." *MSNBC News Online,* June 4, 2003.
http://www.msnbc.com/news/921901.asp
(accessed April 2, 2007).

"Canada Waits for SARS News as Asia Under Control."
Sydney Morning Herald on the Web, June 2,
2003. http://www.smh.com.au/text/articles/
2003/06/01/1054406076596.htm (accessed
April 2, 2007).

Cooke, Robert. "Drugs vs. the Bug of 1918: Virus'
Deadly Code Is Unlocked to Test Strategies to
Fight It." *Newsday,* October 1, 2002.

37 CSE and Other Documentation Styles

37a Using CSE Style

CSE style,* recommended by the Council of Science Editors (CSE), is used in biology, zoology, physiology, anatomy, and genetics. CSE style has two parts—*documentation in the text* and a *reference list.*

1 Documentation in the Text

CSE style permits either of two documentation formats: *citation-sequence format* and *name-year format.*

Citation-Sequence Format. The **citation-sequence format** calls for either **superscripts** (raised numbers) in the text of the paper (the preferred form) or numbers inserted parenthetically in the text of the paper.

    One study[1] has demonstrated the effect of low dissolved

    oxygen.

These numbers refer to a list of references at the end of the paper. Entries are numbered in the order in which they appear in the text of the paper. For example, if **James** is mentioned first in the text, **James** will be number 1 in the reference list. When you refer to more than one source in a single note, the numbers are separated by a hyphen if they are in sequence and by a comma if they are not.

    Some studies[2-3] dispute this claim.

    Other studies[3,6] support these findings.

NOTE: The **citation-name format** is a variation of the citation-sequence format. In the citation-name format, the names in the reference list are listed in alphabetical order. The numbers assigned to the references are used as in-text references, regardless of the order in which they appear in the paper.

---

*CSE style follows the guidelines set in the style manual of the Council of Science Editors: *Scientific Style and Format: The CSE Manual for Authors, Editors, and Publishers,* 7th ed. New York: Rockefeller UP, 2006.

Name-Year Format. The **name-year format** calls for the author's name and the year of publication to be inserted parenthetically in the text. If the author's name is used to introduce the source material, only the date of publication is needed in the parenthetical citation.

> A great deal of heat is often generated during this process (McGinness 1999).

> According to McGinness (1999), a great deal of heat is often generated during this process.

When two or more works are cited in the same parentheses, the sources are arranged chronologically (from earliest to latest) and separated by semicolons.

> Epidemics can be avoided by taking tissue cultures (Domb 1998) and by intervention with antibiotics (Baldwin and Rigby 1984; Martin and others 1992; Cording 1998).

NOTE: The citation **Baldwin and Rigby 1984** refers to a work by two authors; the citation **Martin and others 1992** refers to a work by three or more authors.

2 Reference List

The format of the reference list depends on the documentation format you use. If you use the **name-year** documentation format, your reference list will resemble the reference list for an **APA** paper. If you use the **citation-sequence** documentation style (as in the paper in 37c), your sources will be listed by number, in the order in which they appear in your paper, on a **References** page. Double-space within and between entries. Type each number flush left, followed by a period and one space. Align the second and subsequent lines with the first letter of the author's last name.

See Ch. 35

CSE	PRINT SOURCES: *Entries for Books*

List the author or authors by last name; after one space, list the initial or initials (unspaced) of the first and middle names (followed by a period); the title (not underlined, and with only the first word capitalized); the place of publication; the full name of the publisher (followed by a semicolon); the year (followed by a period); and the total number of pages (including back matter, such as the index).

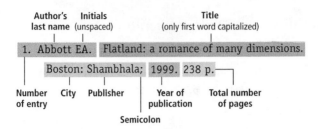

Author's last name | Initials (unspaced) | Title (only first word capitalized)

1. Abbott EA. Flatland: a romance of many dimensions.
Boston: Shambhala; 1999. 238 p.

Number of entry | City | Publisher | Year of publication | Total number of pages

Semicolon

Authors

1. A Book with One Author

1. Hawking SW. Brief history of time: from the big bang to black holes. New York: Bantam; 1995. 198 p.

NOTE: No comma follows the author's last name, and no period separates the initials of the first and middle names.

2. A Book with More Than One Author

2. Horner JR, Gorman J. Digging dinosaurs. New York: Workman; 1988. 210 p.

3. An Edited Book

3. Goldfarb TD, editor. Taking sides: clashing views on controversial environmental issues. 2nd ed. Guilford (CT): Dushkin; 1987. 323 p.

NOTE: The publisher's state, province, or country can be added within parentheses to clarify the location. The two-letter postal service abbreviation can be used for the state or province.

Parts of Books

4. A Chapter or Other Part of a Book with a Separate Title but with the Same Author

4. Asimov I. Exploring the earth and cosmos: the growth and future of human knowledge. New York: Crown; 1984. Part III, The horizons of matter; p. 245-294.

5. A Chapter or Other Part of a Book with a Different Author

    5. Gingerich O. Hints for beginning observers. In: Mallas JH, Kreimer E, editors. The Messier album: an observer's handbook. Cambridge: Cambridge Univ Pr; 1978. p. 194-195.

Religious Works, Classical Literature

6. A Religious Work

    6. The New Jerusalem Bible. Garden City (NY): Doubleday; 1985. Luke 15:11-32; p. 1715-1716.

7. Classical Literature

    7. Homer. Odyssey; Book 17:319-332. In: Lombardo S, translator and editor. The essential Homer: selections from the Iliad and the Odyssey. Indianapolis: Hackett; 2000. p. 391-392.

CSE PRINT SOURCES:
Entries for Articles

List the author or authors (last name first); the title of the article (not in quotation marks, and with only the first word capitalized); the abbreviated name of the journal (with all major words capitalized, but not italicized or underlined); the year (followed by a semicolon); the volume number, the issue number (in parentheses), followed by a colon; and inclusive page numbers. No spaces separate the year, the volume number, and the page numbers. Month names longer than three letters are abbreviated to their first three letters.

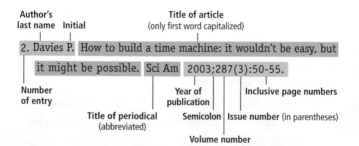

Author's last name — Initial

Title of article (only first word capitalized)

2. Davies P. How to build a time machine: it wouldn't be easy, but it might be possible. Sci Am 2003;287(3):50-55.

Number of entry

Year of publication

Inclusive page numbers

Title of periodical (abbreviated)

Semicolon — Issue number (in parentheses)

Volume number

Articles in Scholarly Journals

8. An Article in a Journal Paginated by Issue

8. Sarmiento JL, Gruber N. Sinks for anthropogenic carbon. Phy Today 2002;55(8):30-36.

9. An Article in a Journal with Continuous Pagination

9. Brazil K, Krueger P. Patterns of family adaptation to childhood asthma. J Pediatr Nurs 2002;17:167-173.

NOTE: Omit the month (and day for weeklies) and issue number for journals with continuous pagination within volumes.

Articles in Magazines and Newspapers

10. A Magazine Article (Signed/Unsigned)

Signed

10. Nadis S. Using lasers to detect E.T. Astronomy 2002 Sep:44-49.

Unsigned

10. Brown dwarf glows with radio waves. Astronomy 2001 Jun:28.

11. A Newspaper Article (Signed/Unsigned)

Signed

11. Husted B. Don't wiggle out of untangling computer wires. Atlanta Journal-Constitution 2002 Jul 21;Sect Q:1(col 1).

Unsigned

11. Scientists find gene tied to cancer risk. New York Times 2002 Apr 22;Sect A:18(col 6).

ENTRIES FOR MISCELLANEOUS PRINT AND NONPRINT SOURCES   CSE

Films, Videotapes, Recordings, Maps

12. An Audiocassette

12. Ascent of man [audiocassette]. Bronowski J. New York: Jeffrey Norton Pub; 1974. 1 audiocassette: 2-track, 55 min.

13. A Film, Videotape, or DVD

13. Stoneberger B, Clark R, editor. Women in science [videocassette]. American Society for Microbiology, producer. Madison (WI): Hawkhill; 1998. 1 videocassette: 42 min., sound, color, 1/2 in. Accompanied by: 1 guide.

14. A Map

A Sheet Map

14. Amazonia: a world resource at risk [ecological map]. Washington: National Geographic Society; 1992. 1 sheet.

A Map in an Atlas

14. Central Africa [political map]. In: Hammond citation world atlas. Maplewood (NJ): Hammond; 1996. p. 114-115. Color, scale 1:13,800,000.

CSE ELECTRONIC SOURCES:
Entries for Sources from Internet Sites

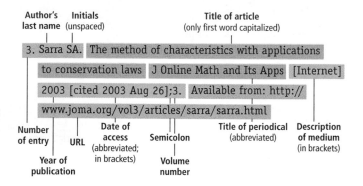

Author's last name | Initials (unspaced) | Title of article (only first word capitalized)

3. Sarra SA. The method of characteristics with applications to conservation laws J Online Math and Its Apps [Internet] 2003 [cited 2003 Aug 26];3. Available from: http://www.joma.org/vol3/articles/sarra/sarra.html

Number of entry | URL | Date of access (abbreviated; in brackets) | Semicolon | Title of periodical (abbreviated) | Description of medium (in brackets)

Year of publication | Volume number

Internet-Specific Sources

15. An Online Book

15. Bohm D. Causality and chance in modern physics [Internet]. Philadelphia: Univ of Pennsylvania Pr; c1999 [cited 2005 Aug 17]. Available from: http://www.netlibrary.com/ebook_info.asp?product_id517169

16. An Online Journal

16. Lasko P. The *Drosophila melanogaster* genome: translation factors and RNA binding proteins. J Cell Biol [Internet]. 2000 [cited 2005 Aug 15];150(2):F51-56. Available from: http://www.jcb.org/search.dtl

37b CSE-Style Manuscript Guidelines

CHECKLIST

TYPING YOUR PAPER

When you type your paper, use the student paper in **37c** as your model.

☐ Type your name, the course, and the date flush left one inch from the top of the first page.

☐ If required, include an **abstract** (a 250-word summary of the paper) on a separate numbered page.

☐ Double-space throughout.

☐ Insert tables and figures in the body of the paper. Number tables and figures in separate sequences (**Table 1**, **Table 2**; **Figure 1**, **Figure 2**; and so on).

☐ Number pages consecutively in the upper right-hand corner; include a shortened title before the number.

☐ When you cite source material in your paper, follow **CSE documentation style**.

See 37a

CHECKLIST

PREPARING THE CSE REFERENCE LIST

When typing your reference list, follow these guidelines:

☐ Begin the reference list on a new page after the last page of the paper, numbered as the next page.

☐ Center the title **References**, **Literature Cited**, or **References Cited** about one inch from the top of the page.

☐ List the entries in the order in which they first appear in the paper—not alphabetically.

(continued)

PREPARING THE CSE REFERENCE LIST
(continued)

☐ Number the entries consecutively; type the note
numbers flush left on (not above) the line, followed
by a period.

☐ Leave one space between the period and the first
letter of the entry; align subsequent lines directly
beneath the first letter of the author's last name.

☐ Double-space within and between entries.

37c Model CSE-Style Research Paper (Excerpts)

The following pages are from a student paper that explores the dangers of global warming for humans and
wildlife. The paper, which cites seven sources and includes a graph, illustrates CSE citation-sequence format.

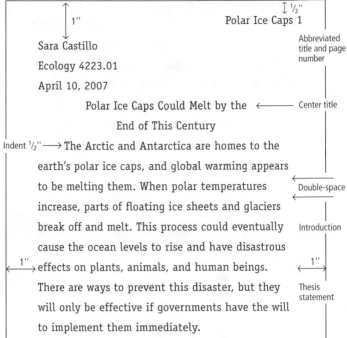

Sara Castillo

Ecology 4223.01

April 10, 2007

Polar Ice Caps Could Melt by the End of This Century

The Arctic and Antarctica are homes to the earth's polar ice caps, and global warming appears to be melting them. When polar temperatures increase, parts of floating ice sheets and glaciers break off and melt. This process could eventually cause the ocean levels to rise and have disastrous effects on plants, animals, and human beings. There are ways to prevent this disaster, but they will only be effective if governments have the will to implement them immediately.

The polar ice caps are melting at a rapid rate, and much of the scientific community agrees that global warming is one of the causes. The greenhouse effect, the mechanism that causes global warming, occurs when molecules of greenhouse gases in the atmosphere reflect the rays of the sun back to the earth. This mechanism enables our planet to maintain a temperature adequate for life. However, as the concentration of greenhouse gases in the atmosphere increases, more heat from the sun is retained, and the temperature of the earth rises.[1]

Greenhouse gases include carbon dioxide (CO_2), methane, and nitrous oxide.[2] Since the beginning of the industrial revolution in the late 1800s, people have been burning fossil fuels that

Polar Ice Caps 2

create CO_2.[3] This CO_2 has led to an increase in the greenhouse effect and has contributed to the global warming that is melting the polar ice caps.

Figure 1 introduced

As Figure 1 shows, the surface temperature of the earth has increased by about 1 degree Celsius (1.8 degrees Fahrenheit) since the 1850s. Some scientists have predicted that temperatures will increase even further.

Figure placed close to where it is discussed

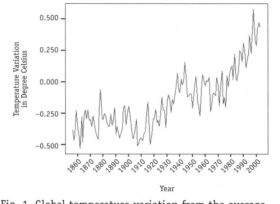

Year

Label, caption, and full source information

Fig. 1. Global temperature variation from the average during the base period 1961-1990 (adapted from Climatic research unit: data: temperature 2003) [Internet]. [cited 2007 Mar 11]. Available from: http://www.cru.uea.ac.uk/cru/data/temperature.

It is easy to see the effects of global warming. For example, the Pine Island Glacier in Antarctica was depleted at a rate of 1.6 meters per year between 1992 and 1999. This type of melting is very likely to increase the fresh water that drains into the oceans each year, thus

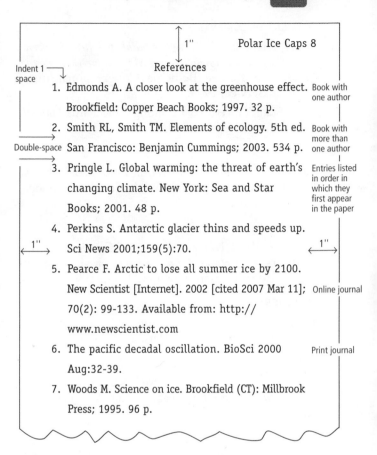

Polar Ice Caps 8

References

Indent 1 space

1. Edmonds A. A closer look at the greenhouse effect. Book with one author
   Brookfield: Copper Beach Books; 1997. 32 p.

2. Smith RL, Smith TM. Elements of ecology. 5th ed. Book with more than one author
   Double-space San Francisco: Benjamin Cummings; 2003. 534 p.

3. Pringle L. Global warming: the threat of earth's Entries listed in order in which they first appear in the paper
   changing climate. New York: Sea and Star
   Books; 2001. 48 p.

4. Perkins S. Antarctic glacier thins and speeds up.
   Sci News 2001;159(5):70.

5. Pearce F. Arctic to lose all summer ice by 2100.
   New Scientist [Internet]. 2002 [cited 2007 Mar 11]; Online journal
   70(2): 99-133. Available from: http://
   www.newscientist.com

6. The pacific decadal oscillation. BioSci 2000 Print journal
   Aug:32-39.

7. Woods M. Science on ice. Brookfield (CT): Millbrook
   Press; 1995. 96 p.

37d Using Other Documentation Styles

The following style manuals describe documentation formats and manuscript guidelines used in various fields.

CHEMISTRY

Dodd, Janet S. American Chemical Society. *The ACS Guide: A Manual for Authors and Editors*. 2nd ed. Washington: Amer. Chemical Soc., 1997.

GEOLOGY

United States Geological Survey. *Suggestions to Authors of the Reports of the United States Geological Survey*. 7th ed. Washington: GPO, 1991.

GOVERNMENT DOCUMENTS

Garner, Diane L. *The Complete Guide to Citing Government Information Resources: A Manual for Writers and Librarians*. Rev. ed. Bethesda: Congressional Information Service, 1993.

United States Government Printing Office. *Style Manual*. Washington: GPO, 2000.

JOURNALISM

Goldstein, Norm, ed. *Associated Press Stylebook and Briefing on Media Law*. 35th ed. New York: Associated P, 2000.

LAW

The Bluebook: A Uniform System of Citation. Comp. Editors of *Columbia Law Review* et al. 16th ed. Cambridge: Harvard Law Rev. Assn., 1996.

MATHEMATICS

American Mathematical Society. *AMS Author Handbook*. Providence: Amer. Mathematical Soc., 1998.

MEDICINE

Iverson, Cheryl. *Manual of Style: A Guide for Authors and Editors*. 9th ed. Chicago: Amer. Medical Assn., 1997.

MUSIC

Holoman, D. Kern, ed. *Writing about Music: A Style Sheet from the Editors of 19th-Century Music*. Berkeley: U California P, 1988.

PHYSICS

American Institute of Physics. *AIP Style Manual*. 5th ed. New York: Am. Inst. of Physics, 1995.

SCIENTIFIC AND TECHNICAL WRITING

Rubens, Philip, ed. *Science and Technical Writing: A Manual of Style*. 2nd ed. New York: Routledge, 2001.

PART 9

Developing Strategies for Academic Success

38 Ten Habits of Successful Students

Successful students have *learned* to be successful: they have developed specific strategies for success, and they apply those strategies to their education. If you take the time, you can learn the habits of successful students and apply them to your own college education—and, later on, to your career.

38a Learn to Manage Your Time Effectively

College makes many demands on your time. It is hard, especially at first, to balance studying, coursework, family life, friendships, and a job. But if you don't take control of your schedule, it will take control of you; if you don't learn to manage your time, you will always be behind, struggling to catch up.

Fortunately, there are two tools that can help you manage your time: a **personal organizer** and a **monthly calendar.** Carry your organizer with you at all times, and post your calendar in a prominent place (perhaps above your desk or on your refrigerator). Remember to record *in both places* school-related deadlines, appointments, and reminders (every due date, study group meeting, conference appointment, and exam) as well as outside responsibilities, such as work hours and medical appointments. (Be sure to record tasks and dates as soon as you learn of them.)

You can also use your organizer to help you plan a study schedule. You can block out times to study or to complete assignment-related tasks—such as a library database search for a research paper—in addition to appointments and deadlines. Make these entries in pencil so you can adjust your schedule as new responsibilities arise.

Remember, your college years can be a very stressful time, but although some degree of stress is inevitable, it can be kept in check. If you are organized, you will be better able to handle the pressures of a college workload.

38b Put Studying First

To be a successful student, you need to understand that studying is something you do *regularly*, not right before an exam. You also need to know that studying does not mean just memorizing facts; it also means reading, rereading, and discussing ideas until you understand them.

To make studying a regular part of your day, set up a study space that includes everything you need (supplies, good light, a comfortable chair) and does not include anything you do not need (clutter, distractions). Then, set up a tentative study schedule that reflects your priorities. Try to designate at least two hours each day to complete assignments due right away, to work on those due later on, and to reread class notes. When you have exams and papers, you can adjust your schedule accordingly.

Successful students often form **study groups,** and you should use this strategy whenever you can—particularly in a course you find challenging. A study group of four or five students who meet regularly (not just the night before an exam) can make studying more focused and effective as well as less stressful. By discussing concepts with your classmates, you can try out your ideas and get feedback, clarify complex concepts, and formulate questions for your instructor.

CHECKLIST

WORKING IN A STUDY GROUP

To get the most out of your study group, you need to set some ground rules:

- ☐ Meet regularly.
- ☐ Decide in advance who will be responsible for particular tasks.
- ☐ Set deadlines.
- ☐ Listen when someone else is speaking.
- ☐ Don't reject other people's ideas and suggestions without considering them very carefully.
- ☐ Have one person take notes to keep a record of the group's activities.
- ☐ Take stock of problems and progress at regular intervals.
- ☐ Be mindful of other students' learning styles and special needs.

38c **Be Sure You Understand School and Course Requirements**

To succeed in school, you need to know what is expected of you—and, if you are not sure, you need to ask.

When you first arrived at school, you probably received a variety of orientation materials—a student handbook, library handouts, and so on—explaining the rules and policies of your school. Read these documents carefully (if you have not already done so). If you do not understand something, ask your peer counselor or your adviser for clarification.

You also need to know the specific requirements of each course you take. Each course has a **syllabus** that explains the instructor's policies about attendance and lateness, assignments and deadlines, plagiarism, and classroom etiquette. In addition, a syllabus may explain penalties for late assignments or missed quizzes, tell how assignments are graded and how much each assignment is worth, or note additional requirements, such as field work or group projects. Requirements vary significantly from course to course, so read each syllabus (as well as any supplementary handouts) carefully.

ESL TIP

If you did not attend high school in the United States, some of your instructors' class policies and procedures may seem strange to you. To learn more about the way US college classes are run, read the syllabus for each of your courses, and talk to your instructors about your concerns.

You may also find it helpful to talk to older students with cultural backgrounds similar to your own. For specific information on adjusting to the US college classroom, **see Chapter 44.**

38d **Be an Active Learner in the Classroom**

Education is not about sitting passively in class and waiting for information and ideas to be given to you. It is up to you to be an active participant in your own education.

First, take as many small classes as you can. Small classes enable you to interact with other students and with your instructor. If a large course has recitation sections, be sure to attend these regularly even if they are not required. Also, be sure to take classes that require writing. Good writing skills are essential to your success as a student (and as a college graduate entering the workforce), and you will need all the practice you can get.

Attend class regularly, and arrive on time. Listen attentively, and take careful, complete notes. (Try to review these notes later with other students to make sure you have not missed anything important.) Do your homework on time, and keep up with the reading. When you read an assignment, interact with the text (for example, underlining the text and making marginal annotations) instead of just looking at what is on the page. If you have time, read beyond the assignment, looking on the Internet and in books, magazines, and newspapers for related information.

Finally, participate in class discussions: ask and answer questions, volunteer opinions, and give helpful feedback to other students. By participating in this way, you learn to consider other points of view, to test your ideas, and to respect the ideas of others.

ESL TIP

Especially in small classes, US instructors usually expect students to participate in class discussion. If you feel nervous about speaking up in class, you might start by expressing your support of a classmate's opinion.

38e Be an Active Learner Outside the Classroom

Taking an active role in your education is also important outside the classroom. Do not be afraid to approach your instructors; visit them during their office hours, and keep in touch with them by email. Get to know your major adviser well, and be sure he or she knows who you are and where your academic interests lie. Make appointments, ask questions, and explore possible solutions to problems: this is how you learn.

In addition, become part of your school community. Read your school newspaper, check the Web site regularly, join clubs, and apply for internships. This participation can help you develop new interests and friendships as well as enhance your education.

Finally, participate in the life of your community outside your school. Try to arrange an **internship,** a job that enables you to gain practical experience. (Many businesses, nonprofit organizations, and government agencies offer internships—paid or unpaid—to qualified students.) Take **service-learning** courses (which combine coursework with community service), if they are offered at your school, or volunteer at a local school or social agency. As successful students know, education is more than just attending classes.

38f Take Advantage of College Services

Colleges and universities offer students a wide variety of support services. For example, if you are struggling with a particular course, you can go to the tutoring service offered by your school's academic support center or by an individual department. If you need help with writing or revising a paper, you can make an appointment with the **writing center,** where tutors will give you advice. If you are having trouble deciding what courses to take or what to major in, you can see your academic adviser. If you are having trouble adjusting to college life, your peer counselor or (if you live in a dorm) your resident adviser may be able to help you. Finally, if you have a personal or family problem you would rather not discuss with another student, you can make an appointment at your school's counseling center, where you can get advice from professionals who understand student problems.

ESL TIP

Many ESL students find using the writing center (sometimes called a writing lab) very helpful. In fact, many writing centers have tutors who specialize in working with ESL students. Most writing centers provide assistance with assignments for any course, and they often assist with writing job application letters and résumés.

Of course, other services are available—for example, at your school's computer center, job placement service, and financial aid office. Your academic adviser or instructors can tell you where to find the help you need, but it is up to you to make the appointment.

38g Use the Library

Because so much material is available on the Internet, you may think your college library is outdated or even obsolete. But learning to use the **library** is an important part of your education. See Ch. 30

First, the library can provide a quiet place to study—something you may need if you have a large family or noisy roommates. The library also contains materials that cannot be found online—rare books, special collections, audiovisual materials—as well as electronic databases that contain material you will not find on the free Internet.

Finally, the library is the place where you have access to the expert advice of your school's reference librarians. These professionals can answer questions, guide your research, and point you to sources that you might never have found on your own.

38h Use Technology

Technological competence is essential to success in college. For this reason, it makes sense to develop good word-processing skills and to be comfortable with the **Internet**. You should also know how to send and receive email from your university account as well as how to attach files to your email. Beyond the basics, you should learn how to manage the files you download, how to evaluate Web sites, and how to use the electronic resources of your library. You might also find it helpful to know how to scan documents (containing images as well as text) and how to paste these files into your documents. See Ch. 31

If you do not already have these skills, you need to locate campus services that will help you get them. Workshops and online tutorials may be available through your school library, and individual assistance with software and hardware is available in computer labs.

Part of being technologically savvy in college involves being aware of the online services your campus has to offer. For example, many campuses rely on customizable information-management systems called **portals.** Not unlike commercial services, such as Yahoo! or America Online, a portal requires you to log in with a user ID and password to access services, such as locating and contacting your academic adviser and viewing your class schedule and grades.

Finally, you need to know not only how to use technology to enhance a project—for example, how to use *Power-Point* for an oral presentation or *Excel* to make a **table**—but also when to use technology (and when not to).

See 40d1

38i Make Contacts

One of the most important things you can do for yourself is to make academic and professional contacts that you can use during college and after you graduate.

Your first contacts are your classmates. Be sure you have the names, phone numbers, and email addresses of at least two students in each of your classes. These contacts will be useful to you if you miss class, if you need help understanding your notes, or if you want to start a study group.

You should also build relationships with students with whom you participate in college activities, such as the college newspaper or the tutoring center. These people are likely to share your goals and interests, so you may want to get feedback from them as you choose a major, consider further education, and make career choices.

Finally, develop relationships with your instructors, particularly those in your major area of study. One of the things cited most often in studies of successful students is the importance of **mentors,** experienced individuals whose advice they trust. Long after you leave college, you will find these contacts useful.

38j Be a Lifelong Learner

Your education should not stop when you graduate from college. To be a successful student, you need to be a lifelong learner.

Get in the habit of reading newspapers or checking the local and national news online; know what is happening in the world outside school. Talk to people outside the college community so that you don't forget there are issues that have nothing to do with courses and grades. Never miss an opportunity to learn: try to get in the habit of attending plays and concerts sponsored by your school or community and lectures offered at your local library or bookstore.

Finally, think about the life you will lead after college. Think about who you want to be and what you have to do to get there. This is what successful students do.

39 Reading Critically

Central to developing effective reading skills is learning the techniques of **active reading:** physically marking the text in order to identify parallels, question ambiguities, distinguish important points from not-so-important ones, and connect causes with effects and generalizations with specific examples. The understanding you gain from active reading prepares you to think (and write) critically about a text.

ESL TIP

When you read a text for the first time, don't worry about understanding every word. Instead, just try to get a general idea of what the text is about and how it is organized. Later on, you can use a dictionary to look up any unfamiliar words.

39a Previewing a Text

Before you actually begin reading a text, you should **preview** it—that is, skim it to get a general sense of its content and emphasis.

When you preview a **book,** start by looking at its table of contents, especially at the sections that pertain to your topic. Then, turn to its index to see how much coverage the book gives to subjects that may be important to you. As you leaf through the chapters, look at any pictures, graphs, and tables, and read the captions that appear with them.

When you preview a **periodical article,** scan the introductory and concluding paragraphs for summaries of the author's main points. (Journal articles in the sciences and social sciences often begin with summaries called **abstracts.**) Thesis statements, topic sentences, repeated key terms, transitional words and phrases, and transitional paragraphs can also help you to identify the points a writer is making. In addition, look for the visual cues—such as **headings and lists**—that writers use to emphasize ideas.

See 40b-c

39b Highlighting a Text

When you have finished previewing a work, you should **highlight** it—that is, use a system of symbols and underlining to identify the writer's key points and their relationships to one another. (If you are working with library material, photocopy the pages you need before you highlight them.)

CHECKLIST

USING HIGHLIGHTING SYMBOLS

- ☐ Underline to indicate information you should read again.
- ☐ Box or circle key words or important phrases.
- ☐ Put question marks next to confusing passages, unclear points, or words you need to look up.
- ☐ Draw lines or arrows to show connections between ideas.
- ☐ Number points that appear in sequence.
- ☐ Draw a vertical line in the margin to set off an important section of text.
- ☐ Star especially important ideas.

39c Annotating a Text

After you have read through a text once, read it again— this time, more critically. At this stage, you should **annotate** the pages, recording your responses to what you read.

Some of your annotations may be relatively straight-forward. For example, you may define new words, identify unfamiliar references, or jot down brief summaries. Other annotations may be more personal: you may identify a parallel between your own experience and one described in the reading selection, or you may record your opinion of the writer's position.

> ## ESL TIP
>
> You may find it useful to use your native language when you annotate a text.

The following excerpt from an article about "white flight" from American public schools illustrates a student's highlighting and annotations.

The main reason the white middle class fled, of course, is race, or more precisely, the complicated admixture of race and class and good intentions gone awry. The fundamental good intention—which even today strikes one as both moral and right—was to integrate the public classroom, and in so doing, to equalize the resources available to all school children. In Boston, this was done through enforced busing. In Washington, it was done through a series of judicial edicts that attempted to spread the good teachers and resources throughout the system. In other big city districts, judges weren't involved; school committees, seeing the handwriting on the wall, tried to do it themselves.

How can he be so sure?

Why does he assume intent was "good" + "moral"? Is he right?

However moral the intent, the result almost always was the same. The white middle class left. The historic parental vigilance I mentioned earlier had had a lot to do with creating the two-tiered system—one in which schools attended by the kids of the white middle class had better teachers, better equipment, better everything than those attended by the kids of the poor. This did not happen because the white middle-class parents were racists, necessarily; it happened because they knew how to manipulate the system and were willing to do so on behalf of their kids. Their neighborhood schools became little havens of decent education, and they didn't much care what happened in the other public schools.

Interesting point—but is it true?

In retrospect, this behavior, though perfectly understandable, was tragically short-sighted. When the judicial fiats made those safe havens untenable, the white middle class quickly discovered what the poor had always known: There weren't enough good teachers, decent equipment, and so forth to go around. For that matter, there weren't even enough good students to go around; along with everything else, middle-class parents had to start worrying about whether their kids were going to be mugged in school.

Slanted language (over-emotional) Generalization

Slanted language (over-emotional)

Faced with the grim fact that their children's education was quickly deteriorating, middle-class parents essentially had two choices: They could stay and pour the energy that had once gone into improving the neighborhood school into improving the entire school system—a frightening task, to be sure. Or they could leave. Invariably, they chose the latter.

Either/or fallacy? Were there other choices?

Oversimplification? No exceptions?

And it wasn't just the white middle class that fled. The black middle class, and even the black poor who were especially ambitious for their children, were getting out as fast as they could too, though not to the suburbs. They headed mainly for the parochial schools, which subsequently became integration's great success story, even as the public schools became integration's great failure. (Joseph Nocera, "The Case Against Joe Nocera: How People Like Me Helped Ruin the Public Schools")

CHECKLIST

READING TEXTS

As you read a text, keep the following questions in mind:

See Ch. 1

See 2b

☐ Does the writer provide any information about his or her background? If so, how does this information affect your reading of the text?

☐ What is the writer's **purpose**? How can you tell?

☐ What **audience** is the text aimed at? How can you tell?

☐ What is the most important idea? What support does the writer provide for that idea?

☐ What information can you learn from the introduction and conclusion?

☐ What information can you learn from the **thesis statement** and topic sentences?

☐ What key words are repeated? What does this repetition tell you about the writer's purpose and emphasis?

☐ How would you characterize the writer's tone?

☐ Where do you agree with the writer? Where do you disagree?

☐ What, if anything, is not clear to you?

40 Designing Effective Documents

Document design refers to the principles that help you determine how to design a piece of written work so that it communicates your ideas clearly and effectively. All well-designed documents share the same general characteristics: an effective format, clear headings, useful lists, and helpful visuals.

40a Creating an Effective Visual Format

An effective document contains visual cues that help readers find, read, and interpret information on a page. For example, wide margins can give a page a balanced, uncluttered appearance; white space can break up a long discussion; and a distinctive type size and typeface can make a word or phrase stand out on a page.

1 Margins

Margins frame a page and keep it from looking overcrowded. Because long lines of text can overwhelm readers and make a document difficult to read, a page should have margins of at least one inch all around. If the material you are writing about is highly technical or unusually difficult, use wider margins (one and a half inches).

Except for documents such as flyers and brochures, where you might want to isolate blocks of text for emphasis, you should **justify** (uniformly align, except for paragraph indentations) the left-hand margin.

2 White Space

White space is the area of a page that is intentionally left blank. Used effectively, white space can isolate material and thereby focus a reader's attention on it. You can use white space around a block of text—a paragraph or a section, for example—or around visuals such as charts, graphs, and photographs.

3 Color

Color (when used in moderation) can help to emphasize and classify information—such as the headings in a résumé or the bars on a graph—while making it visually appealing. Remember, however, that too many colors can distract or confuse readers.

4 Typeface and Type Size

Typefaces are distinctively designed sets of letters, numbers, and punctuation marks. The typeface you choose should be suitable for your purpose and audience. In your

academic writing, avoid fancy or elaborate typefaces—
𝒮𝒸𝓇𝒾𝓅𝓉 or 𝖔𝖑𝖉 𝕮𝖓𝖌𝖑𝖎𝖘𝖍, for example—that call attention to
themselves and distract readers. Instead, select a typeface
that is simple and direct—Courier, Times New Roman,
or Arial, for example. For most of your academic papers,
use 10- or 12-point type (headings will sometimes be
larger).

5 Line Spacing

Line spacing refers to the amount of space between the
lines of a document. If the lines are too far apart, the text
will seem to lack cohesion; if the lines are too close together, the text will appear crowded and be difficult to
read. The type of writing you do may determine line
spacing: the paragraphs of business letters, memos, and
some reports are usually single-spaced and separated by a
double space, but the paragraphs of academic papers are
usually double-spaced.

40b Using Headings

Headings perform some useful functions in a text:

- Headings tell readers that a new idea is being introduced.
- Headings emphasize key ideas.
- Headings indicate how information is organized in a
  text.

1 Number of Headings

The number of headings you use depends on the document. A long, complicated document will need more
headings than a shorter, less complicated one. Keep in
mind that too few headings may not be of much use, but
too many headings will make your document look like
an outline.

2 Phrasing

Headings should be brief, informative, and to the point.
They can be single words—**Summary** or **Introduction**, for
example—or they can be phrases (always stated in **parallel**

See
14a

terms): **Traditional Family Patterns**, **Alternate Family Patterns**, **Modern Family Patterns**. Finally, headings can be questions (**How Do You Choose a Major?**) or statements (**Choose Your Major Carefully**).

3 Indentation

Indenting is one way of distinguishing one level of heading from another. The more important a heading is, the closer it is to the left-hand margin: first-level headings are justified left, second-level headings are indented one-half inch, and third-level headings are indented further. Headings and subheadings may also be centered, placed flush left, or run into the text.

4 Typographical Emphasis

You can emphasize important words in headings by using **boldface**, *italics*, or ALL CAPITAL LETTERS. Used in moderation, these distinctive typefaces make a text easier to read. Used excessively, however, they slow readers down.

5 Consistency

Headings at the same level should have the same typeface, type size, spacing, and color. If one first-level heading is boldfaced and centered, all other first-level headings must be boldfaced and centered. Using consistent patterns reinforces the connection between content and ideas and makes a document easier to understand.

NOTE: Never separate a heading from the text that goes with it. If a heading is at the bottom of one page and the text that goes with it is on the next page, move the heading onto the next page so readers can see the heading and the text together.

40c Constructing Lists

By breaking long discussions into a series of key ideas, a list makes information easier to understand. By isolating individual pieces of information this way and by providing visual cues (such as bullets or numbers), a list also directs readers to important information on a page.

CONSTRUCTING EFFECTIVE LISTS

When constructing lists, you should follow these guidelines:

☐ **Indent each item.** Each item on a list should be indented so that it stands out from the text around it.

☐ **Set off items with numbers or bullets.** Use **bullets** when items (the members of a club, for example) are not organized according to any particular sequence or priority. Use **numbers** when you want to indicate that items (the steps in a process, for example) are organized according to a sequence or priority.

☐ **Introduce a list with a complete sentence.** Introduce a list with a complete sentence (followed by a colon) that tells readers what the list contains.

☐ **Use parallel structure.** Lists are easiest to read when all items are parallel and about the same length.

A number of factors can cause high unemployment:

• a decrease in consumer spending
• a decrease in factory orders
• a decrease in factory output

☐ **Capitalize and punctuate correctly.** If the items on a list are fragments (as in the example above), begin each item with a lowercase letter, and do not end it with a period. However, if the items on a list are complete sentences, begin each item with a capital letter and end it with a period.

☐ **Don't overuse lists.** Too many lists will give readers the impression that you are simply listing points instead of discussing them.

Figure 40.1 shows a page from a student's report that incorporates some of the effective design elements discussed in 40a–c. Notice that the use of different typefaces and type sizes contributes to the document's overall readability.

Different heading formats distinguish levels of importance

Single-spaced paragraphs separated by double space

White space breaks up text

Box isolates quotation

Horizontal rules divide sections

Justified margins contribute to a clean look

Numbered list identifies three subsections of report

WALSH 2

FIELD RESEARCH REPORT
THIRD ANNUAL FAMILY FESTIVAL–SEPTEMBER 27, 2003

OVERVIEW

By observing and participating in the events of the Third Annual Family Festival held on Saturday, September 27, 2003, I came to the conclusion through my discussions with audience members and performers that the interactions of groups were responses to the values and beliefs promoted by the Festival. These responses, in turn, were based upon pre-existing values and beliefs that each group held before attending the Festival. Consequently, those with similar values and beliefs tended to form groups that reinforced such convictions in themselves and, in most cases, in their children.

GROUPS OBSERVED

A TOTAL OF THREE GROUPS WERE OBSERVED, each with its own distinct characteristics:

1) families

2) childless couples

3) observers/other non-participants

FAMILIES

Families comprised the most prevalent group at the Festival. As its name suggests, the Third Annual Family Festival was geared primarily toward families. Each family usually consisted of a mother and a father, at least one child, and occasionally one or more grandparents. Tellingly, most families appeared to be homogeneous with respect to appearance, structural linguistics, sociolinguistics, kinesics, and proxemics. However, the spacing and lack of communication among families and the boundaries each family established distinguished them as distinct groups.

> *"This is first and foremost a family event, a place for parents to spend time with their children in a fun and supportive environment."*
> —Festival Spokesperson

FIGURE 40.1 A well-designed page from a student's report.

40d Using Visuals

Visuals, such as tables, graphs, diagrams, and photographs, can help you convey complex ideas that are difficult to communicate with words; they can also help you attract readers' attention.

1 Tables

Tables present data in rows and columns. Tables may contain numerical data, text, or a combination of the two. When you plan your table, make sure you include only the data that you will need; discard information that is too detailed or difficult to understand. Keep in mind that tables can distract readers, so include only those necessary to support your discussion. (Note that the table in Figure 40.2 on page 316 reports the student writer's original research and therefore needs no documentation.)

As the following table shows, the Madison location now employs more workers in every site than the St. Paul location.

Boldface and shading emphasize column headings

Underlining emphasizes row headings

Table 1
Number of Employees at Each Location

Employees	Location	
	Madison	St. Paul
Plant	461	254
Warehouse	45	23
Outlet Stores	15	9

Reference to table provides context

Heading and descriptive caption

Dividing lines improve readability of data

Because this location has grown so quickly, steps must be taken to

FIGURE 40.2 Sample table from a student paper.

2 Graphs

Like tables, **graphs** present data in visual form. However, whereas tables present specific numerical data, graphs convey the general pattern or trend that the data suggest. Because graphs tend to be more general (and therefore less accurate) than tables, they are frequently accompanied by tables. Figure 40.3 is an example of a bar graph showing data from a source.

Reference to graph provides context

Data

Label and citation

the demographics of college students is changing. According to a 2002 US Department of Education report titled *Nontraditional Undergraduates*, the percentage of students who could be classified as "nontraditional" has increased over the last decade (see fig 1).

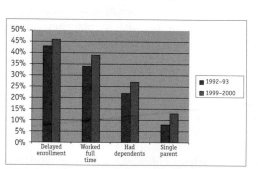

Fig. 1. United States, Dept. of Educ., Office of Educ. Research and Improvement, Natl. Center for Educ. Statistics; *Nontraditional Undergraduates*, by Susan Choy; 2002; National Center for Education Statistics; Web; 27 Feb. 2007.

FIGURE 40.3 Sample graph from a student paper.

3 Diagrams

A **diagram** calls readers' attention to specific details of a mechanism or object. Diagrams are often used in scientific and technical writing to clarify concepts that are difficult to explain in words. Figure 40.4, which illustrates the sections of an orchestra, serves a similar purpose in a music education paper.

Reference to diagram provides context

The sections of an orchestra are arranged precisely to allow for a powerful and cohesive performance. Fig. 1 illustrates the placement of individual sections of an orchestra.

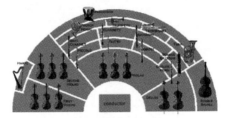

Label, descriptive caption, and citation

Fig. 1. The sections of an orchestra; *The Lyric Opera of Waco: Education Outreach*; Lyric Opera of Waco, 23 Aug. 2002; Web; 11 Nov. 2003.

FIGURE 40.4 Sample diagram from a student paper.

4 Photographs

Photographs enable you to show exactly what something or someone looks like—an animal in its natural habitat, a work of fine art, or an actor in costume, for example. Although it is easy to paste photographs directly into a text, you should do so only when they support or enhance your points. The photograph of a wooded trail in Figure 40.5 (on page 318) illustrates the student writer's description.

CHECKLIST

USING VISUALS

When using visuals in your papers, follow these guidelines:

☐ Use a visual only when it contributes something important to the discussion, not for embellishment.

(continued)

USING VISUALS (*continued*)

☐ Use the visual in the text only if you plan to discuss it in your paper (place the visual in an appendix if you do not).

☐ Introduce each visual with a complete sentence.

☐ Follow each visual with a discussion of its significance.

☐ Leave wide margins around each visual.

☐ Place the visual as close as possible to the section of your document in which it is discussed.

☐ Label each visual appropriately.

☐ Document each visual borrowed from a source.

---

travelers are well advised to be prepared, to always carry water, and to dress for the conditions. Loose fitting, lightweight wicking material covering all exposed skin is necessary in summer, and layers of warm clothing are needed for cold-weather outings. Hats and sunscreen are always a good idea no matter what the temperature, although most of the trails are quite shady with huge oak trees. Fig. 1 shows how nice and shady the trail can be.

Reference to photo provides context

Photo sized and placed appropriately within text with consistent white space above and below

Label and descriptive caption

Fig. 1 Greenbelt Trail in springtime (author photo).

FIGURE 40.5 Sample photograph from a student paper.

---

41 Designing Effective Web Sites

At some point in your college career, you may have to create a Web page or even a full Web site—for example, as a course assignment or as a way of marketing your job skills. Like other documents, Web pages follow the conventions of **document design**. Because so much of the content is meant to be read directly online, your choices of text, color, and navigation strategy are especially important.

See
Ch. 40

CLOSE-UP

COMPONENTS OF A WEB PAGE

A **personal home page** usually contains information about how to contact the author, along with a brief biography. A home page can also be the first page of a **Web site,** a group of related Web pages about a personal, professional, or academic topic. In this case, the home page contains **links** that allow users to move from one page to another or to another Web site.

41a Planning Your Web Site

When you plan your Web site, you should consider your **purpose**, **audience**, and tone, just as you would when planning a print document. In addition, of course, you should consider what content to include. Finally, just as an essay or research paper may have a set page limit, your own Web site may have size and file-type limitations.

See
Ch. 1

Before you create your Web site, you should consider how your Web pages will relate to one another. Beginning with the home page, users will navigate from one part of your Web site to another. For this reason, your home page should provide an overview of your site and give users a clear sense of the material the site contains.

As you plan your Web site, consider how its pages will be organized. One way to do this is to list the information on your Web site under headings or categories, just as you would if you were making an **informal outline**. Later on, you can use this list to create a **site map** (see Figure 41.1 on page 320), a feature that helps users of large Web sites locate and link to relevant content.

See
2c

Site map lists content areas

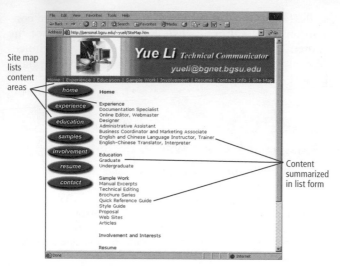

Content summarized in list form

FIGURE 41.1 Sample site map for a student's Web portfolio.

41b Selecting and Inserting Visuals

You can find visuals for your Web site by looking for other sites on the Web that make visuals available for others to use. You can usually find these sites with your search engine—*Google*, for example, has an image directory that you can search. You can also create and upload visuals yourself by using either a digital camera or a scanner. Once a visual has been created and saved electronically, you can use a graphics package such as *Adobe Photoshop* to adjust the visual's size, contrast, or color scheme; to crop the image; or to add text.

41c Planning Navigation

Web sites use a number of design features to make navigation easier. These features are illustrated in Figure 41.2.

- **Navigation Links, Buttons, and Bars** Navigation links, buttons, bars, or other graphic icons, such as arrows or pictures, enable readers to move from one page of a Web site to another.
- **Anchors** Anchors (or **relative links**) enable readers to jump from one part of a Web page to another.
- **Horizontal Rules** Horizontal rules divide sections and parts of a page.
- **Chunking or Clustering** Chunking or clustering means placing related items of text close to one an-

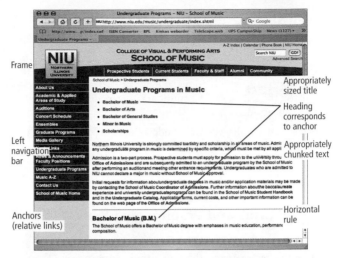

FIGURE 41.2 Sample Web page with navigation links, anchors, and frames.

other. This technique helps users read content easily on the screen.

- **Frames** Frames enable you to divide a single Web page into multiple windows.
- **Text Formatting Features** Like printed texts, Web texts follow the principles of <u>document design</u>, using design elements such as single-spaced text, headings, subheadings, and bulleted lists, as well as boldface and italics to emphasize points. See Ch. 40

41d Linking Your Content

Links are obviously a very important part of Web design. When you provide a link, you are directing people to a particular Web site. For this reason, you should make sure that the site you link to is up and running and that the information appearing there is both accurate and reliable.

CLOSE-UP

WEB SITES AND COPYRIGHT

As a rule, assume that any material on a Web site is copyrighted unless the author makes an explicit statement to

(continued)

41e   Editing and Proofreading Your Web Site

Before you post your Web site, you should proofread and edit it just as you would any other document. (Even if you run a spell check and a grammar check, you must still proofread carefully.)

41f   Posting Your Web Site

Once you have designed a Web site, you will need to upload (post) it so you can view it on the Web.

To get your site up on the Web, you transfer your files to an **Internet server,** a computer that is connected at all times to the Internet. Your Internet service provider will instruct you on how to transfer your files. Once your site is up and running, any mistakes you have made will be apparent as soon as you view your pages on the Web.

CHECKLIST

DESIGNING A WEB SITE

- ☐ Plan the content of your site.
- ☐ Consider how you want your site to be organized.
- ☐ Draw a basic plan of your site.
- ☐ Lay out text and graphics so that they present your ideas clearly and logically.
- ☐ Keep both text and graphics simple.
- ☐ Provide clear and informative links.
- ☐ Proofread your text.
- ☐ Make sure your site looks the way you want it to.

☐ Make sure all your links are active.
☐ Make sure you have acknowledged all material that you have borrowed from a source.
☐ Post your site to an Internet server.

42 Writing for the Workplace

Whether you are writing letters of application, résumés, memos, or email, you should always be concise, avoid digressions, and try to sound as natural as possible.

42a Writing Letters of Application

A **letter of application** summarizes your qualifications for a particular job.

Begin your letter of application by identifying the job you are applying for and telling where you heard about it. In the body of your letter, provide the specific information that will convince readers you are qualified for the position. Conclude by reinforcing your desire for the job and by stating that you have enclosed your résumé and that you will be available for an interview. (Be sure to include your phone number and email address.) Finally, proofread carefully to make sure there are no errors in spelling or punctuation.

NOTE: After you have been interviewed, you should send a **follow-up letter** to the person (or persons) who interviewed you. First, thank your interviewer for taking the time to see you. Then, briefly summarize your qualifications and your interest in the position. Because so few applicants write follow-up letters, such letters can have a very positive effect on the recipient.

Sample Letter of Application

Heading	246 Hillside Drive Urbana, IL 61801 kr237@metropolis.105.com October 20, 2007
Inside address	Mr. Maurice Snyder, Personnel Director Guilford, Fox, and Morris 22 Hamilton Street Urbana, IL 61822
Salutation	Dear Mr. Snyder:

My college advisor, Dr. Raymond Walsh, has told me that you are interested in hiring a part-time accounting assistant. I believe that my academic background and my work experience qualify me for this position.

I am presently a junior accounting major at the University of Illinois. During the past year, I have taken courses in taxation, trusts, and business law. I am also proficient in *Lotus* and *ClarisWorks*. Last spring, I gained practical accounting experience by working in our department's tax clinic.

Double-space →

Single-space →

After I graduate, I hope to get a master's degree in taxation and then return to the Urbana area. I believe that my experience in taxation as well as my familiarity with the local business community will enable me to make a contribution to your firm.

I have enclosed a résumé for your examination. I will be available for an interview any time after midterm examinations, which end October 25. I look forward to hearing from you.

Complimentary close — Sincerely yours,

Written signature — *Sandra Kraft*

Typed signature — Sandra Kraft
Additional data — Enc.: Résumé

42b Designing Résumés

A **résumé** lists relevant information about your education, job experience, goals, and personal interests.

The most common way to arrange the information in your résumé is in **chronological order,** listing your education and work experience in sequence, moving from earliest to latest job. Your résumé should be brief (one page, if possible), clear, and logically organized. Emphasize important information with italics, bullets, boldface, or different fonts. Print your résumé on high-quality paper, and proofread carefully for errors. (If you email your résumé to an employer, send it as an attachment. Do not paste it into the body of your email.)

CLOSE-UP

SCANNABLE RÉSUMÉS

Although the majority of résumés are submitted on paper, an increasing number of résumés are designed to be **scannable;** that is, to be scanned and entered into an electronic database

Because scanners will not pick up columns, bullets, or italics, you should not use them in a scannable résumé. Whereas in print résumés you use strong action verbs to describe your accomplishments (*performed computer troubleshooting,* for example), in a scannable résumé you use key nouns and adjectives (*computer troubleshooter,* for example) to attract employers who carry out a keyword search for applicants with certain skills. (To facilitate such a search, you should include a Skills or Keyword section on your scannable résumé.)

Sample Résumé: Print

KAREN L. OLSON

SCHOOL	HOME
3812 Hamilton St. Apt. 18	110 Ascot Ct.
Philadelphia, PA 19104	Harmony, PA 16037
215-382-0831	412-452-2944
olsont@dunm.ocs.drexel.edu	

EDUCATION

Drexel University, Philadelphia, PA 19104
Bachelor of Science in Graphic Design
Anticipated Graduation: June 2009
Cumulative Grade Point Average: 3.2 on a 4.0 scale

COMPUTER SKILLS

Hardware: Familiar with both Macintosh and PC systems
Software: *Adobe Illustrator, Photoshop,* and *Type Align;*
QuarkXPress; CorelDRAW; Micrografx Designer

EMPLOYMENT EXPERIENCE

The Triangle, Drexel University, Philadelphia, PA 19104
January 2006–present
Graphics Editor. Design all display advertisements submitted to
Drexel's student newspaper.

Unisys Corporation, Blue Bell, PA 19124
June–September 2006, Cooperative Education
Graphic Designer. Designed interior pages as well as covers for target marketing brochures. Created various logos and spot art designed for use on interoffice memos and departmental publications.

Charming Shoppes, Inc., Bensalem, PA 19020
June–December 2005, Cooperative Education
Graphic Designer/Fashion Illustrator. Created graphics for future
placement on garments. Did some textile designing. Drew flat
illustrations of garments to scale in computer. Prepared presentation boards.

Design and Imaging Studio, Drexel University, Philadelphia, PA
19104
October 2005–June 2006
Monitor. Supervised computer activity in studio. Answered telephone. Assisted other graphic design students in using computer
programs.

ACTIVITIES AND AWARDS

Kappa Omicron Nu Honor Society, vice president: 2007–present;
Dean's List: 2005–2006; Graphics Group, vice president:
2006–present

REFERENCES AND PORTFOLIO

Available upon request.

Sample Résumé: Scannable

CONSTANTINE G. DOUKAKIS

2000 Clover Lane
Fort Worth, TX 76107

Phone: (817) 735-9120
Email: Douk@aol.com

Employment Objective: Entry-level position in an organization that will enable me to use my academic knowledge and the skills that I learned in my work experience.

EDUCATION:

University of Texas at Arlington, Bachelor of Science in Civil Engineering, June 2007. Major: Structural Engineering. Graduated Magna Cum Laude. Overall GPA: 3.75 on a 4.0 base.

SCHOLASTIC HONORS AND AWARDS:

Member of Phi Eta Sigma First-Year Academic Honor Society, Chi Epsilon Civil Engineering Academic Society, Tau Beta Pi Engineering Academic Society, Golden Key National Honor Society.

Jack Woolf Memorial Scholarship for Outstanding Academic Performance.

COOPERATIVE EMPLOYMENT EXPERIENCE:

Johnson County Electric Cooperative, Cleburne, TX, Jan. to June 2006. Junior Engineer in Plant Dept. of Maintenance and Construction Division. Inspected and supervised in-plant construction. Devised solutions to construction problems. Estimated costs of materials for small construction projects. Presented historical data relating to the function of the department.

Dallas-Fort Worth International Airport, Tarrant County, TX, Dec. 2004 to June 2005. Assistant Engineer. Supervised and inspected airfield paving, drainage, and utility projects as well as terminal building renovations. Performed on-site and laboratory soil tests. Prepared concrete samples for load testing.

Dallas-Fort Worth International Airport, Tarrant County, TX, Jan. to June 2004. Draftsman in Design Office. Prepared contract drawings and updated base plans as well as designed and estimated costs for small construction projects.

SKILLS:

Organizational and leadership skills. Written and oral communication skills, C++, IBM, Macintosh, DOS, Windows 2000, and Mac OS. Word, Excel, FileMakerPro, PowerPoint, WordPerfect, Internet client software. Computer model development. Technical editor.

42c Writing Memos

Memos communicate information within an organization. Begin your memo with a purpose statement, followed by a background section. In the body of your memo, support your main point. If your memo is short, use bulleted or numbered lists to emphasize information. If it is more than two or three paragraphs, use headings to designate individual sections. End your memo by stating your conclusions and recommendations.

Sample Memo

TO: Ina Ellen, Senior Counselor
FROM: Kim Williams, Student Tutor Supervisor   Opening
SUBJECT: Construction of a Tutoring Center   component
DATE: November 10, 2007

This memo proposes the establishment of a tutor-   Purpose
ing center in the Office of Student Affairs.   statement

BACKGROUND
Under the present system, tutors must work with
students at a number of facilities scattered across the
university campus. As a result, tutors waste a lot of
time running from one facility to another and are
often late for appointments.

NEW FACILITY
I propose that we establish a tutoring facility adjacent to the Office of Student Affairs. The two empty
classrooms next to the office, presently used for   Body
storage of office furniture, would be ideal for this use.
We could furnish these offices with the desks and file
cabinets already stored in these rooms.

BENEFITS
The benefits of this facility would be the centraliz-
ing of the tutoring services and the proximity of the
facility to the Office of Student Affairs. The tutoring
facility could also use the secretarial services of the
Office of Student Affairs.

RECOMMENDATIONS
To implement this project, we would need to do   Conclusion
the following:

1. Clean up and paint rooms 331 and 333
2. Use folding partitions to divide each room into
   five single-desk offices
3. Use stored office equipment to furnish the
   center

I am certain these changes would do much to improve the tutoring service. I look forward to discussing
this matter with you in more detail.

42d Writing Emails

In many workplaces, virtually all internal (and some external) communications are transmitted as email. Although personal email tends to be informal, business email observes the conventions of standard written communication.

CLOSE-UP

WRITING EMAILS

The following rules can help you communicate effectively in an electronic business environment:

- Write in complete sentences. Avoid the slang, imprecise diction, and abbreviations that are common in personal email.
- Use an appropriate tone. Address readers with respect, just as you would in a standard business letter.
- Include a subject line that clearly identifies your content. If your subject line is vague, your email may be deleted without being read.
- Make your message as short as possible. Because most emails are read on the screen, long discussions are difficult to follow.
- Use short paragraphs, leaving an extra space between paragraphs.
- Use lists and internal headings to focus your discussion and to break it into manageable parts. This strategy will make your message easier to understand.
- Take the time to edit your email after you have written it. Delete excess words and phrases.
- Proofread carefully before sending your email. Look for errors in grammar, spelling, and punctuation.
- Make sure that your list of recipients is accurate and that you do not send your email to unintended recipients.
- Do not send your email until you are absolutely certain that your message says exactly what you want it to say.
- Do not forward an email unless you have the permission of the sender.
- Watch what you write. Keep in mind that email written at work is the property of the employer, who has the legal right to access it—even without your permission.

43 Making Oral Presentations

At school and on the job, you may sometimes be called upon to make oral presentations. The guidelines that follow can make the experience easier and less stressful.

43a Getting Started

Just as with writing an essay, the preparation phase of an oral presentation is as important as the speech itself.

Identify Your Topic. The first thing you should do is identify the topic of your speech. Once you have a topic, you should decide how much information, as well as what kind of information, you will need.

Consider Your Audience. The easiest way to determine what kind of information you will need is to consider the nature of your **audience**. Is your audience made up of experts or of people who know very little about your topic? How much background information will you have to provide? Can you use technical terms, or should you avoid them? Do you think your audience will be interested in your topic, or will you have to create interest? See 1b

Consider Your Purpose. Your speech should have a specific **purpose** that you can sum up concisely—for example, *to suggest ways to make registration easier for students.* To help you zero in on your purpose, ask yourself what you are trying to accomplish with your presentation. See 1a

Consider Your Constraints. How much time do you have for your presentation? (Obviously a ten-minute presentation requires more information and preparation than a three-minute presentation.) Do you already know enough about your topic, or will you have to do research?

43b Planning Your Speech

In the planning phase, you focus your ideas about your topic and develop a thesis; then, you decide what specific points you will discuss and divide your speech into a few manageable sections.

Develop a Thesis Statement. Before you can actually plan your speech, you should develop a thesis statement that clearly and concisely communicates your main idea to your audience. If you know a lot about your topic, you can develop a thesis on your own. If you do not, you will have to gather information and review it before you can decide on a thesis.

Decide on Your Points. Once you have developed a thesis, you can decide what points you will discuss. Unlike readers, who can reread a passage until they understand it, listeners must understand information the first time they hear it. For this reason, speeches usually focus on points that are clear and easy to follow.

Outline the Individual Parts of Your Speech. Every speech has a beginning, a middle, and an end. Your **introduction** should introduce your subject, engage your audience's interest, and state your thesis—but it should not include an in-depth discussion or a summary of your topic. The **body,** or middle section, of your speech should present the points that support your thesis. It should also include the facts, examples, and other information that will clarify your points and help convince listeners that your thesis is reasonable. Your **conclusion** should bring your speech to a definite end and reinforce your thesis.

43c Preparing Your Notes

Most people use notes of some form when they give a speech.

Full Text. Some people like to write out the full text of their speech and refer to it during their presentation. If the type is large enough, and if you triple-space, this strategy can be useful. One disadvantage of using the full text of your speech is that it is easy to lose your place and become disoriented; another is that you may find yourself simply reading.

Notecards. Some people write parts of their speech—for example, a list of key points or definitions—on notecards. If these cards are small, they can be placed inconspicuously on a podium or a table. With some practice, you can use notecards effectively. You have to be careful, however, not to become so dependent on the cards that you lose eye contact with your audience or begin fidgeting with the cards as you give your speech.

Outlines. Some people like to refer to an outline when they give a speech. As they speak, they can glance down at the outline to get their bearings or to remind themselves of a point they may have forgotten. Because an outline does not contain the full text of a speech, the temptation to read is eliminated. However, if for some reason you draw a blank, an outline gives you very little to fall back on.

43d Using Visual Aids

Visual aids—such as overhead transparencies or posters—can reinforce important information and make your speech easier to understand. For a simple speech, a visual aid may be no more than a definition or a few key terms, names, or dates written on the board. For a more complicated presentation, you might need charts, graphs, diagrams, or photographs—or even objects.

If you are using equipment (such as a laptop) to display visuals, make sure you know how to operate it—and have a contingency plan in case the equipment doesn't work the way it should. In addition, make sure that the visual you use is large enough for everyone in your audience to see. Printing or typing should be neat and free of errors.

Microsoft PowerPoint, the most commonly used **presentation software** package, enables you to prepare attractive, professional slides (see Figure 43.1 on page 334). This program contains many options for backgrounds, color schemes, and special effects, and also lets you supplement your slides with sound and video.

COMPUTER TIP   academic.cengage.com/eng/kirsznermandell

USING *POWERPOINT*

If possible, use the same computer that you used to prepare your *PowerPoint* slides when you deliver your speech.

(continued)

> **USING *POWERPOINT*** *(continued)*
>
> That way, you will be sure that you will be able to open your files and that all the multimedia effects you included with your slides will work.

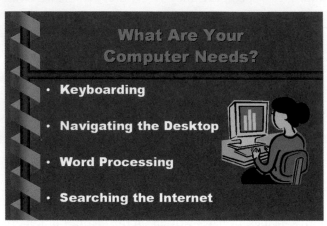

FIGURE 43.1 Sample *PowerPoint* slide.

USING VISUAL AIDS IN YOUR PRESENTATIONS		
Visual Aid	Advantages	Disadvantages
Computer presentations	Clear Easy to read Professional Graphics, video, sound, and animated effects Portable (disk or CD-ROM)	Special equipment needed Expertise needed Special software needed Software might not be compatible with all computer systems
Overhead projectors	Transparencies are inexpensive Transparencies are easily prepared with computer or copier Transparencies are portable	Transparencies can stick together Transparencies can be placed upside down Transparencies must be placed on projector by hand Some projectors are noisy

Visual Aid	Advantages	Disadvantages
Overhead projectors (continued)	Transparencies can be written on during presentation Projector is easy to operate	Speaker must avoid projector's power cord during presentation
Slide projector	Colorful Professional Projector is easy to use Order of slides can be reversed during presentation Portable (slide carousel)	Slides are expensive to produce Special equipment needed for lettering and graphics Dark room needed for presentation Slides can jam in projector
Posters or flip charts	Low-tech Good for small-group presentations Portable	May not be large enough to be seen in some rooms Artistic ability needed May be expensive if prepared professionally Must be secured to an easel
Chalkboards or whiteboards	Available in most rooms Easy to use Easy to erase or change information during presentation	Difficult to draw complicated graphics Handwriting must be legible Must catch errors as you write Cannot face audience when writing or drawing Very informal

CHECKLIST

DESIGNING VISUALS

☐ Do not put more than three or four points on a single visual.
☐ Use single words or short phrases, not sentences or paragraphs.
☐ Limit the number of visuals. For a three- to five-minute presentation, five or six visuals are enough.

(continued)

DESIGNING VISUALS (continued)

☐ Use type that is large enough for your audience to see (50-point type for major headings and 30–34 point type for text).

☐ Do not use elaborate graphics or special effects just because your computer software enables you to do so (this is especially relevant for users of *Microsoft Power-Point*).

☐ Check your visuals for correctness. Make sure your graphics do not contain typos, mislabelings, or other errors.

43e Rehearsing Your Speech

You should practice your speech often—at least five times. Do not try to memorize your entire speech, but be sure you know it well enough so that you can move from point to point without constantly looking at your notes. Finally, time yourself. Make certain that your three-minute speech actually takes three minutes to deliver.

43f Delivering Your Speech

The most important part of your speech is your delivery. Keep in mind that a certain amount of nervousness is normal, so try not to focus on it too much. While you are waiting to begin, take some deep breaths to help you calm down. Once you get to the front of the room, do not start right away. Take the time to make sure that everything you will need is there and that all your equipment is positioned properly.

When you begin speaking, pace yourself. Speak slowly and clearly, and look at the entire audience. Even though your speech is planned, it should sound natural and conversational. Try using pauses to emphasize important points and to give listeners time to consider what you have said. Finally, sound enthusiastic about your subject.

How you look will be the first thing that listeners notice about you, so dress appropriately for the occasion. (Although shorts and a T-shirt may be appropriate for an afternoon in the park, they are not suitable for a classroom presentation.)

PART 10

Resources for Bilingual and ESL Writers

44 Adjusting to the US Classroom

If you went to school outside of the United States, you may not be familiar with the way writing is taught in US composition classes.

CLOSE-UP

ADJUSTING TO THE US CLASSROOM

Here are some aspects of US classrooms that may be unfamiliar to you:

- **Punctuality** Students are expected to be in their seats and ready to begin class at the scheduled time. If you are late repeatedly, your grade may be lowered.
- **Student–Instructor Relationships** The relationship between students and instructors may be more casual or friendly than you are used to. However, instructors still expect students to abide by the rules they set.
- **Class Discussion** Instructors typically expect students to volunteer ideas in class and may even enjoy it when students disagree with their opinions (as long as the students can make good arguments for their positions). Rather than being a sign of disrespect, this is usually considered to be evidence of interest and involvement in the topic under discussion.

44a Understanding the Writing Process

See Ch. 2 Typically, US composition instructors teach writing as a **process**. This process usually includes the following components:

- **Planning and shaping your writing** Your instructor will probably help you get ideas for your writing by assigning relevant readings, conducting class discussions, and asking you to keep a journal or engage in See 2a2 **freewriting** and **brainstorming**.
- **Writing multiple drafts** After you write your paper for the first time, you will probably get feedback from your instructor or your classmates so that you can **revise** (improve) your paper before receiving a grade on it. Instructors expect students to use the suggestions they receive to make significant improvements to their papers. (For more information on the drafting process, **see 2d.**)

■ **Looking at sample papers** Your instructor may provide the class with sample papers of the type that he or she has assigned. Such samples can help you understand how to complete the assigned paper. Sometimes the samples are strong papers that can serve as good examples of what to do. However, most samples will have both strengths and weaknesses, so be sure you understand your instructor's opinion of the samples he or she provides.

■ **Engaging in peer review** (sometimes called peer editing) Your instructor may ask the class to work in small groups or in pairs to exchange ideas about an assigned paper. You will be expected to provide other students with feedback on the strengths and weaknesses of their papers. Afterward, you should think carefully about your classmates' comments and make changes to improve your paper. See 29h3

■ **Attending conferences** Your instructor may schedule one or more appointments with you to discuss your writing and may ask you to bring a draft of the paper you are working on. Your instructor may also be available to help you with your paper without an appointment during his or her office hours. In addition, many educational institutions have **writing centers,** where tutors help students get started on their papers or improve their drafts. When you meet with your instructor or writing center tutor, bring a list of specific questions about your paper, and be sure to make careful notes about what you discuss. You can refer to these notes when you revise your paper.

CLOSE-UP

USING YOUR NATIVE LANGUAGE

Depending on your language background and skills, you may find it helpful to use your native language in some stages of your writing.

When you are making notes about the content of your paper, you may be able to generate more ideas and record them more quickly if you do some of the work in your native language. Additionally, when you are drafting your paper and cannot think of a particular word in English, it

(continued)

USING YOUR NATIVE LANGUAGE *(continued)*

may be better simply to write the word in your native language (and come back to it later) so you do not lose your train of thought.

However, if you use another language a great deal as you draft your writing and then try to translate your work into English, the English may sound awkward or be hard for readers to understand. The best strategy when you draft your papers is to write in English as much as you can, using the vocabulary and structures that you already know.

44b Understanding English Language Basics

Getting used to writing and editing your work in English will be easier if you understand a few basic principles:

ESL
45a

■ **In English, words may change their form according to their function.** For example, <u>verbs</u> change form to communicate whether an action is taking place in the past, present, or future.

■ **In English, context is extremely important to understanding function.** In the following sentences, for instance, the very same words can perform different functions according to their relationships to other words.

> Juan and I are taking a <u>walk</u>. (*Walk* is a noun, a direct object of the verb *taking*, with an article, *a*, attached to it.)

> If you <u>walk</u> instead of driving, you will help conserve the Earth's resources. (*Walk* is a verb, the predicate of the subject *you*.)

See
Ch. 23

■ **Spelling in English is not always phonetic and sometimes may seem illogical.** <u>Spelling</u> in English may be related more to the history of the word and to its origins in other languages than to the way the word is pronounced. Therefore, learning to spell correctly is often a matter of memorization, not sounding out the word phonetically. For example, "ough" is pronounced differently in *tough*, *though*, and *thought*.

ESL
45f

■ <u>Word order</u> **is extremely important in English sentences.** In English sentences, word order may indicate which word is the subject of the sentence and which is the object, whether the sentence is a question or a statement, and so on.

44c Learning to Edit Your Work

See
2e

<u>Editing</u> your papers involves focusing on grammar, spelling, punctuation, and mechanics. The approach you take to editing for grammar errors should depend on your strengths and weaknesses in English.

If you learned English mostly by speaking it, if you have strong oral skills, and if you usually make correct judgments about English by instinct, the best approach for you may be reading your paper aloud and listening for mistakes, correcting them by deciding what sounds right. You may even find that as you read aloud, you automatically correct your written mistakes as you speak. (Be sure to transfer those corrections to your paper.) In addition to proofreading your paper from beginning to end, you might find it helpful to start from the end of the paper, reading and proofreading sentence by sentence. This strategy can keep you from being distracted by your ideas, allowing you to focus on grammar alone.

If you learned English mostly by reading, studying grammar rules, and/or translating between your native language and English, you may not feel that you have good instincts about what sounds right in English. If this is the case, you should take a different approach to editing your papers. First, identify the errors you make most frequently by looking at earlier papers your instructor has marked or by asking your instructor for help. Once you have identified your most common errors, read through your paper, checking each sentence for these errors. Try to apply the grammar and mechanics rules you already know, or check the relevant grammar explanations in **Chapter 45** for help.

After you check your paper for grammar errors, you should check again to make sure that you have used proper punctuation, capitalization, and spelling. If you have difficulty with spelling, you can use a spell checker to help you, but remember that spell checkers cannot catch every error. After you have made grammar and mechanics corrections on your own, you can seek outside help in identifying errors you might have missed. You should also keep a notebook with a list of your most frequent grammatical errors and review it often.

45 Grammar and Style for ESL Writers

For ESL writers (as for many native English writers), grammar can be a persistent problem. Grammatical knowledge in a second language usually develops slowly, with time and practice, and much about English is idiomatic (not subject to easy-to-learn rules). This chapter is designed to provide you with the tools you will need to address some of the most common grammatical errors made by ESL writers.

45a Using Verbs

1 Subject-Verb Agreement

See
A1.3   English **verbs** change their form according to person, number, and tense. The verb in a sentence must agree with the subject in person and number. **Person** refers to
See
13a4   *who* or *what* is performing the action of the verb (for example, *myself*, *you*, or someone else), and **number** refers to *how many* people or things are performing the action
See
7a   (one or more than one).

   In English, the rules for **subject-verb agreement** are very important. Unless you use the correct person and number in the verbs in your sentences, you will confuse your English-speaking audience by communicating meanings you do not intend.

2 Tense

In English, the form of a verb changes according to when the action of the verb takes place—in the past, present, or future. One problem that many nonnative speakers of English have with English verb tenses results from the
See
8a   large number of **irregular verbs** in English. For example, the first-person singular present tense of *be* is not "I be" but "I am," and the past tense is not "I beed" but "I was."

CLOSE-UP

CHOOSING THE SIMPLEST VERB FORMS

Some nonnative English speakers use verb forms that are more complicated than they need to be. They may do this because their native language uses more complicated verb forms than English does or because they "overcorrect" their verbs into complicated forms. Specifically, nonnative speakers tend to use progressive and perfect verb forms instead of simple verb forms. To communicate your ideas clearly to an English-speaking audience, choose the simplest possible verb form.

3 Auxiliary Verbs

The **auxiliary verbs** (also known as **helping verbs**) *be*, *have*, and *do* are used to create some present, past, and future forms of verbs in English: "Julio *is taking* a vacation"; "I *have been* tired lately"; "He *does* not *need* a license." The auxiliary verbs *be*, *have*, and *do* change form to reflect the time frame of the action or situation and to agree with the subject; however, the main verb remains in simple present or simple past form.

CLOSE-UP

AUXILIARY VERBS

Only auxiliary verbs, not the verbs they "help," change form to indicate person, number, and tense.

Present perfect: They <u>have gone</u> to the movies.

Past perfect: They <u>had gone</u> to the movies.

<u>Modal auxiliaries</u> (such as *can* and *should*) do not change form to indicate tense, person, or number.

See
A1.3

4 Negative Verbs

The meaning of a verb may be made negative in English in a variety of ways, chiefly by adding the words *not* or *does not* to the verb (is, is *not*; can ski, *cannot* ski; drives a car, *does not* drive a car).

CLOSE-UP

CORRECTING DOUBLE NEGATIVES

A **double negative** is an error that occurs when the meaning of a verb is made negative not just once but twice in a single sentence.

Henry doesn't have ~~no~~ friends. (*or* Henry ~~doesn't have~~
no friends.)
any above "no"; *has* above "doesn't have"

I looked for articles in the library, but there ~~weren't~~
none. (*or* I looked for articles in the library, but there
weren't ~~none~~.)
were above "weren't"; *any* below "weren't"

5 Phrasal Verbs

Many verbs in English are composed of two or more words that are combined to create a new idiomatic expression—for example, *check up on*, *run for*, *turn into*, and *wait on*. These verbs are called **phrasal verbs.** It is important to become familiar with phrasal verbs and their definitions so you will recognize these verbs as phrasal verbs instead of as verbs that are followed by prepositions. Knowing the definitions of the individual words that make up these verbs is not always enough to enable you to define the phrasal verbs accurately. Even after consulting a dictionary, you will need to pay close attention to the use of these verbs in speech and writing.

Separable Phrasal Verbs. Often, the words that make up a phrasal verb can be separated by a direct object. In these **separable phrasal verbs,** the object can come either before or after the preposition. For example, "<u>Ellen turned down</u> the job offer" and "<u>Ellen turned</u> the job offer <u>down</u>" are both correct. However, when the object is a pronoun, the pronoun must come before the preposition. Therefore, "<u>Ellen turned</u> it <u>down</u>" is correct; "<u>Ellen turned down</u> it" is incorrect.

CLOSE-UP

SEPARABLE PHRASAL VERBS

Verb	Definition
call off	cancel

Verb	Definition
carry on	continue
cheer up	make happy
clean out	clean the inside of
cut down	reduce
figure out	solve
fill in	substitute
find out	discover
give back	return something
give up	stop doing something or stop trying
leave out	omit
pass on	transmit
put away	place something in its proper place
put back	place something in its original place
put off	postpone
start over	start again
talk over	discuss
throw away/out	discard
touch up	repair

Inseparable Phrasal Verbs. Some phrasal verbs—such as *look into* and *break into*—consist of words that can never be separated. With these **inseparable phrasal verbs,** you do not have a choice about where to place the object; the object must always follow the preposition. For example, "<u>Anna</u> <u>cared for</u> her niece" is correct, but "<u>Anna</u> <u>cared</u> her niece <u>for</u>" is incorrect.

CLOSE-UP

INSEPARABLE PHRASAL VERBS

Verb	Definition
come down with	develop an illness
come up with	produce
do away with	abolish
fall behind in	lag
get along with	be congenial with
get away with	avoid punishment

(continued)

INSEPARABLE PHRASAL VERBS (continued)	
Verb	**Definition**
keep up with	maintain the same achievement or speed
look up to	admire
make up for	compensate
put up with	tolerate
run into	meet by chance
see to	arrange
show up	arrive
stand by	wait or remain loyal to
stand up for	support
watch out for	beware of or protect

6 Voice

See
8d Verbs may be in either active or passive <u>**voice**</u>. When the subject of a sentence performs the action of the verb, the verb is in **active voice.** When the action of the verb is performed on the subject, the verb is in **passive voice.**

> <u>Karla and Miguel</u> <u>purchased</u> the plane tickets. (active voice)

> <u>The plane tickets</u> <u>were purchased</u> by Karla and Miguel. (passive voice)

Because your writing will usually be clearer and more concise if you use the active voice, you should use the passive voice only when you have a good reason to do so. For example, in scientific writing, it is common for writers to use the passive voice in order to convey the idea of scientific objectivity (lack of bias).

7 Transitive and Intransitive Verbs

Many nonnative English speakers find it difficult to decide whether or not a verb needs an object and in what order direct and indirect objects should appear in a sentence. Learning the difference between transitive verbs and intransitive verbs can help you with such problems.

A **transitive verb** is a verb that has a direct object: "<u>My father</u> <u>asked</u> a question" (subject + verb + direct object). In this example, *asked* is a transitive verb; it needs an object to complete its meaning.

An **intransitive verb** is a verb that does not take an object: "<u>The doctor</u> <u>smiled</u>" (subject + verb). In this example, *smiled* is an intransitive verb; it does not need an object to complete its meaning.

A transitive verb may be followed by a direct object or by both an indirect object and a direct object. (An indirect object answers the question "To whom?" or "For whom?") The indirect object may come before or after the direct object. If the indirect object follows the direct object, the preposition *to* or *for* must precede the indirect object.

<u>Keith</u> <u>wrote</u> a letter. (subject + verb + direct object)

<u>Keith</u> <u>wrote</u> his friend a letter. (subject + verb + indirect object + direct object)

<u>Keith</u> <u>wrote</u> a letter *to* his friend. (subject + verb + direct object + *to/for* + indirect object)

Some verbs in English look similar and have similar meanings, except that one is transitive and the other is intransitive. For example, *lie* is intransitive, *lay* is transitive; *sit* is intransitive, *set* is transitive; *rise* is intransitive, *raise* is transitive. Knowing whether a verb is transitive or intransitive can help you with troublesome verb pairs like these and also help you place the words in the correct order.

NOTE: It is also important to know whether a verb is transitive or intransitive because only transitive verbs can be used in the **passive voice**. To determine whether a verb is transitive or intransitive—that is, to determine whether or not it needs an object—consult the example phrases in a dictionary.

See 8d

8 Infinitives and Gerunds

In English, two verb forms may be used as nouns: **infinitives,** which always begin with *to* (as in *to work, to sleep, to* *eat*), and **gerunds,** which always end in *-ing* (as in *working, sleeping, eating*).

> To bite into this steak requires better teeth than mine. (infinitive used as a noun)

> Cooking is one of my favorite hobbies. (gerund used as a noun)

Sometimes the gerund and the infinitive form of the same verb can be used interchangeably. For example, "He continued *to sleep*" and "He continued *sleeping*" convey the same meaning. However, this is not always the case. Saying, "Marco and Lisa stopped *to eat* at Julio's Café" is not the same as saying, "Marco and Lisa stopped *eating* at Julio's Café." In this example, the meaning of the sentence changes depending on whether a gerund or infinitive is used.

9 Participles

In English, verb forms called **present participles** and **past participles** are frequently used as adjectives. Present participles usually end in *-ing*, as in *working, sleeping,* and *eating*, and past participles usually end in *-ed*, *-t*, or *-en*, as in *worked, slept,* and *eaten*.

> According to the Bible, God spoke to Moses from a burning bush. (present participle used as an adjective)

> Some people think raw fish is healthier than cooked fish. (past participle used as an adjective)

A **participial phrase** is a group of words consisting of the participle plus the noun phrase that functions as the object or complement of the action being expressed by the participle. To avoid confusion, the participial phrase must be placed as close as possible to the noun it modifies.

> Having visited San Francisco last week, Jim and Lynn showed us pictures from their vacation. (The participial phrase is used as an adjective that modifies *Jim and Lynn*.)

10 Verbs Formed from Nouns

In English, nouns can sometimes be used as verbs, with no change in form (other than the addition of an *-s* for agreement with third-person singular subjects or the addition of past tense endings). For example, the nouns *chair*, *book*, *frame*, and *father* can all be used as verbs.

She <u>chairs</u> a committee on neighborhood safety.

We <u>booked</u> a flight to New York for next week.

I will <u>frame</u> my daughter's diploma after she graduates.

He <u>fathered</u> several children before he was thirty.

45b Using Nouns

See 23b7

<u>Nouns</u> name things: people, animals, objects, places, feelings, ideas. If a noun names one thing, it is **singular;** if a noun names more than one thing, it is **plural.**

1 Recognizing Noncount Nouns

Some English nouns do not have a plural form. These are called **noncount nouns** because what they name cannot be counted. (**Count nouns** name items that can be counted, such as *woman* or *desk*.)

CLOSE-UP

NONCOUNT NOUNS

The following commonly used nouns are noncount nouns. These words have no plural forms. Therefore, you should never add -*s* or -*es* to them.

advice	homework
clothing	information
education	knowledge
equipment	luggage
evidence	merchandise
furniture	revenge

---

2 Using Articles with Nouns

English has two **articles,** *indefinite* and *definite.*

Use an **indefinite article** (*a* or *an*) with a noun when readers are not familiar with the noun you are naming—for example, when you are introducing the noun for the first time. To say "Jatin entered *a* building" signals to the audience that you are introducing the idea of the building for the first time. The building is indefinite, or not specific, until it has been identified.

The indefinite article *a* is used when the word following it (which may be a noun or an adjective) begins with a consonant or with a consonant sound: *a* tree, *a* onetime offer. The indefinite article *an* is used if the word following it begins with a vowel (*a, e, i, o,* or *u*) or with a vowel sound: *an* apple, *an* honor.

Use the **definite article** (*the*) when the noun you are naming has already been introduced, when the noun is already familiar to readers, or when the noun to which you refer is specific. To say "Jatin entered *the* building" signals to readers that you are referring to the same building you mentioned earlier. The building has now become specific and may be referred to by the definite article.

CLOSE-UP

USING ARTICLES WITH NOUNS

There are two exceptions to the rules governing the use of articles with nouns:

1. **Plural nouns** do not require indefinite articles: "I love horses," not "I love <u>a</u> horses." (Plural nouns do, however, require definite articles: "I love <u>the</u> horses in the national park near my house.")
2. **Noncount nouns** may not require articles: "Love conquers all," not "<u>A</u> love conquers all" or " <u>The</u> love conquers all."

---

3 Using Other Determiners with Nouns

ESL
45d **Determiners** are words that function as **<u>adjectives</u>** to limit or qualify the meaning of nouns. In addition to articles, **demonstrative pronouns, possessive nouns and pronouns, numbers** (both **cardinal** and **ordinal**), and other words indicating amount or order can function in this way.

CLOSE-UP

USING OTHER DETERMINERS WITH NOUNS

■ **Demonstrative pronouns** (*this, that, these, those*) communicate the following:
1. the relative nearness or farness of the noun from the speaker's position (*this* and *these* for things that are *near; that* and *those* for things that are *far*): *this* book on my desk, *that* book on your desk; *these* shoes on my feet, *those* shoes in my closet.
2. the number of things indicated (*this* and *that* for *singular* nouns, *these* and *those* for *plural* nouns): *this* (or *that*) flower in the vase, *these* (or *those*) flowers in the garden.

■ **Possessive nouns** and **possessive pronouns** (*Ashraf's, his, their*) show who or what the noun belongs to: *Maria's* courage, *everybody's* fears, the *country's* natural resources, *my* personality, *our* groceries.

■ **Cardinal** numbers (*three, fifty, a thousand*) indicate how many of the noun you mean: *seven* continents. **Ordinal** numbers (*first, tenth, thirtieth*) indicate in what order the noun appears among other items: *third* planet.

■ Words other than numbers may indicate **amount** (*many, few*) and **order** (*next, last*) and function in the same ways as cardinal and ordinal numbers: *few* opportunities, *last* chance.

45c Using Pronouns

Any English noun may be replaced by a **pronoun**. For example, *doctor* may be replaced by *he* or *she*, *books* by *them*, and *computer* by *it*.

See A1.2

1 Pronoun Reference

Pronoun reference is very important in English sentences, where the noun the pronoun replaces (the **antecedent**) must be easily identified. In general, you should place the pronoun as close as possible to the noun it replaces so the noun to which the pronoun refers is clear. If this is impossible, use the noun itself instead of replacing it with a pronoun.

See 9c

Unclear: When Tara met Emily, she was nervous.
(Does *she* refer to Tara or to Emily?)

Clear: When Tara met Emily, Tara was nervous.

Unclear: Stefano and Victor love his DVD collection.
(Whose DVD collection—Stefano's, Victor's, or
someone else's?)

Clear: Stefano and Victor love Emilio's DVD collection.

2 Pronoun Placement

Never use a pronoun immediately after the noun it replaces. For example, do not say, "Most of my classmates
they are smart"; instead, say, "Most of my classmates are
smart." The only exception to this rule occurs with an
intensive pronoun, which ends in *-self* and emphasizes
the preceding noun or pronoun: "Marta *herself* was eager
to hear the results."

3 Indefinite Pronouns

Unlike **personal pronouns** (*I, you, he, she, it, we, they, me,
him, her, us,* and *them*), **indefinite pronouns** do not refer
to a particular person, place, or thing. Therefore, an
indefinite pronoun does not require an antecedent. **Indefinite pronoun subjects** (*anybody, nobody, each, either, someone,
something, all, some*), like personal pronouns, must **agree** in
number with the sentence's verb.

See
7b

Nobody ~~have~~ has failed the exam. (*Nobody* is a singular
subject and requires a singular verb.)

4 Appositives

Appositives are nouns or noun phrases that identify or
rename an adjacent noun or pronoun. An appositive
usually follows the noun it identifies or renames but can
sometimes precede it.

My parents, Mary and John, live in Louisiana. (*Mary
and John* identifies *parents*.)

See
9a **NOTE:** The **case** of a pronoun in an appositive depends
on the case of the word it describes.

If an appositive is *not* necessary to the meaning of the
sentence, use commas to set off the appositive from the

rest of the sentence. If an appositive *is* necessary to the meaning of the sentence, do not use commas.

> His aunt Trang is in the hospital. (*Trang* is necessary to the meaning of the sentence because it identifies which aunt is in the hospital.)

> Akta's car, a 1994 Jeep Cherokee, broke down last night. (*a 1994 Jeep Cherokee* is not necessary to the meaning of the sentence.)

5 Pronouns and Gender

A pronoun must agree in **gender** with the noun to which it refers.

> My *sister* sold *her* old car.

> Your *uncle* is walking *his* dog.

NOTE: In English, most nonhuman nouns are referred to as *it* because they do not have grammatical gender. However, exceptions are sometimes made for pets, ships, and countries. Pets are often referred to as *he* or *she*, depending on their gender, and ships and countries are sometimes referred to as *she*.

45d Using Adjectives and Adverbs

<u>Adjectives and adverbs</u> are words that **modify** (describe, limit, or qualify) other words.

See A1. 4–5; Ch. 10

1 Position of Adjectives and Adverbs

Adjectives in English usually appear *before* the nouns they modify. A native speaker of English would not say, "*Cars red and black* are involved in more accidents than *cars blue or green*" but would say instead, "*Red and black cars* are involved in more accidents than *blue or green cars*."

However, adjectives may appear *after* linking verbs ("The name seemed *familiar*."), *after* direct objects ("The coach found them *tired* but *happy*."), and *after* indefinite pronouns ("Anything *sad* makes me cry.").

Adverbs may appear before or after the verbs they describe, but they should be placed as close to the verb as possible: not "I *told* John that I couldn't meet him for lunch *politely*," but "I *politely told* John that I couldn't meet him for lunch" or "I *told* John *politely* that I couldn't meet him for lunch." When an adverb describes an adjective or another adverb, it usually comes *before* that adjective or adverb: "The essay has *basically* sound logic"; "You must express yourself *absolutely clearly*." Never place an adverb between the verb and the direct object.

Incorrect: Rolf drank *quickly* the water.

Correct: Rolf drank the water *quickly* (or, Rolf *quickly* drank the water).

2 Order of Adjectives

A single noun may be modified by more than one adjective, perhaps even by a whole list of adjectives. Given a list of three or four adjectives, most native speakers would arrange them in a sentence in the same order. If, for example shoes are to be described as *green* and *big*, numbering *two*, and of the type worn for playing *tennis*, a native speaker would say "two big green tennis shoes." Generally, the adjectives that are most important in completing the meaning of the noun are placed closest to the noun.

CLOSE-UP

ORDER OF ADJECTIVES

1. Articles (*a*, *the*), demonstratives (*this*, *those*), and possessives (*his*, *our*, *Maria's*, *everybody's*)
2. Amounts (*one*, *five*, *many*, *few*), order (*first*, *next*, *last*)
3. Personal opinions (*nice*, *ugly*, *crowded*, *pitiful*)
4. Sizes and shapes (*small*, *tall*, *straight*, *crooked*)
5. Age (*young*, *old*, *modern*, *ancient*)
6. Colors (*black*, *white*, *red*, *blue*, *dark*, *light*)
7. Nouns functioning as adjectives to form a unit with the noun (*soccer* ball, *cardboard* box, *history* class)

45e Using Prepositions

See
A1.6 In English, **prepositions** (such as *to*, *from*, *at*, *with*, *among*, *between*) give meaning to nouns by linking them with other words and other parts of the sentence. Prepositions convey several different kinds of information:

■ Relations to **time** (*at* nine o'clock, *in* five minutes, *for* a month)

- Relations of **place** (*in* the classroom, *at* the library, *beside* the chair) and **direction** (*to* the market, *onto* the stage, *toward* the freeway)
- Relations of **association** (go *with* someone, the tip *of* the iceberg)
- Relations of **purpose** (working *for* money, dieting *to* lose weight)

1 Commonly Used Prepositional Phrases

In English, the use of prepositions is often idiomatic rather than governed by grammatical rules. In many cases, therefore, learners of English as a second language need to memorize which prepositions are used in which phrases.

In English, some prepositions that relate to time have specific uses with certain nouns, such as days, months, and seasons:

- *On* is used with days and specific dates: *on* Monday, *on* September 13, 1977.
- *In* is used with months, seasons, and years: *in* November, *in* the spring, *in* 1999.
- *In* is also used when referring to some parts of the day: *in* the morning, *in* the afternoon, *in* the evening.
- *At* is used to refer to other parts of the day: *at* noon, *at* night, *at* seven o'clock.

CLOSE-UP

DIFFICULT PREPOSITIONAL PHRASES

The following phrases (accompanied by their correct prepositions) sometimes cause difficulties for ESL writers:

according *to*	*at* least	relevant *to*
apologize *to*	*at* most	similar *to*
appeal *to*	refer *to*	subscribe *to*
different *from*		

---

2 Commonly Confused Prepositions

The prepositions *to*, *in*, *on*, *into*, and *onto* are very similar to one another and are therefore easily confused:

- *To* is the basic preposition of direction. It indicates movement toward a physical place: "She went *to* the restaurant"; "He went *to* the meeting." *To* is also used to form the infinitive of a verb: "He wanted *to deposit* his paycheck before noon"; "Irene offered *to drive* Maria to the baseball game."

■ *In* indicates that something is within the boundaries of a particular space or period of time: "My son is *in* the garden"; "I like to ski *in* the winter"; "The map is *in* the car."

■ *On* indicates position above or the state of being supported by something: "The toys are *on* the porch"; "The baby sat *on* my lap"; "The book is *on* top of the magazine."

■ *Into* indicates movement to the inside or interior of something: "She walked *into* the room"; "I threw the stone *into* the lake"; "He put the photos *into* the box." Although *into* and *in* are sometimes interchangeable, note that usage depends on whether the subject is stationary or moving. *Into* usually indicates movement, as in "I jumped *into* the water." *In* usually indicates a stationary position relative to the object of the preposition, as in "Mary is swimming *in* the water."

■ *Onto* indicates movement to a position on top of something: "The cat jumped *onto* the chair"; "Crumbs are falling *onto* the floor." Both *on* and *onto* can be used to indicate a position on top of something (and therefore they can sometimes be used interchangeably), but *onto* specifies that the subject is moving to a place from a different place or from an outside position.

CLOSE-UP

PREPOSITIONS IN IDIOMATIC EXPRESSIONS

Many nonnative speakers use incorrect prepositions in idiomatic expressions. Compare the incorrect expressions in the left-hand column below with the correct expressions in the right-hand column.

Common Nonnative Speaker Usage	Native Speaker Usage
according *with*	according *to*
apologize *at*	apologize *to*
appeal *at*	appeal *to*

Common Nonnative Speaker Usage	Native Speaker Usage
believe *at*	believe *in*
different *to*	different *from*
for least, *for* most	*at* least, *at* most
refer *at*	refer *to*
relevant *with*	relevant *to*
similar *with*	similar *to*
subscribe *with*	subscribe *to*

45f Understanding Word Order

Word order is extremely important in English sentences. For example, word order may indicate which word is the subject of a sentence and which is the object, or it may indicate whether a sentence is a question or a statement.

1 Standard Word Order

Like Chinese, English is an "SVO" language, or one in which the most typical sentence pattern is "subject-verb-object." (Arabic, by contrast, is an example of a "VSO" language.)

2 Word Order in Questions

Word order in questions can be particularly troublesome for speakers of languages other than English because there are so many different ways to form questions in English.

CLOSE-UP

WORD ORDER IN QUESTIONS

1. To create a **yes/no question** from a statement whose verb is a form of *be* (*am, is, are, was, were*), move the verb so it precedes the subject.

   <u>Rasheem is</u> in his laboratory.

   <u>Is</u> <u>Rasheem</u> in his laboratory?

   (continued)

WORD ORDER IN QUESTIONS (*continued*)

When the statement is *not* a form of *be*, change the verb to include a form of *do* as a helping verb, and then move that helping verb so it precedes the subject.

<u>Rasheem</u> <u>researched</u> the depletion of the ozone level.

<u>Did</u> <u>Rasheem</u> <u>research</u> the depletion of the ozone level?

2. To create a **yes/no question** from a statement that includes one or more helping verbs, move the first helping verb so it precedes the subject.

<u>Rasheem</u> <u>is researching</u> the depletion of the ozone layer.

<u>Is</u> <u>Rasheem</u> <u>researching</u> the depletion of the ozone layer?

<u>Rasheem</u> <u>has been researching</u> the depletion of the ozone layer.

<u>Has</u> <u>Rasheem</u> <u>been researching</u> the depletion of the ozone layer?

3. To create a **question asking for information,** replace the information being asked for with an **interrogative** word (*who, what, where, why, when, how*) at the beginning of the question, and invert the order of the subject and verb as with a yes/no question.

<u>Rasheem</u> <u>is</u> in his laboratory.

Where <u>is</u> <u>Rasheem</u>?

<u>Rasheem</u> <u>is researching</u> the depletion of the ozone layer.

What <u>is</u> <u>Rasheem</u> <u>researching</u>?

<u>Rasheem</u> <u>researched</u> the depletion of the ozone level.

What <u>did</u> <u>Rasheem</u> <u>research</u>?

If the interrogative word is the subject of the question, however, do *not* invert the subject and verb.

<u>Who</u> <u>is researching</u> the depletion of the ozone level?

4. You can also form a question by adding a **tag question** (such as *won't he?* or *didn't I?*) to the end of a statement. If the verb of the main statement is *positive*, then the verb of the tag question is *negative;* if the verb of the main statement is *negative*, then the verb of the tag question is *positive*.

<u>Rasheem</u> <u>is</u> researching the depletion of the ozone layer, <u>isn't</u> <u>he</u>?

<u>Rasheem</u> <u>doesn't</u> intend to write his dissertation about the depletion of the ozone layer, <u>does</u> <u>he</u>?

A Grammar Review

A1 Parts of Speech

The **part of speech** to which a word belongs depends on its function in a sentence.

1 Nouns

Nouns name people, animals, places, things, ideas, actions, or qualities.

A **common noun** names any of a class of people, places, or things: *artist, judge, building, event, city.*

A **proper noun,** always <u>capitalized</u>, refers to a particular person, place, or thing: *Mary Cassatt, World Trade Center, Crimean War.*

See 24a

A **collective noun** designates a group thought of as a unit: *committee, class, family.*

An **abstract noun** refers to an intangible idea or quality: *love, hate, justice, anger, fear, prejudice.*

2 Pronouns

Pronouns are words used in place of nouns. The noun for which a pronoun stands is called its **antecedent.**

If you use a <u>quotation</u> in your paper, you must document <u>it</u>. (Pronoun *it* refers to antecedent *quotation*.)

Although different types of pronouns may have the same form, they are distinguished from one another by their function in a sentence.

A **personal pronoun** stands for a person or thing: *I, me, we, us, my, mine, our, ours, you, your, yours, he, she, it, its, him, his, her, hers, they, them, their, theirs.*

The firm made Debbie an offer, and <u>she</u> couldn't refuse <u>it</u>.

An <u>indefinite pronoun</u> does not refer to any particular person or thing, so it does not require an antecedent. Indefinite pronouns include *another, any, each, few, many, some, nothing, one, anyone, everyone, everybody, everything, someone, something, either,* and *neither.*

<u>Many</u> are called, but <u>few</u> are chosen.

A **reflexive pronoun** ends with *-self* and refers to a recipient of the action that is the same as the actor: *myself, yourself, himself, herself, itself, oneself, themselves, ourselves, yourselves.*

They found <u>themselves</u> in downtown Pittsburgh.

Intensive pronouns have the same form as reflexive pronouns. An intensive pronoun emphasizes a preceding noun or pronoun.

Darrow <u>himself</u> was sure his client was innocent.

A **relative pronoun** introduces an adjective or noun clause in a sentence. Relative pronouns include *which, who, whom, that, what, whose, whatever, whoever, whomever,* and *whichever.*

Gandhi was the man <u>who</u> led India to independence. (introduces adjective clause)

<u>Whatever</u> happens will be a surprise. (introduces noun clause)

An **interrogative pronoun** introduces a question. Interrogative pronouns include *who, which, what, whom, whose, whoever, whatever,* and *whichever.*

<u>Who</u> was at the door?

A **demonstrative pronoun** points to a particular thing or group of things. *This, that, these,* and *those* are demonstrative pronouns.

<u>This</u> is one of Shakespeare's early plays.

A **reciprocal pronoun** denotes a mutual relationship. The reciprocal pronouns are *each other* and *one another. Each other* indicates a relationship between two individuals; *one another* denotes a relationship among more than two.

Cathy and I respect <u>each other</u> for our differences.

Many of our friends do not respect <u>one another</u>.

3 Verbs

Verbs can be classified into two groups: *main verbs* and *auxiliary verbs.*

Main Verbs. **Main verbs** carry most of the meaning in a sentence or clause. Some main verbs are action verbs.

He <u>ran</u> for the train. (physical action)

He <u>thought</u> about taking the bus. (emotional action)

Other main verbs are linking verbs. A **linking verb** does not show any physical or emotional action. Its function is to link the subject to a **subject complement,** a word or phrase that renames or describes the subject.

Carbon disulfide <u>smells</u> bad.

FREQUENTLY USED LINKING VERBS				
appear	believe	look	seem	taste
be	feel	prove	smell	turn
become	grow	remain	sound	

Auxiliary Verbs. **Auxiliary verbs** (also called **helping verbs**), such as *be* and *have*, combine with main verbs to form **verb phrases.** Auxiliary verbs indicate tense, voice, or mood.

[auxiliary] [main verb] [auxiliary] [main verb]

The train <u>has started</u>. We <u>are leaving</u> soon.

[verb phrase] [verb phrase]

Certain auxiliary verbs, known as **modal auxiliaries,** indicate necessity, possibility, willingness, obligation, or ability.

MODAL AUXILIARIES			
can	might	ought [to]	will
could	must	shall	would
may	need [to]	should	

Verbals. **Verbals,** such as *known* or *running* or *to go*, are verb forms that act as adjectives, adverbs, or nouns. A verbal can never serve as a sentence's main verb unless it is used with one or more auxiliary verbs (*He <u>is</u> running*). Verbals include *participles, infinitives,* and *gerunds.*

PARTICIPLES

Virtually every verb has a **present participle,** which ends in *-ing* (*loving, learning*) and a **past participle,** which

See
8a usually ends in *-d* or *-ed* (*agreed, learned*). Some verbs have **irregular** past participles (*gone, begun, written*). Participles may function in a sentence as adjectives or as nouns.

> Twenty brands of <u>running</u> shoes were on display. (participle serves as adjective)

> The <u>wounded</u> were given emergency first aid. (participle serves as noun)

INFINITIVES

An **infinitive** is made up of *to* and the base form of the verb (*to defeat*). An infinitive may function as an adjective, an adverb, or a noun.

> Ann Arbor was clearly the place <u>to be</u>. (infinitive serves as adjective)

> Carla went outside <u>to think</u>. (infinitive serves as adverb)

> <u>To win</u> was everything. (infinitive serves as subject)

GERUNDS

Gerunds, which like present participles end in *-ing*, always function as nouns.

> <u>Seeing</u> is <u>believing</u>.

> Andrew loves <u>skiing</u>.

4 Adjectives

Adjectives describe, limit, qualify, or in some other way modify nouns or pronouns.

    Descriptive adjectives name a quality of the noun or pronoun they modify.

> After the game, they were <u>exhausted</u>.

> They ordered a <u>chocolate</u> soda and a <u>butterscotch</u> sundae.

    When articles, pronouns, numbers, and the like function as adjectives, limiting or qualifying nouns or pronouns, they are referred to as <u>**determiners**</u>.

ESL
45b3

5 Adverbs

Adverbs describe the action of verbs or modify adjectives or other adverbs (or complete phrases, clauses, or sentences). They answer the questions "How?" "Why?" "When?" "Under what conditions?" and "To what extent?"

He walked <u>rather hesitantly</u> toward the front of the room.

Let's meet <u>tomorrow</u> for coffee.

Adverbs that modify other adverbs or adjectives limit or qualify the words they modify.

He pitched an <u>almost</u> perfect game yesterday.

Interrogative Adverbs. The **interrogative adverbs** (*how, when, why,* and *where*) introduce questions.

<u>How</u> are you doing?

<u>Why</u> did he miss class?

Conjunctive Adverbs. **Conjunctive adverbs** act as <u>transitional words</u>, joining and relating independent clauses.

See 3b

FREQUENTLY USED CONJUNCTIVE ADVERBS			
accordingly	furthermore	meanwhile	similarly
also	hence	moreover	still
anyway	however	nevertheless	then
besides	incidentally	next	thereafter
certainly	indeed	nonetheless	therefore
consequently	instead	now	thus
finally	likewise	otherwise	undoubtedly

6 Prepositions

A **preposition** introduces a noun or pronoun (or a phrase or clause functioning in the sentence as a noun), linking it to other words in the sentence. The word or word group that the preposition introduces is its **object.**

       prep   obj   prep   obj

They received a postcard <u>from</u> Bobby telling <u>about</u> his trip.

FREQUENTLY USED PREPOSITIONS			
about	after	among	at
above	against	around	before
across	along	as	behind

(continued)

FREQUENTLY USED PREPOSITIONS *(continued)*

below	except	on	to
beneath	for	onto	toward
beside	from	out	under
between	in	outside	underneath
beyond	inside	over	until
by	into	past	up
concerning	like	regarding	upon
despite	near	since	with
down	of	through	within
during	off	throughout	without

7 Conjunctions

Conjunctions connect words, phrases, clauses, or sentences.

Coordinating Conjunctions. **Coordinating conjunctions** (*and, or, but, nor, for, so, yet*) connect words, phrases, or clauses of equal weight.

> Should I order chicken <u>or</u> fish?

> Thoreau wrote *Walden* in 1854, <u>and</u> he died in 1862.

Correlative Conjunctions. Always used in pairs, **correlative conjunctions** also link items of equal weight.

> <u>Both</u> Hancock <u>and</u> Jefferson signed the Declaration of Independence.

> <u>Either</u> I will renew my lease, <u>or</u> I will move.

FREQUENTLY USED CORRELATIVE CONJUNCTIONS

both . . . and	neither . . . nor
either . . . or	not only . . . but also
just as . . . so	whether . . . or

Subordinating Conjunctions. Words such as *since, because,* and *although* are **subordinating conjunctions.** A subordinating conjunction introduces a dependent (subordinate) clause, connecting it to an independent (main) clause to form a **complex sentence.**

See
11a2

> <u>Although</u> people may feel healthy, they can still have medical problems.

> It is best to diagram your garden <u>before</u> you start to plant.

8 Interjections

Interjections are words used as exclamations to express emotion: *Oh! Ouch! Wow! Alas! Hey!*

A2 Sentences

1 Basic Sentence Elements

A **sentence** is an independent grammatical unit that contains a <u>subject</u> (a noun or noun phrase) and a <u>predicate</u> (a verb or verb phrase) and expresses a complete thought.

<u>The quick brown fox</u> <u>jumped over the lazy dog</u>.

<u>It</u> <u>came from outer space</u>.

2 Basic Sentence Patterns

A **simple sentence** consists of at least one subject and one predicate. Simple sentences conform to one of five patterns.

Subject + Intransitive Verb (s + v)

$\quad$ s $\qquad$ v

<u>Stock prices</u> <u>may fall</u>.

Subject + Transitive Verb + Direct Object
(s + v + do)

$\quad$ s $\qquad$ v $\qquad$ do

<u>Van Gogh</u> <u>created</u> *The Starry Night*.

$\quad$ s $\qquad$ v $\quad$ do

<u>Caroline</u> <u>saved</u> Jake.

Subject + Transitive Verb + Direct Object + Object
Complement (s + v + do + oc)

$\quad$ s $\quad$ v $\qquad$ do $\quad$ oc

<u>I</u> <u>found</u> the exam easy.

$\quad$ s $\qquad$ v $\qquad$ do $\qquad$ oc

<u>The class</u> <u>elected</u> Bridget treasurer.

Subject + Linking Verb + Subject Complement
(s + v + sc)

$\quad$ s $\qquad$ v $\quad$ sc

<u>The injection</u> <u>was</u> painless.

$\quad$ s $\qquad$ v $\qquad$ sc

<u>Nancy Pelosi</u> <u>became</u> House Democratic Leader.

Subject + Transitive Verb + Indirect Object + Direct Object (s + v + io + do)

<u>Cyrano</u> <u>wrote</u> Roxanne a poem. (Cyrano wrote a poem *for* Roxanne.)

<u>Hester</u> <u>gave</u> Pearl a kiss. (Hester gave a kiss *to* Pearl.)

3 Phrases and Clauses

Phrases. A **phrase** is a group of related words that lacks a subject or predicate or both and functions as a single part of speech. It cannot stand alone as a sentence.

- A **verb phrase** consists of a **main verb** and all its auxiliary verbs. (Time *is flying*.)
- A **noun phrase** includes a noun or pronoun plus all related modifiers. (I'll climb *the highest mountain*.)
- See A1.6
  A **prepositional phrase** consists of a <u>preposition</u>, its object, and any modifiers of that object. (They considered the ethical implications *of the animal studies*.)
- See A1.3
  A **verbal phrase** consists of a <u>verbal</u> and its related objects, modifiers, or complements. A verbal phrase may be a **participial phrase** (*encouraged by the voter turnout*), a **gerund phrase** (*taking it easy*), or an **infinitive phrase** (*to evaluate the evidence*).
- An **absolute phrase** usually consists of a noun and a participle, accompanied by modifiers. It modifies an entire independent clause rather than a particular word or phrase. (*Their toes tapping*, they watched the auditions.)

Clauses. A **clause** is a group of related words that includes a subject and a predicate. An **independent** (main) **clause** may stand alone as a sentence, but a **dependent** (subordinate) **clause** cannot. It must always be combined with an independent clause to form a <u>complex sentence</u>.
See 11a2

[Lucretia Mott was an abolitionist.] [She was also a pioneer for women's rights.] (two independent clauses)

[Lucretia Mott was an abolitionist] [who was also a pioneer for women's rights.] (independent clause, dependent clause)

Dependent clauses may be *adjective*, *adverb*, or *noun* clauses:

- **Adjective clauses,** sometimes called **relative clauses,** modify nouns or pronouns and always follow the nouns or pronouns they modify. They are introduced by relative pronouns—*that, what, which, who,* and so on—or by the adverbs *where* and *when.*

  Celeste's grandparents, who were born in Romania, speak little English.

- **Adverb clauses** modify verbs, adjectives, adverbs, entire phrases, or independent clauses. They are always introduced by subordinating conjunctions.

  Mark will go wherever there's a party.

- **Noun clauses** function as subjects, objects, or complements. A noun clause may be introduced by a relative pronoun or by *whether, when, where, why,* or *how.*

  What you see is what you get.

4 Types of Sentences

A **simple sentence** is a single independent clause. A simple sentence can consist of just a subject and a predicate.

Jessica fell.

Or, a simple sentence can be expanded with modifying words and phrases.

Jessica fell in love with the mysterious Henry Goodyear on Halloween.

A **compound sentence** consists of two or more simple sentences linked by a coordinating conjunction (preceded by a comma), by a semicolon (alone or followed by a transitional word or phrase), by correlative conjunctions, or by a colon. See 11a1

[The moon rose in the sky], <u>and</u> [the stars shone brightly].

[José wanted to spend a quiet afternoon]; <u>however,</u> [his aunt surprised him with a new set of plans.]

A **complex sentence** consists of one independent clause and at least one dependent clause. See 11a2

    independent clause   dependent clause
[It was hard for us to believe] [that anyone could be so cruel].

A **compound-complex sentence** is a compound sentence—made up of at least two independent clauses—that also includes at least one dependent clause.

[My mother always worried] [when my father had to work late], and [she could rarely sleep more than a few minutes at a time].

CLOSE-UP

CLASSIFYING SENTENCES

Sentences can also be classified according to their function:

- **Declarative sentences** make statements; they are the most common.
- **Interrogative sentences** pose questions, usually by inverting standard subject-verb order (often with an interrogative word) or by adding a form of *do* (*Is Maggie at home? Where is Maggie? Does Maggie live here?*).
- **Imperative sentences** express commands or requests, using the second-person singular of the verb and generally omitting the pronoun subject *you* (*Go to your room. Please believe me.*).
- **Exclamatory sentences** express strong emotion and end with an exclamation point (*The killing must stop now!*).

B Usage Review

This usage review lists words and phrases that writers often find troublesome.

a, an   Use *a* before words that begin with consonants and words that have initial vowels that sound like consonants: *a* person, *a* one-horse carriage, *a* uniform. Use *an* before words that begin with vowels and words that begin with a silent *h*: *an* artist, *an* honest person.

accept, except   *Accept* is a verb that means "to receive"; *except* can be a preposition, a conjunction, or a verb. As a preposition or conjunction, *except* means "other than," and as a verb, it means "to leave out": The auditors will *accept* all your claims *except* the last two. Some businesses are *excepted* from the regulation.

affect, effect   *Affect* is a verb meaning "to influence"; *effect* can be a verb or a noun. As a verb it means "to bring about," and as a noun it means "result": We know how the drug *affects* patients immediately, but little is known of its long-term *effects*. The arbitrator tried to *effect* a settlement between the parties.

all ready, already   *All ready* means "completely prepared"; *Already* means "by or before this or that time": I was *all ready* to help, but it was *already* too late.

all right, alright   Although the use of *alright* is increasing, current usage calls for *all right*.

a lot   *A lot* is always two words.

among, between   *Among* refers to groups of more than two things; *between* refers to just two things: The three parties agreed *among* themselves to settle the case. There will be a brief intermission *between* the two acts.

amount, number   *Amount* refers to a quantity that cannot be counted; *number* refers to things that can be counted: Even a small *amount* of caffeine can be harmful. Seeing their commander fall, a large *number* of troops ran to his aid.

an, a   See **a, an**.

and/or   In business or technical writing, use *and/or* when either or both of the items it connects can apply. In college writing, however, the use of *and/or* should generally be avoided.

as . . . as . . .   In such constructions, *as* signals a comparison between two items; therefore, you must always use the second *as*: *East of Eden* is *as* long *as* *The Grapes of Wrath*.

as, *like* *As* can be used as a conjunction (to introduce a complete clause) or as a preposition; *like* should be used as a preposition only: In *The Scarlet Letter,* Hawthorne uses imagery *as* (not *like*) he does in his other works. After classes, Amy works *as* a manager of a fast-food restaurant. Writers *like* her appear only once in a generation.

at, *to* Many people use the prepositions *at* and *to* after *where* in conversation: *Where* are you working *at? Where* are you going *to?* This usage is redundant and should not appear in college writing.

bad, *badly* *Bad* is an adjective, and *badly* is an adverb: The school board decided that *Huckleberry Finn* was a *bad* book. American automobile makers did *badly* this year. After verbs that refer to any of the senses or after any other linking verb, use the adjective form: He looked *bad.* He felt *bad.* It seemed *bad.*

being as, *being that* These awkward phrases add unnecessary words and weaken your writing. Use *because* instead.

between, *among* See **among, between.**

bring, *take* *Bring* means to transport from a farther place to a nearer place; *take* means to carry or convey from a nearer place to a farther one: *Bring* me a souvenir from your trip. *Take* this message to the general, and wait for a reply.

can, *may* *Can* denotes ability, and *may* indicates permission: If you *can* play, you *may* use my piano.

capital, *capitol* *Capital* refers to a city that is an official seat of government; *capitol* refers to a building in which a legislature meets: Washington, DC, is the *capital* of the United States. When we were there, we visited the *Capitol* building.

center around This imprecise phrase is acceptable in speech and informal writing but not in college writing. Use *center on* instead.

cite, *site* *Cite* is a verb meaning "to quote as an authority or example"; *site* is a noun meaning "a place or setting": Jeff *cited* five sources in his research paper. The builder cleared the *site* for the new bank.

climactic, *climatic* *Climactic* means "of or related to a climax"; *climatic* means "of or related to climate": The *climactic* moment of the movie occurs unexpectedly. If scientists are correct, the *climatic* conditions of Earth are changing.

coarse, *course* *Coarse* is an adjective meaning "inferior" or "having a rough, uneven texture"; *course* is a noun meaning "a route or path," "an area on which a sport is played," or "a unit of study": *Coarse* sandpaper is used to smooth the surface. The *course* of true love never runs smoothly. Last semester I had to drop a *course*.

complement, compliment *Complement* means "to complete or add to"; *compliment* means "to give praise": A double-blind study would *complement* their preliminary research. My instructor *complimented* me on my improvement.

conscious, conscience *Conscious* is an adjective meaning "having one's mental faculties awake"; *conscience* is a noun that means the moral sense of right and wrong: The patient will remain *conscious* during the procedure. His *conscience* wouldn't allow him to lie.

could of, should of, would of The contractions *could've*, *should've*, and *would've* are often misspelled as the nonstandard constructions *could of, should of,* and *would of.* Use *could have, should have,* and *would have* in college writing.

council, counsel A *council* is "a body of people who serve in a legislative or advisory capacity"; *counsel* means "to offer advice or guidance": The city *council* argued about the proposed ban on smoking. The judge *counseled* the couple to settle their differences.

couple of *Couple* means "a pair," but *couple of* is used colloquially to mean "several" or "a few." In your college writing, specify "four points" or "two examples" rather than using "a couple of."

criterion, criteria *Criteria*, from the Greek, is the plural of *criterion,* meaning "standard for judgment": Of all the *criteria* for hiring graduating seniors, class rank is the most important *criterion.*

data *Data* is the plural of the Latin *datum,* meaning "fact." In everyday speech and writing, *data* is used for both singular and plural. In college writing, you should use *data* only for the plural: The *data* discussed in this section *are* summarized in Appendix A.

different from, different than *Different than* is widely used in American speech. In college writing, use *different from.*

disinterested, uninterested *Disinterested* means "objective" or "capable of making an impartial judgment"; *uninterested* means "indifferent or unconcerned": The American judicial system depends on *disinterested* jurors. Finding no treasure, Hernando de Soto was *uninterested* in going farther.

don't, doesn't *Don't* is the contraction of *do not; doesn't* is the contraction of *does not.* Do not confuse the two: My dog *doesn't* (not *don't*) like to walk in the rain.

effect, affect See **affect, effect.**

e.g. *E.g.* is an abbreviation for the Latin *exempli gratia*, meaning "for example" or "for instance." In college writing, do not use *e.g.* Instead, use its English equivalent.

emigrate from, immigrate to To *emigrate* is "to leave one's country and settle in another"; to *immigrate* is "to come to another country and reside there." The noun forms of these words are *emigrant* and *immigrant*: My great-grandfather *emigrated from* Warsaw along with many other *emigrants* from Poland. Many people *immigrate* to the United States for economic reasons, but such *immigrants* still face great challenges.

etc. *Etc.*, the abbreviation of *et cetera*, means "and the rest." Do not use it in your college writing. Instead, say "and so on" or, better, specify exactly what *etc.* stands for.

everyday, every day *Everyday* is an adjective that means "ordinary" or "commonplace"; *every day* means "occurring daily": In the Gettysburg Address, Lincoln used *everyday* language. She exercises almost *every day.*

everyone, every one *Everyone* is an indefinite pronoun meaning "every person"; *every one* means "every individual or thing in a particular group": *Everyone* seems happier in the spring. *Every one* of the packages had been opened.

except, accept See **accept, except.**

explicit, implicit *Explicit* means "expressed or stated directly"; *implicit* means "implied" or "expressed or stated indirectly": The director *explicitly* warned the actors to be on time for rehearsals. Her *implicit* message was that lateness would not be tolerated.

farther, further *Farther* designates distance; *further* designates degree: I have traveled *farther* from home than any of my relatives. Critics charge that welfare subsidies encourage *further* dependence.

fewer, less Use *fewer* with nouns that can be counted: *fewer* books, *fewer* people, *fewer* dollars. Use *less* with quantities that cannot be counted: *less* pain, *less* power, *less* enthusiasm.

firstly (secondly, thirdly, . . .) Archaic forms meaning "in the first . . . second . . . third place." Use *first, second, third.*

further, farther See **farther, further.**

good, well *Good* is an adjective, never an adverb: She is a *good* swimmer. *Well* can function as an adverb or as an adjective. As an adverb it means "in a good manner": She swam *well* (not *good*) in the meet. *Well* is used as an adjective with verbs that denote a state of being or feeling. Here *well* can mean "in good health": I feel *well*.

got to   *Got to* is not acceptable in college writing. To indicate obligation, use *have to, has to,* or *must.*

hanged, hung   Both *hanged* and *hung* are past participles of *hang. Hanged* is used to refer to executions; *hung* is used to mean "suspended": Billy Budd was *hanged* for killing the master-at-arms. The stockings were *hung* on the mantel.

he, she   Traditionally *he* has been used in the generic sense to refer to both males and females. To acknowledge the equality of the sexes, however, avoid the generic *he.* Use plural pronouns whenever possible. **See 16c2.**

hopefully   The adverb *hopefully,* meaning "in a hopeful manner," should modify a verb, an adjective, or another adverb. Do not use *hopefully* as a sentence modifier meaning "it is hoped." Rather than "*Hopefully,* scientists will soon discover a cure for AIDS," write, "Scientists *hope* they will soon discover a cure for AIDS."

i.e.   The abbreviation *i.e.* stands for the Latin *id est,* meaning "that is." In college writing, do not use *i.e.* Instead, use its English equivalent.

illusion, allusion   See **allusion, illusion.**

immigrate to, emigrate from   See **emigrate from, immigrate to.**

implicit, explicit   See **explicit, implicit.**

imply, infer   *Imply* means "to hint" or "to suggest"; *infer* means "to conclude from": Mark Antony *implied* that the conspirators had murdered Caesar. The crowd *inferred* his meaning and called for justice.

infer, imply   See **imply, infer.**

inside of, outside of   *Of* is unnecessary when *inside* and *outside* are used as prepositions. *Inside of* is colloquial in references to time: He waited *inside* (not *inside of*) the coffee shop. He could run a mile in *under* (not *inside of*) eight minutes.

irregardless, regardless   *Irregardless* is a nonstandard version of *regardless.* Use *regardless* instead.

is when, is where   These constructions are faulty when they appear in definitions: A playoff *is* an additional game played to establish the winner of a tie. (not "A playoff *is when* an additional game is played. . . . ")

its, it's *Its* is a possessive pronoun; *it's* is a contraction of *it is: It's* no secret that the bank is out to protect *its* assets.

kind of, sort of *Kind of* and *sort of* to mean "rather" or "somewhat" are colloquial and should not appear in college writing: It is well known that Napoleon was *rather* (not *kind of*) short.

lay, lie See **lie, lay.**

leave, let *Leave* means "to go away from" or "to let remain"; *let* means "to allow" or "to permit": *Let* (not *leave*) me give you a hand.

less, fewer See **fewer, less.**

let, leave See **leave, let.**

lie, lay *Lie* is an intransitive verb (one that does not take an object) that means "to recline." Its principal forms are *lie, lay, lain, lying:* Each afternoon she would *lie* in the sun and listen to the surf. *As I Lay Dying* is a novel by William Faulkner. By 1871, Troy had *lain* undisturbed for two thousand years. The painting shows a nude *lying* on a couch.

Lay is a transitive verb (one that takes an object) meaning "to put" or "to place." Its principal forms are *lay, laid, laid, laying:* The Federalist Papers *lay* the foundation for American conservatism. In October of 1781, the British *laid* down their arms and surrendered. He had *laid* his money on the counter before leaving. We watched the stonemasons *laying* a wall.

like, as See **as, like.**

loose, lose *Loose* is an adjective meaning "not rigidly fastened or securely attached"; *lose* is a verb meaning "to misplace": The marble facing of the building became *loose* and fell to the sidewalk. After only two drinks, most people *lose* their ability to judge distance.

lots, lots of, a lot of These words are colloquial substitutes for *many, much,* or *a great deal of.* Avoid their use in college writing: This point of view has many (not *lots of* or *a lot of*) advantages.

man Like the generic pronoun *he, man* has been used in English to denote members of both sexes. This usage is being replaced by *human beings, people,* or similar terms that do not specify gender. **See 16c2.**

may, can See **can, may.**

media, medium *Medium,* meaning a "means of conveying or broadcasting something," is singular; *media* is the plural form and requires a plural verb: The *media* have distorted the issue.

might have, might of *Might of* is a nonstandard spelling of the contraction of *might have* (*might've*).

number, amount See **amount, number.**

OK, O.K., okay All three spellings are acceptable, but this term should be avoided in college writing. Replace it with a more specific word or words: The lecture was *adequate* (not *okay*), if uninspiring.

outside of, inside of See **inside of, outside of.**

passed, past *Passed* is the past tense of the verb *pass; past* is a noun or adjective meaning "belonging to a former time" or "no longer current": The car must have been going eighty miles per hour when it *passed* us. The man had a mysterious *past.* I ran *past* the other runners.

percent, percentage *Percent* indicates a part of a hundred when a specific number is referred to: "*10 percent* of his salary." *Percentage* is used when no specific number is referred to: "a *percentage* of next year's receipts." In technical and business writing, it is permissible to use the % sign after percentages you are comparing. In other college writing, % is acceptable only when used with a numeral (6%).

principal, principle As a noun, *principal* means "a sum of money (minus interest) invested or lent" or "a person in the leading position"; as an adjective it means "most important." A *principle* is a rule of conduct or a basic truth: He wanted to reduce the *principal* of the loan. The *principal* of the high school is a talented administrator. Women are the *principal* wage earners in many American households. The Constitution embodies certain fundamental *principles.*

quote, quotation *Quote* is a verb. *Quotation* is a noun. In college writing, do not use *quote* as a shortened form of *quotation:* Scholars attribute those *quotations* (not *quotes*) to Shakespeare.

raise, rise *Raise* is a transitive verb, and *rise* is an intransitive verb—that is, *raise* takes an object, and *rise* does not: My grandparents *raised* a large family. The sun will *rise* at 6:12 this morning.

real, really *Real* means "genuine" or "authentic"; *really* means "actually." In your college writing, do not use *real* as an adjective meaning "very."

reason is that, reason is because *Reason* should be used with *that* and not with *because,* which is redundant: The *reason* he left *is that* (not *is because*) you insulted him.

regardless, irregardless See **irregardless, regardless.**

rise, raise See **raise, rise.**

set, sit *Set* means "to put down" or "to lay." Its principal forms are *set* and *setting:* After rocking the baby to sleep, he *set* her down carefully in her crib. *Sit* means "to assume a sitting position." Its principal forms are *sit, sat, sat,* and *sitting:* Many children *sit* in front of the television five to six hours a day.

shall, will *Will* has all but replaced *shall* to express all future action.

should of See **could of, should of, would of.**

sit, set See **set, sit.**

so Avoid using *so* alone as a vague intensifier meaning "very" or "extremely." Follow *so* with *that* and a clause that describes the result: She was *so* pleased with their work *that* she took them out to lunch.

sometime, sometimes, some time *Sometime* means "at some time in the future"; *sometimes* means "now and then"; *some time* means "a period of time": The president will address Congress *sometime* next week. All automobiles, no matter how reliable, *sometimes* need repairs. It has been *some time* since I read that book.

sort of, kind of See **kind of, sort of.**

take, bring See **bring, take.**

than, then *Than* is a conjunction used to indicate a comparison; *then* is an adverb indicating time: The new shopping center is bigger *than* the old one. He did his research; *then,* he wrote a report.

that, which, who Use *that* or *which* when referring to a thing; use *who* when referring to a person: It was a speech *that* inspired many. The movie, *which* was a huge success, failed to impress her. Anyone *who* (not *that*) takes the course will benefit.

their, there, they're *Their* is a possessive pronoun; *there* indicates place and is also used in the expressions *there is* and *there are; they're* is a contraction of *they are:* Watson and Crick did *their* DNA work at Cambridge University. I love Los Angeles, but I wouldn't want to live *there. There* is nothing we can do to resurrect an extinct species. When *they're* well treated, rabbits make excellent pets.

themselves; theirselves, theirself *Theirselves* and *theirself* are nonstandard variants of *themselves.*

then, than See **than, then.**

till, until, 'til   *Till* and *until* have the same meaning, and both are acceptable. *Until* is preferred in college writing. *'Til*, a contraction of *until*, should be avoided.

to, at   See **at, to.**

to, too, two   *To* is a preposition that indicates direction; *too* is an adverb that means "also" or "more than is needed"; *two* expresses the number 2: Last year we flew from New York *to* California. "Tippecanoe and Tyler, *too*" was Harrison's campaign slogan. The plot was *too* complicated for the average reader. Just north of *Two* Rivers, Wisconsin, is a petrified forest.

try to, try and   *Try and* is the colloquial equivalent of *try to:* He decided to *try to* (not *try and*) do better.

-type   Deleting this empty suffix eliminates clutter and clarifies meaning: Found in the wreckage was an *incendiary* (not *incendiary-type*) device.

uninterested, disinterested   See **disinterested, uninterested.**

unique   Because *unique* means "the only one," not "remarkable" or "unusual," you should never use constructions like "the most unique" or "very unique."

until   See **till, until, 'til.**

utilize   In most cases, it is best to replace *utilize* with *use* (*utilize* often sounds pretentious).

wait for, wait on   To *wait for* means "to defer action until something occurs." To *wait on* means "to act as a waiter": I am *waiting for* (not *on*) dinner.

weather, whether   *Weather* is a noun meaning "the state of the atmosphere"; *whether* is a conjunction used to introduce an alternative: The *weather* is chilly for April. It is doubtful *whether* we will be able to ski tomorrow.

well, good   See **good, well.**

were, we're   *Were* is a verb; *we're* is the contraction of *we are:* The Trojans *were* asleep when the Greeks attacked. We must act now if *we're* going to succeed.

whether, if   See **if, whether.**

which, who, that   See **that, which, who.**

who, whom   When a pronoun serves as the subject of its clause, use *who* or *whoever*; when it functions in a clause as an object, use *whom* or *whomever*: Sarah, *who* is studying ancient civilizations, would like to visit Greece. Sarah, *whom* I met in France, wants me to travel to Greece with her.

who's, whose *Who's* means "who is"; *whose* indicates possession: *Who's* going to take calculus? The writer *whose* book was in the window was autographing copies.

will, shall See **shall, will.**

would of See **could of, should of, would of.**

your, you're *Your* indicates possession, and *you're* is the contraction of *you are:* You can improve *your* stamina by jogging two miles a day. *You're* certain to be the winner.

Credits

This page constitutes an extension of the copyright page. We have made every effort to trace the ownership of all copyrighted material and to secure permission from copyright holders. In the event of any question arising as to the use of any material, we will be pleased to make the necessary corrections in future printings. Thanks are due to the following authors, publishers, and agents for permission to use the material indicated.

Part Openers

Part and Chapter opener graphic: Robert Stahl/Getty Images.

Text and Illustrations

p. 143: Excerpt from "Freedom of Hate Speech?" by Phil Sudo from *Scholastic Update*, 124.14 (1992), pp. 17–20. Copyright © 1992 by Scholastic Inc. Reprinted by permission of Scholastic Inc.

p. 194: From "A Song in the Front Yard" by Gwendolyn Brooks. Reprinted by consent of Brooks Permissions.

p. 223: U.S. Dept. of Commerce, Economics and Statistics Admin., Natl. Telecommunications and Info. Admin., A Nation Online: How Americans Are Expanding Their Use of the Internet, Washington: GPO, 2002, p. 43.

p. 296: Global temperature variation from the average during the base period 1961–1990 (adapted from Climatic research unit: data: temperature 2003) cited 2007, March 11. Available from http://www.cru.uea.ac.uk/cru/data/temperature.

pp. 309–310: Joe Nocera, "The Case Against Joe Nocera: How People Like Me Helped Ruin the Public Schools," *Washington Monthly*, September/October 1989. Reprinted with permission from *The Washington Monthly*. Copyright by Washington Monthly Publishing, LLC, 1319 F St., NW, Suite 710, Washington DC 20004. (202) 393-5155. www.washingtonmonthly.com.

Photos

Index

Note: Page numbers in blue refer to definitions.

Correction Symbols

abbr	Incorrect abbreviation: **27a–c;** *editing misuse,* **27d**	**p**	Punctuation error: **Pt. 4**
ad	Incorrect adjective: **45d; 10a–b;** *comparative/ superlative forms,* **10c**	**par** *or* **¶**	New paragraph: **3a–d**
		no ¶	No paragraph: **3a–d**
adv	Incorrect adverb: **45d; 10b;** *comparative/superlative forms,* **10c**	**¶ coh**	Paragraph not coherent: **3b**
		¶ dev	Paragraph not developed: **3c**
		¶ un	Paragraph not unified: **3a**
agr	Faulty agreement: *subject/ verb,* **7a;** *pronoun/antecedent,* **7b**	**plan**	Lack of planning: **2a; 41a**
		purp	Purpose not clear: *determining purpose,* **1a;** *purpose checklist,* **p. 3**
aud	Audience not clear: *identifying audience,* **1b**	**ref**	Incorrect pronoun reference: **9c**
awk	Awkward: **13a–c**		
ca	Incorrect case: **9a;** *case in special situations,* **9b**	**rep**	Unnecessary repetition: *eliminating,* **12b**
cap	Incorrect capitalization: **24a–b**	**rev**	Revise: **2d; 29h**
		run-on	Run-on sentence: *correcting,* **5b**
coh	Lack of coherence: *paragraphs,* **3b**	**shift**	Unwarranted shift: **13a**
con	Be more concise: **12a–c**	**sp**	Spelling error: **23a–b**
cs	Comma splice: *correcting,* **5b**	**sxt**	Sexist or offensive language: **16c**
d	Inappropriate diction: *appropriate words,* **16a;** *inappropriate language,* **16b;** *offensive language,* **16c**	**thesis**	Unclear or unstated thesis: **2b; 29d; 29g**
		var	Lack of sentence variety: **11a–c**
dead	Deadwood: **12a1**	**w**	Wordiness: *eliminating,* **12a**
det	Use concrete details: **16a3–4**	**ꞌ**	Apostrophe: **20a–c**
dev	Inadequate development: **3c**	**[ ]**	Brackets: **22d**
dm	Dangling modifier: **15c**	**:**	Colon: **22a1–3;** *editing misuse,* **22a4**
doc	Incorrect or inadequate documentation: *MLA,* **34a;** *APA,* **35a;** *Chicago,* **36a;** *CSE,* **37a**	**⌃**	Comma: **18a–f;** *editing misuse,* **18g**
		—	Dash: **22b**
exact	Use more exact word: **16a**	**. . .**	Ellipsis: **22f**
frag	Sentence fragment: *correcting,* **6b**	**!**	Exclamation point: **17c**
		//	Faulty parallelism: *using parallelism,* **14a;** *revising,* **14b**
fs	Fused sentence: *correcting,* **5b**		
ital	Use italics: **25a–c;** *for emphasis or clarity,* **25d**	**-**	Hyphen: **26a–b**
		( )	Parentheses: **22c**
log	Incorrect or faulty logic: **13c**	**.**	Period: **17a**
mix	Mixed construction: **13b**	**?**	Question mark: **17b;** *editing misuse,* **17b**
mm	Misplaced modifier: **15a**		
ms	Incorrect manuscript form: *MLA,* **34b;** *APA,* **35b;** *Chicago,* **36b;** *CSE,* **37b**	**" "**	Quotation marks: **21a–c;** *with other punctuation,* **21d;** *editing misuse,* **21e**
num	Incorrect use of numeral or spelled-out number: **20b; 28a–b**	**;**	Semicolon: **19a–b;** *editing misuse,* **19c**
		/	Slash: **22e**

Contents